A HERITAGE OF NONSENSE

JIM GARRISON'S TALES OF MYSTERY AND IMAGINATION

FRED LITWIN

CONTENTS

ALSO BY FRED LITWIN

Conservative Confidential: Inside the Fabulous Blue Tent
I Was a Teenage JFK Conspiracy Freak
On the Trail of Delusion — Jim Garrison: The Great Accuser
Oliver Stone's Film-Flam: The Demagogue of Dealey Plaza

First North American edition published in 2024 by NorthernBlues Books.

Cover design by Kathleen Lynch

Edited by Michael J. Totten

Manufactured in the United Stated on acid-free paper.

First North American Edition

Litwin, Fred

A Heritage of Nonsense: Jim Garrison's Tales of Mystery and Imagination

ISBN 978-0-9948630-7-2

This photo was taken at Hugh and Paula's house in November 2019.

Dedicated to the memory of Hugh Aynesworth, who passed away in 2023 at the age of ninety-two. Hugh was very supportive of my work and even supplied a blurb for my book On the Trail of Delusion. *I enjoyed every minute I could spend with Hugh—after all, he witnessed the assassination itself, the arrest and murder of Lee Harvey Oswald, and Jack Ruby's funeral, and he was one of the first to realize that Jim Garrison was dangerous. And Hugh didn't just cover the JFK assassination—he also worked on many other important stories, including the Henry Lee Lucas case and the serial murderer Ted Bundy, which were both turned into Netflix miniseries.*

RIP, Hugh. You will be missed.

ABOUT THE AUTHOR

Fred at the Old Red Courthouse in Dallas.

A Heritage of Nonsense is Fred Litwin's fifth book. In 2023, he published *Oliver Stone's Film-Flam: The Demagogue of Dealey Plaza*, which debunked the director's documentary series *JFK: Destiny Betrayed*. In 2020, he published *On the Trail of Delusion—Jim Garrison: The Great Accuser*, which chronicled Garrison's persecution of Clay Shaw. In 2018, Fred published *I Was a Teenage JFK Conspiracy Freak*, detailing his journey from believing in a JFK assassination conspiracy at eighteen to slowly moving to believe that Lee Harvey Oswald was the lone assassin. Fred's first book, *Conservative Confidential: Inside the Fabulous Blue Tent*, was a memoir about his move from left-wing antinuclear activist to Conservative Party campaigner. Fred lives in Ottawa, Canada, with his partner, Andrew.

Fred.Litwin@gmail.com

Please visit www.onthetrailofdelusion.com for photographs, documents, and updates related to this book.

INTRODUCTION

This book was made possible by COVID-19. In March of 2020, I visited Dallas to examine the papers of author Patricia Lambert at the Sixth Floor Museum and to have fun with my JFK buddies. On our last day, Sunday, March 8, we had our usual dinner at Campisi's, the restaurant where Jack Ruby ate dinner on the evening of November 21, 1963. COVID-19 was starting to hit North America, and I could see from the news on my phone that we were in for turbulent times.

I flew back to Canada the next morning and breezed right through security. The plane was half-full. The next day I went to the airport in Ottawa to pick up my partner, Andrew, who had been visiting his sister in Europe. He went back to work on Wednesday, but that was it. The Canadian government shut down that week, and the city of Ottawa was in lockdown.

But I had a job to do, and that was to finish my book *On the Trail of Delusion—Jim Garrison: The Great Accuser*, which was about Clay Shaw, the innocent gay man whom Garrison prosecuted in 1967 for conspiring to kill JFK. The case was bogus from start to finish, and the only evidence against Shaw was a witness's recovered memory that was manufactured using hypnosis and sodium pentothal, a purported truth serum. The case took two years to go to trial, and the jury acquitted Shaw in fifty minutes. It would have happened faster, but the jurors took a bathroom break. Garrison then indicted Shaw for perjury, and it took another two years for those charges to be quashed. Shaw was forced to sell his house and come out of retirement to earn a living. He sued Garrison for five million dollars in damages but died of cancer before his case could be heard.

My book also included six other stories about Jim Garrison's malfeasance, his paranoia, and his conspiratorial mindset, and—believe me—there was no shortage of material. But I still had to write the last chapter and get the manuscript in shape to send to my editor, Michael Totten. So I was grateful to have lots of time to devote to the project.

I published my book in September 2020 along with a new website. I decided to write a daily blog to post reviews and podcasts. I also decided to tell additional stories that were not included in my book. I was fortunate to have thousands of pages of documents from visits to archives across the United States, which provided a rich source of material.

I had all the time I needed for additional research, and my website soon became a valuable repository of JFK assassination documentation. Fast forward to August 2024, and I had published over 925 articles, not only debunking all sorts of conspiracy nonsense but digging deep into areas few researchers have touched. I even solved a mystery that has perplexed researchers for years (see the Bolton Ford chapter).

But my blog now had the raw material for another book. And so *A Heritage of Nonsense* is a companion book to *On the Trail of Delusion*. There is a commonality that runs through these chapters: the insidious nature of conspiratorial thinking, gullibility that stretches the imagination, and a smattering of mental illness.

The subtitle of my book refers to Edgar Allan Poe's collection *Tales of Mystery and Imagination*. The major difference is that Poe's book was fiction presented as fiction.

Here is what I have chosen for this book:

- Larry Crafard was a drifter who briefly worked for Jack Ruby as a handyman at his nightclub. Right after the assassination, Crafard hitchhiked to Michigan to visit his sister. Garrison came to believe that Crafard was a gunman on the grassy knoll and the killer of officer J. D. Tippit, a Dallas policeman murdered on the afternoon of November 22, 1963.

- Breck Wall was an entertainer who was friends with Jack Ruby. On the evening of November 23, Ruby called him in Galveston, Texas, where he was visiting his stepparents. Jim Garrison thought this was suspicious and made Wall a suspect in his investigation. He even spied on Wall in Las Vegas.

- Bootsie Gay was a client of G. Wray Gill, a New Orleans lawyer who employed David Ferrie, a Garrison suspect in the assassination, as an investigator. In 1967, she told Jim Garrison that right after the assassination, she saw a map of Dealey Plaza on Ferrie's desk. In 1977, he passed this lead to the House Select Committee on Assassinations (HSCA).

- Raymond Broshears was a gay rights activist in San Francisco known for his militant views. He was also a fabulist who spun incredible tales. He told a Los Angeles television audience that he had channeled Lee Harvey Oswald in a séance and was a roommate with David Ferrie. This caught the attention of Garrison's investigators, and Broshears was brought to New Orleans for questioning. He told them more silly stories and even testified before the HSCA.

- Arthur Strout was a dishwasher in Boston. In 1967 he called Jim Garrison's office and told them he had explosive information about the case. They sent him a plane ticket to New Orleans. Along the way, he reconsidered and turned back to Boston. He could have been a star witness.

- Rose Cherami was a drug-addicted prostitute who was found dead on a roadside in 1965. There were rumors that she mentioned the JFK assassination while hospitalized in Louisiana a few days before it happened. Garrison decided to find her to learn exactly what she had said and what she knew. The opening scene in Oliver Stone's film *JFK* features her.

- Richard Case Nagell was a decorated Korean War veteran who transferred into military intelligence. In 1954, he was the sole survivor of a plane cash and suffered organic brain damage. He became extremely paranoid and had to leave the service. In

September 1963, Nagell walked into a bank in El Paso with a gun, demanded traveler's checks, and fired two shots into the ceiling on the way out. He was arrested trying to flee the scene. He later inserted himself into the JFK assassination.

- *Farewell America* was an amateurish book supposedly written by French intelligence about the JFK assassination. It was delivered to Jim Garrison in 1968, and he sent an investigator to Europe to find out who was behind it.
- In 1961, a man named Joseph Moore stopped in at the Bolton Ford truck dealership to buy trucks for an anti-Castro Cuban organization. After the assassination, the salesman remembered that the order form also listed "Oswald" as the person accompanying Moore. Conspiracy theorists believe this person was impersonating Lee Harvey Oswald, who was then in the Soviet Union. I believe I have solved the mystery by identifying the man who accompanied Joseph Moore.

Unfortunately, some of the more popular conspiracy books accept this nonsense without the bat of an eye. Their natural skepticism, assiduously applied to the Warren Commission, dissipates when it comes to many of the stories in this book.

Every story in *A Heritage of Nonsense* stands on its own, so feel free to start anywhere you want. And don't worry—I will publish many more conspiracy tales in future books. So dig in and enjoy.

1

WAS LARRY CRAFARD THE GRASSY KNOLL ASSASSIN?

Larry Crafard in a picture taken by the FBI in late November 1963,
when he was just twenty-two years old. He rarely smiled because
his front teeth had been knocked out in a fight.

Right after Clay Shaw's acquittal on March 1, 1969, Jim Garrison charged him with two counts of perjury. Shaw's lawyers went to court, and in May 1971, Judge Herbert Christenberry granted a permanent injunction against further prosecution. He noted in his ruling:

Garrison states he was interested in the "forces responsible for the assassination, rather than individuals." Notwithstanding this statement by Garrison, this court, considering all of the evidence, finds that Garrison undertook his baseless investigation with the specific intent to deprive Shaw of his rights under the First, Fifth, and Fourteenth Amendments to the Constitution of the United States.

Garrison appealed, and it went all the way to the Supreme Court, which in November 1972 refused to hear the case. Clay Shaw was finally free from his ordeal.

But Garrison was furious, and he composed a nine-page press release claiming that the assassination "was instigated by the powerful military chieftains of the Pentagon ... in concert with dominant elements of the Central Intelligence Agency." The "entire operation" was "carried out by the domestic espionage apparatus of the United States government." Garrison concluded that the Supreme Court decision "puts the final nail in John Kennedy's coffin."

He also included this paragraph:

On November 22, 1963, the President of the United States was murdered in a professionally executed guerilla ambush at Dealey Plaza in Dallas, Texas. He was killed by riflemen located on the grassy knoll in front of the limousine and in two buildings located behind the limousine. The first shot, fired by riflemen in the front, went through the knot of his tie and entered his neck. The following two shots, fired by two riflemen at the rear, struck President Kennedy and Governor Connally each in the back. The fourth shot—fired once more form the grassy knoll in front of the limousine—fatally wounded the President in the head. The Cause of Death Certificate made out by a civilian doctor at Parkland Hospital, is still recorded in Dallas and certifies that the President died from a gunshot wound of the temple—which customarily is located in the front of the head.

While Garrison knew the exact details of the assassination—a professionally executed guerilla ambush—he couldn't even get it right about JFK's death certificate.

CERTIFICATE OF DEATH
NAVMED N (REV. 4-58) FRONT

See *NAVMED DEPT.* for *instructions regarding number of copies and submission.*

FROM *(Ship or Station)*
The White House, Washington, D.C.

IF UNIDENTIFIED INDICATE BY USING "X" AND CONSECUTIVE NUMBER HERE

1. NAME	2. SEX	3. RACE
President John Fitzgerald Kennedy	☒ MALE ☐ FEMALE	☒ CAUCA-SIAN ☐ NEGROID ☐ OTHER *(Specify)*

4. STATUS						5. LENGTH OF SERVICE *(Years and months)*	6. AVIATION
President of the United States						2 years	
☐ REGULAR ACTIVE ☐ RESERVE ACTIVE ☐ RETIRED ☐ DEPENDENT ☐ NOP ☒ OTHER *(Specify)*						11 Months	☐ YES ☒ NO

7. FILE OR SERVICE	8. RANK/RATE	9. CORPS	10. BRANCH OF SERVICE	11. PLACE OF BIRTH *(City and State or Country)*		14. RELIGION
NA	NA	NA	NA	Brookline, Massachusetts		Catholic

12. DATE OF BIRTH *(Month, day and year)*	13. AGE *(Years, months) (Days, if under 1 year)*	
May 29, 1917	46 years 6 months	

15. COLOR OF EYES	16. COLOR OF HAIR	17. COMPLEXION	18. HEIGHT	19. WEIGHT
Blue	Auburn	Ruddy	72"	172

20. MARKS AND SCARS *(Noted in health record)*

4" scar 2nd, 3rd and 4th lumbar spine
4" scar upper left leg, well healed

21. FINGERPRINT - STATE WHICH FINGER *(Right index preferred)*

22. NEXT OF KIN OR FRIEND *(Relation, name and address)*

Mrs. John Fitzgerald Kennedy, The White House, Washington, D.C.

23. ADMITTED TO SICK LIST FROM *(If on active duty, last duty station before current admission to sick list)*	24. DATE ADMITTED TO SICK LIST *(Month, day, year)*
The White House, Washington, D.C.	November 22, 1963

25. PLACE OF DEATH	26. TIME OF DEATH *(Month, day, year, hour)*
Parkland Memorial Hospital, Dallas, Texas	November 22, 1963 1:00p.m

27.	I. DISEASE OR CONDITION DIRECTLY LEAD-ING-TO DEATH. *(This does not mean the mode of dying, e.g. heart failure, asthenia, etc. It means the disease, injury or complication which caused death.)*	(a)		APPROXIMATE INTERVAL BETWEEN ONSET AND DEATH
		Gunshot wound, skull		
		DUE TO *(b)*		

The certificate did not specify that Kennedy was hit in the temple, just that he suffered a gunshot wound to the skull.

After reading Garrison's press release, journalist Ron Rosenbaum, who has written about the origins of Adolf Hitler and the controversies surrounding Shakespeare, called him up and asked about the four hired killers:

Garrison: Well actually there were more than four. You had four gunmen, but each one had an assistant gunman, and you had to have a man in charge, and you had to have a communications man, and—I didn't bother to go into it, but you had two people who created a diversion just as the parade rounded from Main.

Rosenbaum: Well, what about the man who fired the fatal shot? What was his name and what became of him?

Garrison: Well, I have no way of hunting any of them down now. If I gave you, off the record, the name of one of the two who was firing from the grassy knoll, which is where the fatal shot came from maybe you could track him down all right?

Rosenbaum: Okay.

Garrison: All right?

Rosenbaum: Uh huh.

Garrison: I don't want it surfacing.

Rosenbaum: Okay.

Garrison: All right. One of the men on the grassy knoll was named

_____ .

Rosenbaum: Uh hum.

Garrison: _____ is a nickname. His full name is _____ .

Rosenbaum did not include the man's name in his January 1973 *Village Voice* article, "The Assassination Labyrinth." But Garrison told him that the man was Curtis LaVerne Crafard, known simply as Larry. He also wasn't sure if Crafard was still alive or had been eliminated by the government:

Garrison: You see it's customary, at least through history it has happened that in really major assassinations, the government has subsequently disposed of the actual assassins—put an end to them. But that would only be conjecture. I would think there would be an equal chance he's retired comfortably for life.

For good measure, Garrison told him there were no mysteries left:

Garrison: Well, I'm finished really. Finished investigating long ago. There's no mysteries. Oh no, there are really none. When I began investigating, I thought the problem was going to be to find out who killed Kennedy. I thought the problem was going to be to find out who killed him and that's not the problem at all. It wasn't that hard. You didn't have to be a genius to solve it. We just dug into this thing real deep. It wasn't so much we were geniuses it was ... we were the only game in the country. There just wasn't anyone else trying, so we have to end up finding out what happened. To make a long story short, for example, we came across—just to give you a rough idea—such things that seemed mysterious, like the Tippit slaying, ceases to be mysterious. That was _____ again."

Rosenbaum: _____ again?

Garrison: Not Oswald. That was _____. And they describe him perfectly. But the people who describe _____ are not brought down to the identification to see Oswald …

Rosenbaum: Was _____ the one who fired the fatal shot?

Garrison: I cannot say. Because I only know that he was one of the two riflemen at the front.

So just who was Larry Crafard? And was there any evidence linking him to the JFK assassination or the murder of officer J. D. Tippit?

Larry Crafard was born on March 10, 1941, in Farwell, Michigan. His family moved several times when he was growing up, and Crafard ended up dropping out of high school in 1958.

He then enlisted in the armed forces and after thirteen months was discharged for medical reasons. His separation code was 264, which indicated "unsuitability, character and behavioral disorders." Some conspiracy theorists have speculated that this was for homosexuality, but there is no evidence that Crafard was gay, and he did not elaborate on his discharge during his testimony before the Warren Commission. Incidentally, Crafard's actual last name was Craford, but the Army misspelled his name when he enlisted, and he decided it was easier to use that name.

Crafard picked up his family's itinerant habits and moved so many times that even he found it all too hazy.

Here is an excerpt from his testimony before the Warren Commission:

Mr. Hubert: Can you tell us anything about your employment with Stewart-Hill in Berkeley, Calif., 1052 Dwight Way, Berkeley, Calif?

Mr. Crafard: I don't remember even.

Mr. Hubert: That would have been between July and September of 1960?

Mr. Crafard: I don't remember.

Mr. Hubert: Do you remember working for the Teer Plating Co., Dallas, Tex.?

Mr. Crafard: Yes.

Mr. Hubert: Tell us about it, please.

Mr. Crafard: I believe I worked for them for 2 or 3 weeks, something like that.

Mr. Hubert: How much did you make with them?

Mr. Crafard: I was making a dollar and a quarter an hour while I worked for them. I believe hen I left there my last check was either $65 or $85.

Mr. Hubert: Is that the first time you had ever been in Dallas, Tex.?

Mr. Crafard: Let's see, I believe it was, I am not certain of that.

Mr. Hubert: That was between April and June of 1961, was it not?

Mr. Crafard: I believe so. The way I have traveled around, I had a lot of jobs I even forgot about almost.

Crafard then picked fruit, worked in a cannery, and even joined a carnival. He had so many places of work that it was hard to keep track.

Mr. Hubert: Judging by the time schedule you had mentioned that would have been around the middle of September, is that correct?

Mr. Crafard: I believe so; I am not sure.

Mr. Hubert: Where did you go?

Mr. Crafard: Let's see, I went to California. I went down on the coast and I worked for a Chinese man down there raising strawberries.

Mr. Hubert: How long did you stay there?

Mr. Crafard: I was there for about a week. And from there I went to Long Beach, Calif. I went to work on the new Playland down on Long Beach. I was there for about a month, I believe it was. Then I went to Barstow, Calif., where I went to work for produce out there.

Mr. Hubert: What was the name of that?

Mr. Crafard: I don't remember the name of that outfit.

Mr. Hubert: How long did you stay there?

Mr. Crafard: I was with him for about 3 or 4 weeks, I believe it was.

Mr. Hubert: I take it that these jobs simply gave you enough money to live on and save up a little so you could move to the next place?

Mr. Crafard: That is right.

Crafard got married in June of 1962, and he and his wife lived in Dallas, Oregon, for about six months. She left him in December before the birth of their son. Crafard wasn't sure if he was the father.

Mr. Hubert: She was pregnant then, was she not?

Mr. Crafard: To my knowledge, as far as I know; yes.

Mr. Hubert: The child was born in March of 1963.

Mr. Crafard: Well, I will tell you the truth, the doctor has some doubts himself so I couldn't say.

Mr. Hubert: I mean she was pregnant when she left is what I mean in December. I think we are thinking about two different things.

Mr. Crafard: No, I believe we are thinking about the same thing.

Mr. Hubert: I am not asking you whether she was pregnant when you married her.

Mr. Crafard: No; I know that.

Mr. Hubert: I am asking you whether she was pregnant when she left you in December of 1962, because you have just told us the child was born in March of 1963.

Mr. Crafard: I will put it this way. When the doctor was informed she had a child, her doctor was then informed she had a child, he was very shocked and surprised that she had had a child, and she was his patient in May of 1962. He operated on her in May of 1962. So in other words, there is some doubt as to the fact that the child was mine and actually there is a little doubt as to the child is actually hers.

Mr. Hubert: Well, I wish you would explain that latter part. How can there be some doubt that the child is hers?

Mr. Crafard: I don't really understand it entirely myself. But the doctor that performed the operation when he was informed she had had the child he was very shocked and very surprised that she had had a child. He wouldn't say any reason for being so but he was. But I took him —I had understood from him that she wouldn't be able to have a child for about 2 years after the operation.

Crafard went back to Dallas, Texas, and reconciled with his wife, and they moved to Washington and then to California. She left him in the summer of 1963, and he then picked strawberries and joined another carnival.

In the fall of 1963 (it's hard to know exactly when), Crafard moved back to Dallas, Texas and got a job at the State Fair. He worked as a barker for a show called "How Hollywood Makes Movies." During the carnival, Crafard got into a fight and had several teeth knocked out. Jack Ruby came by a few times to talk to the people running the show about marketing an exercise twist board he was promoting. When the state fair ended, Ruby bought some of the lumber from the booth and paid Crafard to deliver it to his club.

On November 1, 1963, Ruby hired Crafard to clean his nightclub daily, work the stage lights, and answer the phone. Crafard lived in the club on a cot in an office. He was not even on a salary; he just took money from the till and left chits.

Crafard wanted to see the JFK motorcade but made no definite plans to attend. Unfortunately, he slept in that day. He was awakened just after the assassination by Andy Anderson, the manager of the Carousel Club. He got dressed, and the two of them watched television and listened to the radio. At about 2:30 p.m., Ruby showed up and told them that he was going to close his clubs for the weekend. He then left and came back later in the afternoon. He told Crafard to make a sign about the closure and to post it outside at about 6:30 p.m. He didn't want to signal too early to his competition that he was closing for the weekend.

Crafard went to bed about 9:30 p.m. and received a phone call at about midnight from a girl who wanted to be a dancer. He talked to her for about three hours—he knew that dancers tended to be good looking —so he tried hard to get her phone number for a date. He was unsuccessful.

At about 3:45 a.m., Ruby phoned Crafard and asked to meet him downstairs with the club's Polaroid camera, flash bulbs, and some extra film. Ruby was with his roommate, George Senator, and their first job was to take a picture of an "Impeach Earl Warren" sign. It was a John Birch Society advertisement, listing their "Box 1757" Belmont, Massachusetts, headquarters.

The three of them then went to a coffee shop, and Ruby commented on the similarity between the PO box on the sign and the PO box that appeared in an ad in the *Dallas Morning News* the day before. It was a full-page ad criticizing JFK's foreign policy, and it was signed by a Bernard Weissman, which Ruby recognized to be a Jewish name. Ruby wondered if the two ads were the work of either the Communists or the John Birchers and were perhaps designed to discredit the Jews.

They then dropped Crafard back at the club while Ruby and Senator went to the Dallas post office on Ervay Street to find out more about Weissman. Ruby asked the clerk for information, who refused for privacy reasons. Ruby did note that the box was full of mail.

At 8:30 a.m. Crafard called Jack Ruby about dog food. Ruby kept three dachshunds at the club, and Crafard was out of dog food. Ruby was annoyed at being woken up so early, and he chewed him out. Crafard went out for breakfast, hung around the club for a while, then just plain took off.

He hitchhiked to Clare, Michigan, where he stayed with his cousin for a day, then he went to Harrison to visit his aunt, and he finally arrived on the twenty-seventh of November, in Kalkaska to stay with his sister.

The next day was Thanksgiving, and the FBI, who had been trying to find him for what he knew about Jack Ruby, tracked him down. They talked to him for about five hours. On Friday, he was interviewed for another two hours, and they also took some photographs of Crafard (including the one at the beginning of this chapter).

After staying with his sister for a couple of days, he was on the move again. He started hitchhiking to Florida but was picked up by a man who told him it was too cold to be waiting for lifts. The man managed an oil-drilling crew in Mt. Pleasant, Michigan, just south of Clare, and he offered Crafard a job. He worked there until mid-February 1964.

Crafard then spent a few more weeks in Clare and in March hitchhiked to Dallas, Texas, to try and find his wife and child. He stayed at the Dallas City Mission for three nights but was then turned away because he had stayed the maximum time allowed and because he appeared to be drunk. He then slept one night at the former Carousel Club (now the Big D Copa Night Club).

He testified at Jack Ruby's trial for murder on March 12, 1964. The following week he left for California to visit a family friend, and then he went back to Dallas, Oregon. In April 1964, he testified before the Warren Commission in Washington, DC. They were extremely anxious to question him, to learn more about Jack Ruby and, of course, to understand why Crafard had left so precipitously.

Burt Griffin, an assistant counsel for the Warren Commission, emailed me and said that that "his sudden departure from Dallas after Ruby took the photo of the Impeach Earl Warren billboard caused us to suspect Ruby had done or said something that might get Crafard in trouble. So, he left."

Mark Lane, the leading conspiracy theorist and author of *Rush to Judgment*, also had suspicions. He told his readers that Crafard "left Dallas suddenly and mysteriously" and said "the flight of Larry Crafard" was proof that Ruby's shooting of Oswald was premeditated.

But Ruby told Crafard after the assassination that the nightclub business in Dallas would be hurt and that the assassination "would ruin the city of Dallas." Many people considered leaving for a while. as did Ruby, who called his sister Eileen in Chicago and told her he was coming to visit. She calmed him down as she had just had an operation and was not up for company. Breck Wall, a local entertainer you will meet in Chapter Two, left to visit his stepparents in Galveston. A few of Ruby's dancers also left town.

More importantly, on November 17, Crafard told Ruby he was leaving. He wasn't that fond of the work, and he wasn't busy enough at the club. In addition, he had written a letter to one of his sisters, which she hadn't answered, so he was worried. He wanted to find out what was going on. He only decided to hang around after Ruby promised to put him on a salary.

But Ruby's irritation on the morning of November 23 put him off, and he decided it was finally time to leave. And as is readily apparent, leaving abruptly was completely in character for Crafard.

At Jack Ruby's trial, Crafard testified that "I had discussed leaving with Jack before, and he had asked me to stay for a while, and I'm kind of a footloose character anyhow, I move around quite a bit. When I get ready to go someplace, I go. I was ready to go, so I left."

There wasn't anything really suspicious about Crafard leaving Dallas.

But there was something else that led to speculation about his possible involvement. Mark Lane told the Warren Commission about a purported meeting at Ruby's Carousel Club on November 14, 1963, between Bernard Weissman (the signer of the ad criticizing JFK on November 22), Jack Ruby, and police officer J. D. Tippit (whom Oswald murdered on November 22). It was all nonsense: Weissman and Tippit had never been in Ruby's club. But Lane mentioned that Crafard told the FBI that he had served Weissman drinks at the club. What Lane did not tell his readers was that Crafard's description of "Weissman" was nowhere close to the real person and that he later admitted that he had his "recollection of a Mr. Weissman mixed up with someone else."

In fact, there were several reports of Oswald having been seen in the Carousel Club. The Warren Commission examined this issue and noted that Crafard looked a bit like Oswald. Since there was no evidence that Oswald was ever there, it was logical to assume that some people perhaps mistook Crafard for Oswald. And this would later become grist for the mill for conspiracy theorists.

Not surprisingly, Jim Garrison took a keen interest in Larry Crafard.

He annotated Crafard's Warren Commission testimony. At one point, Garrison commented on Crafard's "remarkable memory," and next to his testimony about working at the carnival in Oroville, California, Garrison wrote "As what? A sharpshooter?"

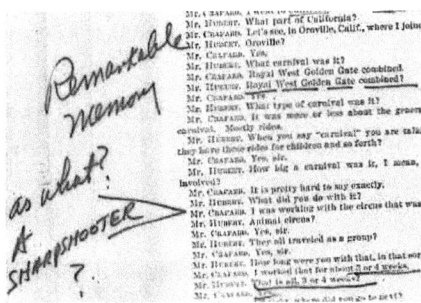

Garrison then noted that Crafard was "unaccounted for during the shooting."

Crafard was not really unaccounted for—he was sleeping. And Andy Anderson testified that he woke Crafard up right after the assassination.

Garrison also put his cryptologic skills to work by examining Crafard's notebook, which contained phone messages from Ruby's nightclub. Garrison then compared these numbers to Oswald's address book.

Here is an entry from a September 1967 entry from the diary of Tom Bethell, a Garrison staffer:

Garrison has been doing a great deal of research into the various Ruby or Crafard notebooks published in the 26 vols [Warren Commission's 26 volumes of evidence], and the Oswald address book. He's quite proud of this research, and reckons he's probably the world expert in this sub-topic. (He probably is.) He says the annotation "Midland 2550" occurs in the Crafard book and "Newton 2550" in the Oswald book. Garrison suggest these are "Callsigns" on some radio frequency.

Newton 2550 did appear in Crafard's notebook, and he was asked about it. He said someone else wrote it down. I don't see a notation for Midland 2550 in Oswald's notebook. Not that it matters since the suggestion that these are "callsigns" is crazy.

One of Garrison's investigators, Bill Boxley, wrote a memo about Crafard's Warren Commission testimony. I don't know which came first, this memo or Garrison's annotations.

2 October 1968

TO: JIM GARRISON, DISTRICT ATTORNEY

FROM: Wm. C. Boxley

RE: LARRY CRAFARD: References to BOEING Insurance; UNION DRILLING CO.,

1. LARRY CRAFARD's entire testimony is textbook quality for any intelligence service's course in "Resistance to Interrogation." It is a classic in the art of selective recall.

2. Attached are a few examples of facets which fascinate me in his testimony, although all 200 pages of it are full of them. On the whole, CRAFARD seems extremely sharp at detecting and avoiding the nuances of HUBERT's questions. His handling of the English language is nothing less than expert for a lad who barely compiled three years of high school and who was given a "general under honorable conditions" discharge out of the Army--from Germany, after 13 months service--in 소요 1959 when H.O.W. Bockelman was leaving Germany for an intelligence assignment in the U.S., etc.

3. CRAFARD is able to remember job details in his past which no other itenerant I've ever known could recall; at the same time he appears able to anticipate HUBERT's heading into an area where a memory blackout would seem beneficial to him. (WASHINGTON)

4. On the whole, CRAFARD appears to me to be travelling in the off-beat church league, perhaps as a courier or better. He refers to his church several times in the testimony, and once identifies it as the General Assembly and Church of the First Born in Dallas. (Naturally, no such church is listed in the 1963 Dallas telephone directory). He hits all the key spots in his travels--from West Coast Washington to Long Beach to Dallas to Memphis. He seems to maintain fantastic communications for a drifter relying only on what friends write relatives who write to him.

5. HUBERT calls recesses and even goes off the record at two or three key points in the testimony, but overall, CRAFARD has to pull HUBERT out of more holes than HUBERT does CRAFARD. e.g. when GRIFFIN asks of UNION DRILLING COMPANY'S predecessors "Were they Michigan companies or were they people--" CRAFARD rescues him with a quick "Michigan companies. Period." and GRIFFIN recesses until the next day (Last page of Volume 13).

6. What CRAFARD's role may have been is impossible to speculate, but on the facts of his testimony it appears at least as interesting as JACK LAWRENCE's. He actually was unaccounted for during the morning of the assassination until God-knows-when in the afternoon, for there is only his word, and possibly that of ANDY ARMSTRONG, Jack RUBY'S faithful slave. And, one of the most unbelievable elements of his testimony covers the period of 1 to-3:30 a.m. on Saturday morning Nov. 23, when he allegedly kept the phone tied up talking to a female he'd never seen or heard from before. Could this have been cover to have accounted for the telephone having been busy that length of time in case reporters or others may have tried to call RUBY and learned it was busy, while RUBY was supposed to have been out of the club? We don't REALLY know where CRAFARD was ALL DAY AND NIGHT Friday Nov. 22, before he could be quested by any Dallas police or newsmen--and he did not surface until the FBI talked with him in Michigan on Thanksgiving Day.

7. Finally, his hitch-hiking toward Florida from Clare, Mich. and being picked up by an unknown benefactor who gave him lodging and a job right there in Michigan until the RUBY trial is too Horatio Alger. And then he gets mixed up on why he went back to Dallas in time for the RUBY trial,....

Q: Where is Crafard now? Doing what?

You can see the Garrison notation at the bottom: "Q: Where is Crafard now? Doing what?"

This is an insane memo. Right at the start, Boxley writes that Crafard's testimony is "textbook quality for any intelligence service's course in 'Resistance to Interrogation.'" Crafard is "travelling in the off-beat church league, perhaps as a courier or better." And that phone call with that girl he was trying to get a date with, well, "Could this have been cover to have accounted for the telephone having been busy that length of time in case reporters or others may have tried to call RUBY and learned it was busy, while RUBY was supposed to be out of the club?"

Other conspiracy theorists went further. Joachim Joesten, an early JFK conspiracy theorist, wrote that Crafard impersonated Oswald "for the purpose of planting false clues that would incriminate Oswald after the assassination and thus divert attention from the real murderers of the President."

In his 1967 book, *Oswald: The Truth*, Joesten wrote that "the man who fired from the Dal-Tex Building was, I believe, Larry Crafard and he didn't know either, that Kennedy was being assassinated. He was just doing his job for which he had gotten $5,000 from Ruby. He was shooting at Governor Connally."

The notion that Crafard was shooting at Connally didn't really catch on. But maybe Crafard killed police officer J. D. Tippit.

Several witnesses identified Oswald as the perpetrator who fled the scene of the Tippit murder. But conspiracy theorists like to believe that Oswald was completely innocent. So one way to explain the incriminating evidence against Oswald is to believe that he was being impersonated.

Penn Jones, a conspiracy theorist whose specialty was writing about mysterious deaths, wrote this article in 1972 in his *Midlothian Mirror* newspaper:

LARRY CRAFARD

While taping a second TV show in Chicago last week, we were asked: "If Oswald did not kill

Officer Tippit, who did?" And we went blank. For the life of us, the name Larry Crafard would not come out. For the rest of that thirty minute show, we struggled, unsuccessfully.

Now, we want to print his name. It is the opinion of this editor Larry Crafard was one of the two gunmen who shot Officer J. D. Tippit. Crafard fitted the description given by most of the witnesses. Only two wittnesses claimed the Tippit killer was 'Oswald.

Crafard was missing for several hours that day. He was living at the Carousel Club, and left Dallas two days later, about the time Ruby was killing Oswald.

Crafard's testimony is that of a trained agent. If the question was important, Crafard could remember nothing. If it was a trivial question, Crafard remembered every minute detail.

The evidence points towards Crafard's escape after shooting Tippit by going into a church, but the police, instead, searched a branch library.

Chicago, we are sorry we could not recall his name.

Wherever you are, little punk Crafard, if you are still alive, come forward, if you are not guilty.

Jim Garrison's suspicions grew over the years, and in July of 1977 he wrote Jonathan Blackmer of the HSCA with some leads he thought were important. He told Blackmer that Crafard was perhaps "one of the men on the grassy knoll" as well as "an excellent candidate as the man who killed Tippit." Needless to say, the HSCA didn't think much of this idea.

Larry Crafard remarried in 1964 and seems to have settled down. But in 1988, author David Scheim published his book *Contract on America*, which pinned JFK's murder on the mafia. He wrote that "Carousel employee Larry Crafard also behaved strangely after the assassination."

And several pages later, Scheim writes:

In any event, it was clear that "someone in the police department," as Ruby intimated in his testimony, was "guilty of giving information as to when Lee Harvey Oswald was coming down." Also assisting the plot was Karen Carlin, so instrumental in establishing Ruby's alibi, whom Ruby again described with his thin hypothetical façade as "part of the conspiracy." Another who lent a hand was the man in Ruby's apartment who impersonated him in the telephone conversation with Elnora Pitts. And the conspirators included whoever secured the perjured testimony of the terrified Karen Carlin, murdered soon after; of the equally terrified George Senator; of the frightened Kathy Kay, who left Dallas with Harry Olsen after his auto accident; and of the fleeing Larry Crafard, who hitchhiked to Michigan on November 23, with $7 in his pocket.

A conspirator had "secured the perjured testimony" of "the fleeing Larry Crafard."

Researcher Peter Whitmey tracked down Crafard and spoke to him in 2001. He had become slightly paranoid:

> I also learned from Curtis that in 1980 he and his wife, along with two of their four children, were involved in a serious car accident, caused by faulty steering, even though the vehicle was quite new. Curtis was convinced that someone had tampered with the steering, which has made him fearful for his safety ever since. After his wife read *Contract on America*, by David Scheim, which I had recommended, she too seemed suspicious of the accident. I also recall when I was speaking to Craford in the late 1990s on the phone, apparently my voice was fading in and out, which caused Curtis to believe that the line was tapped.

Crafard's former girlfriend asked Whitmey not to reveal their address because she didn't want "the Mafia coming around."

This wasn't uncommon. Kerry Thornley, a Marine buddy of Oswald's, also became paranoid and started believing that he and Oswald were products of genetic tests carried out by a secret proto-Nazi sect of eugenicists. Roger Craig, a Dallas deputy sheriff, also became paranoid and believed that assassins were after him. He ended up committing suicide.

Crafard also had become a fabulist. He told Whitmey that he had been a "hit man" when living in San Francisco in the early 1960s. He said he got involved with the granddaughter of the local "don" and got her pregnant. Crafard promised to leave town and never speak to her again. Whitmey was skeptical about these claims, but he spoke to Crafard's older brother, "who appeared to confirm" them. I am not sure what that means, but it sure doesn't sound like corroboration.

He also told Whitmey that while serving in the military in West Germany, "he claimed to have been selected for several covert operations as a demolition expert, which took him over the Berlin Wall as well as into southeast Asia." Crafard showed Whitmey some scars on his leg, which he claimed were related to these operations. Of course, Crafard admitted that "there would be no written records related to his covert operations."

Conspiracy theorist Joan Mellen also spoke to Crafard, and he told her that he had seen Rose Cherami (see Chapter Six) dance at the Carousel Club. This is just plain ridiculous—Cherami was a forty-year-old drug-addicted prostitute and would hardly have been a stripper at the Carousel Club.

Here is what Crafard's first cousin Gale Cascaddan told the FBI in 1964:

> He was conceited and frequently bragged of his muscular strength and his "excellent" physique. He claimed to have an extensive knowledge of judo. To support this latter claim, on occasions he would use a "judo chop" on the interior wall of a house to show the power of his blow. He told Mrs. Cascaddan's mother that by continuously snapping his finger on a certain spot on a woman's breast he would cause the woman so much pain that she would beg him to kill her rather than be further tortured.

Crafard was a gift that kept on giving. Even comedian Mort Sahl got into the act, and he mentioned Crafard in his act "Mort Sahl's America." Here is an excerpt from *The New Yorker* of April 25, 1994:

His America turns out to be talk shows, movie studios, cocktail parties, and Presidential banquets, with an occasional detour into the Warren Report. In fact, he reads verbatim a snatch of Earl Warren and the then Representative Gerald Ford interviewing a barman, Curtis LaVerne Crafard, who had worked at Jack Ruby's Carousel Club before he was seized by F.B.I. men as he hightailed it out of town the day after the Kennedy assassination, saying, "They are not going to pin this on me." In the interview, Warren asks him what he did before he was a bartender. "I was a master sniper in the Marine Corps," Crafard says. Warren's next question is "What kind of entertainment did they have at the club? It's the one pure moment of political comedy in a show that otherwise bears out one of Sahl's best quips: "An intellectual in show business is like the smartest bear in the zoo."

Of course, this is not verbatim testimony from the Warren Commission. Crafard never said anything about being a master sniper, and he never thought that anything was being pinned on him.

It's bad enough that a comedian would write something like that. But how about Gaeton Fonzi, a well-respected critic who worked as an investigator for the HSCA? In 1998, JFK Lancer, a conspiracy organization based in Dallas, gave him a lifetime achievement award for his research. In his speech, Fonzi quoted this imaginary testimony in making a point about the Warren Commission's supposed deliberate deceit of the American people.

There is a brief glimpse, an illustration of the level at which that deceit was carried out, in an incident that occurred during the Warren Commission's investigation. Commission chairman Earl Warren himself, with then Representative Gerald Ford at his side, was interviewing a barman, Curtis Laverne Crafard. Crafard had worked at Jack Ruby's Carousel Club before he was seized by FBI men as he was hightailing it out of town the day after the assassination, having told someone, "They are not going to pin this on me."

In the interview, Warren asks Crafard what he did before he was a bartender.

"I was a Master sniper in the Marine Corps," Crafard answered.

The next question that Warren immediately asked was: "What kind of entertainment did they have at the club?"

And conspiracy theorists are still writing about Larry Crafard:

Did Larry Crafard kill J.D. Tippit?

[Please note: The following essay was proofread and edited by researcher Jim DiEugenio prior to it being published on this blog].

Headline from a 2014 article on the blog of Hasan Yusuf.

A quick internet search will find additional YouTube videos and podcasts alleging that Crafard was the man who killed Tippit.

Ep. 67 ~ The Ballad Of Larry Crafard

From The Lone Gunman Podcast : JFK Assassination

♡0 ♡0   ⏱ 60 minutes

Description

This week we take a closer look at the man himself, Larry Crafard. Classified by the Warren Commision as Jack Ruby's barman, we learn he was much more than that...likely the man who killed Officer J.D. Tippit, and possibly one of JFK's assassins.

A 2015 podcast on Crafard.

Interestingly, Jim Garrison didn't mention Larry Crafard in his 1988 book *On the Trail of the Assassins*. Gee, I wonder why.

Burt Griffin of the Warren Commission never thought that Crafard was a suspect. But perhaps he might have been the key to understanding more about Jack Ruby.

For many years, I thought that Crafard might be the Rosetta Stone to Jack Ruby and that someday he would tell a story that we had not heard. He died on April 19, 2011, at age seventy without writing a book or telling a different story to other investigators. I suspect that after nearly forty-eight years of silence, he was not withholding anything of importance.

Larry Crafard tried to run away from the JFK assassination. Unfortunately, it kept running after him.

2

GALVESTON, OH GALVESTON

Breck Wall courtesy of Ken Owens.

On the evening of November 23, 1963, Jack Ruby was fuming. He had closed the Carousel, his strip club in Dallas, for the weekend, but his competitors were still open. It was not right, and it wasn't decent. So he picked up the phone and called the one person he thought could help: Billy Ray Wilson, who went by his stage name Breck Wall.

Wall was a Dallas entertainer who was operating a musical revue, *Bottoms Up,* at the Adolphus Hotel, right across the street from Ruby's club. He was also the newly elected president of the Dallas Council of the American Guild of Variety Artists (AGVA), the union that represented the strippers and entertainers.

Bottoms Up at the Adolphus Hotel, courtesy of Ken Owens.

Like many people in Dallas, Breck Wall decided that Saturday afternoon to get out of town, and the best place to chill out was Galveston, Texas, where he could stay with his stepparents. He left his phone number with the Adolphus Hotel operator (where he was living with his partner Joe Peterson), and at 11:44 p.m., Ruby called him from Dallas.

Ruby was still terribly upset about the assassination, and he was glad Wall had closed his show at the Adolphus Hotel. However, he called his competitors names for staying open. He was also having trouble with the scheduling of the stripper and comedian acts at his club, and he wanted Wall to help plead his case to the union. Wall told Ruby that he would help ensure everything would be presented properly. Ruby asked Wall to call him as soon as he got back to Dallas.

The phone call lasted two minutes.

Little did Breck Wall know that this phone call would later make him a suspect in the JFK assassination. To figure this all out, we must go back to the afternoon of the previous day, just after JFK had been killed in Dallas. Fortunately, there are multiple FBI and Secret Service reports to tell us exactly what happened. In addition, the unpublished manuscript by Stephen Roy (the undisputed expert on David Ferrie) helps fill in all the details.

David Ferrie was an Eastern Airlines pilot who was fired in 1961 because of morals charges regarding affairs with teenage boys in New Orleans. In March of 1962, Ferrie became an investigator for G. Wray Gill, a lawyer in New Orleans who was representing mobster Carlos Marcello. On November 22, they were all in court for the closing arguments in the trial of Marcello, who had been indicted for conspiring to get a false Guatemalan birth certificate to evade deportation. At about 2:00 p.m., Judge Herbert Christenberry was given a note about JFK's assassination, and he sent the case to the jury and declared a recess. The trial reconvened at 2:30 p.m., and at 3:15 p.m., a not-guilty verdict was delivered. Ferrie then went to a victory party at the Royal Orleans Hotel.

Now that the trial was over, he could take a few days off to relax. Ferrie picked up his friend Al Beauboeuf at 4:30 p.m. and they drove back to his apartment to watch TV reports on the assassination.

Ferrie also had some business for Gill to take care of. One of his clients, Marion James "Buster" Johnson, had been convicted of perjury, and Gill needed Ferrie to visit him in Vinton, Louisiana, to get payment for a trial transcript needed for his appeal. Why not combine some pleasure with some work?

At about 6:30 p.m., Ferrie and Beauboeuf picked up Mel Coffey, a twenty-three-year-old who was working for Chrysler at Michoud (just east of New Orleans), where the space industry was located. Beauboeuf was an expert roller skater but wanted to try his hand at ice-skating. They thought about going to a rink in Baton Rouge, but it was closed because of the assassination. Ferrie knew about the Winterland skating rink in Houston, and he phoned and found it would be open on Saturday afternoon. They decided to drive to Houston, skate at the rink, and then stop at Vinton on the way back for Ferrie to conduct his business. They might also stop in Alexandria, where Beauboeuf had family or go geese hunting near Galveston.

The three of them left New Orleans at about 7:00 p.m. Their first stop was a restaurant in Kenner, Louisiana. It was raining, and by the time they left the restaurant at 9:15, the storm had passed to the east. They arrived in Houston at 5:00 a.m. and checked into the Alamotel Hotel. They got up at noon, purchased some clothes at Sears Roebuck, and headed to the Winterland Skating Rink at 3:30 p.m.

All three of them went out to skate, but Ferrie left the rink when he found it a little more difficult than he had expected. When the manager of the rink, Chuck Rolland, arrived at about 4:00 p.m., Ferrie went to talk to him about operating a skating rink. Ferrie had a hefty fee coming to him from his work in the Marcello trial, and he was looking for an investment.

ICE SKATING RINK
MAY OPEN HERE

"I have all machinery and equipment including skates for a large ice rink to be located in New Orleans," announces a Business Opportunity ad.

"I need a partner, active or inactive, with $15,000 to finance moving and setting up. For details, write C. A. Bass, Iceland, Inc., 4306 Laurel dr., Houston 21, Tex."

Excerpt from a column in the *New Orleans Times-Picayune* from July 16, 1963. One of Ferrie's friends thought he might have seen this article.

Ferrie also used a pay phone to call Gill to tell him that he was in Houston but could not reach him. At 5:30 p.m., they left the rink and returned to their hotel. Ferrie once again tried unsuccessfully to reach Gill. They checked out at 7:30 p.m., had dinner, headed for Galveston, and checked into the Driftwood Motor Hotel at 11:00 p.m.

They checked out the next morning and headed to Port Arthur. They arrived at 11:15 a.m. and got new spark plugs for Ferrie's car. While there, they saw Ruby shoot Oswald on TV. Just after noon, the car was ready, and they headed out toward Vinton. Ferrie spoke to Johnson for about twenty minutes, and they then left for Alexandria. They arrived at about 3:00 p.m., stopped at a gas station, and Ferrie once again unsuccessfully tried to reach Gill. He then called home to speak to Layton Martens, a young friend who was staying there.

Martens said that reporters had been calling and that Ferrie was being accused of involvement in the assassination by Jack Martin, a former felon who held a personal grudge. Martin had heard on the TV that Oswald had been in the Civil Air Patrol (CAP) in the mid-1950s when he was fifteen years old, and he knew that Ferrie had once been a CAP instructor. Martin phoned everybody he could think of to say that there might be a connection between Ferrie and Oswald.

Ferrie was stunned. He denied any involvement with Oswald, and he realized that his feud with Jack Martin had turned ugly. At 4:30 p.m., they headed back to New Orleans. They stopped at 6:00 p.m., and Ferrie finally reached Gill, who told him that Martin had contacted the DA's office, the FBI, the Secret Service, and the press. He was even intimating that Ferrie had perhaps flown Oswald to Texas.

Gill instructed Ferrie to return to New Orleans, and the three of them arrived at his apartment at 9:30 p.m. While Ferrie and Coffey were grocery shopping, police busted in the door, waved their guns around, and arrested Martens and Beauboeuf for vagrancy.

When Ferrie and Coffey returned, they sensed that something was wrong and took off. Ferrie dropped Coffey off at home and went to visit a friend at Southeastern Louisiana College. The next afternoon, Ferrie headed to the district attorney's office.

Ferrie told Garrison's assistant district attorney about their trip to Houston and Galveston. They showed him a photograph of Lee Harvey Oswald, and Ferrie denied ever seeing him. However, he did admit that Oswald might have gone to some CAP meetings when he was an instructor in the 1950s but that he could not remember him.

Martens and Beauboeuf were released on November 25, and Ferrie was released on November 26. His story had checked out, and there was nothing to charge him with.

Mystery Probe Pair Released, Another Held

Two men arrested by investigators of the district attorney's of f i c e on unspecified charges were released today, but a third was still being held.

New Orleans Times-Picayune, November 26, 1963.

I spoke to Al Beauboeuf in 2020, and he said it was his idea to go ice-skating. He told me that he was an expert roller skater and that he really wanted to get on the ice. The entire story is that Ferrie, Coffey, and Beauboeuf drove to Houston and Galveston. They went ice-skating. Ferrie conducted some business. That's it.

So what is the connection between Ruby's phone call to Breck Wall and David Ferrie's trip to Houston?

Only someone like Jim Garrison could link the two events. He had a particularly unique investigative technique to get at the truth: his theory of propinquity. What a great word! But not so great a concept. Here's how staffer Tom Bethell described it:

> If two people lived near one another, say within two or three blocks, it's suspicious. If any closer—they are 'linked.' If, on the other hand, they live at opposite ends of the city, get a list of friends of each (from their address books). Two such friends are very likely to live in the same block, or even know each other. Presto—the link.

Garrison wrote two memos titled, "Time and Propinquity; Factors in Phase 1." His concept of propinquity went beyond geography. Any sort of relationship—numerical, even sexual—was enough to set off alarm bells. Garrison told Bethell that "sooner or later, because people are lazy, you catch them out on propinquity."

And so here you have a homosexual (David Ferrie) in Galveston on the evening of November 23 at the same time another homosexual (Breck Wall) was in Galveston being phoned by Jack Ruby.

Could anything be more suspicious?

In early March 1967, Garrison traveled to Las Vegas, where he met journalist James Phelan:

> **Garrison**: You're aware that I had Ferrie picked up a few days after the assassination in 1963, on a tip that tied him to Oswald. We questioned him and then turned him over to the federal authorities. That was our big mistake. We had our hands on a key figure right at the beginning but didn't know it. The FBI made a cursory check and turned Ferrie loose. The FBI blew the investigation right there, only I didn't know it at the time.
>
> **Phelan**: But Ferrie was in New Orleans when Kennedy was killed.
>
> **Garrison**: That's right. But that night he left by car for Texas, with two other men. It was a curious trip, a most curious trip, by a curious man to a curious place at a curious time. With the whole nation sitting glued to their television sets for news about the assassination, Ferrie headed for Texas and drove all night through a rainstorm. When I picked him up on his return, he claimed he had gone to Houston to go ice-skating at a rink there. Can you imagine, driving all night through a rainstorm to go ice-skating?

Of course, the rainstorm had mostly moved to the east before a major part of the drive. When I spoke to Beauboeuf, he told me that it would not have mattered anyway since David Ferrie was the kind of pilot who would fly into storms. A drive through some rain would not have bothered him one bit.

> **Garrison**: When we came back into the case, a few months ago, we went into it deeper. We interviewed the rink manager and we picked up what the FBI had missed. *Ferrie never put on his ice skates.* He was at the rink all afternoon and *never put on his ice skates.* [emphasis by Phelan]

Of course, Ferrie only skated for a few minutes and was off the ice when the rink manager, Chuck Rolland, arrived.

The story confused Phelan:

Phelan: I'm sorry, but I don't follow you. Ferrie went to Houston to go ice-skating but didn't go ice-skating. How does this put him into a conspiracy to kill Kennedy?

Garrison: It broke down his story about why he went to Houston. It showed he had lied to us and to the FBI.

Of course, Ferrie had not lied. But Garrison was on to something far more insidious:

Phelan: Okay, why did he go to Houston?

Garrison: Let me tell you the rest of it. The rink manager told us that Ferrie made a great point of impressing his name on him. Ferrie said, 'I'm Dave Ferrie' four or five times, as if he wanted everyone to remember that he had been there. Now we come to the important part. The manager told us that the rink had a pay telephone, and Ferrie stuck by the telephone instead of going ice-skating. The manager remembered that distinctly. So it was obvious.

Ferrie phoned Gill but did not reach him. He probably tried to get Gill to call him back at the rink, so he was waiting by the pay phone. Rolland later testified that he was terribly busy and didn't pay much attention to Ferrie.

Phelan asked Garrison what was "obvious."

Garrison: The skating rink was the message center.

Phelan: I see. After the assassination, Ferrie drove from New Orleans over to Houston to get a phone message at the skating rink. Who was the message from?

Garrison: We don't know that. But the skating rink had to be the message center.

Phelan: But you don't know who called him or what they said.

Garrison: No.

If you think this could not get any wackier, you'd be wrong. Because propinquity was in play—and only Garrison knew how to apply the theory.

Garrison: Let me tell you about the phone call Jack Ruby made down to Galveston. Then you'll see the pattern. And where do you think Dave Ferrie went when he left the skating rink in Houston? To Galveston.

Phelan: He met Breck Wall there?

Garrison: We haven't established that. But look at the pattern. Ferrie leaves New Orleans and drives all night in a heavy rainstorm to go ice-skating. Breck Wall, close friend of Jack Ruby, takes off from Dallas after Kennedy is killed, drives through Houston to Galveston and gets a phone call from Ruby. Ferrie's on stand-by at the message center—the rink in Houston—and he takes off and drives down to Galveston, too. And the Warren Commission would have you believe that all this was just coincidence.

Garrison told journalist Lawrence Schiller that Breck Wall ordered Jack Ruby to kill Lee Harvey Oswald.

Does any of this make any sense?

The propinquity went even further. Garrison had a keen interest in homosexuality since many of his suspects were gay. And when his investigator, Andrew Sciambra, interviewed Chuck Rolland, the manager of the skating rink, homosexuality came up:

```
ROLLAND said there is a Follies Club which is operated by a KEITH
RICHARDS a few blocks from his rink, which is a gay club. Two
or three guys did female impersonations at this club. RICHARDS
lived in Mexico City for a while and worked as a tourist guide.
He was a bullfighter and could fly. His wife, SALLY, worked at
Gus Stevens in Biloxi. KEITH RICHARDS and the three gay kids
who used to do the female impersonations for him used to come
over to ROLLAND's skating rink quite often and skate. ROLLAND
said the three kids who did the impersonations had spent a lot
of time in New Orleans and talked about New Orleans all the time.
He said one also talked a lot about Washington, D.C.
```

How this is relevant is beyond me. Rolland's wife also remembered Brett [sic] Wall "because *Bottoms Up* once played at Houston-Continental."

By this time, Wall's show *Bottoms Up* was playing in Las Vegas at the Thunderbird Hotel, so Garrison sent Bill Gurvich, one of his investigators, to tape the show. He took a photographer who, according to Gurvich, had a camera rigged up to a pack of cigarettes. Gurvich told Phelan, "When Wall came bounding onstage, the photographer stood up, put the cigarette pack up to his eye, and started snapping pictures. I expected some bouncer to come over and ask him why he was pointing his cigarettes at Wall, and then he'd spot my tape recorder. I kept thinking about what I could say if he asked what we were doing. I could hardly have told him, 'Well, sir, we're investigating the assassination of President Kennedy.'"

And while some conspiracy theorists might question the recollections of Bill Gurvich or James Phelan, there is proof that these photographs were taken. There are references in the papers of Richard Billings, a *Life* magazine editor who helped the Garrison investigation, of photographs of Garrison listening to Gurvich's tape recording, and to several shots taken at the Thunderbird Hotel of the *Bottoms Up* show.

In his oral history interview for the Sixth Floor Museum, Wall said he was followed for a week in Las Vegas by Garrison and Gurvich. He said the possibility of being named as a suspect was a "fear that I lived with."

At one point, Hank Greenspun, editor of the *Las Vegas Sun*, and James Phelan called up Wall and told him he would be named in the next couple of days as being part of the conspiracy to assassinate Kennedy. Wall was "terrified." He agreed to give the *Sun* the exclusive story if he were named but wouldn't mention anything until then. Wall understood that he "could have been dragged into it really bad" and that "it would have ruined the show." He knew that "if someone said, well I think Breck is guilty, then most everybody in the country will think I'm guilty. And I'm totally innocent."

Garrison did not name Wall, but he remained a target for Garrison's investigators. In 1961, Wall became the owner of the Playbill Club in Dallas, and in the bankruptcy transaction he listed as references his stepfather Thomas McKenna, Forest Windell, and Earle Cabell, the mayor of Dallas.

Once again, Garrison thought this was suspicious because Cabell's brother Charles was formerly the deputy director of the CIA.

> BRECK WALL: On Saturday night, November 23rd, Breck Wall drove from Dallas down to Galveston, arriving there the same night that David Ferrie arrived, by way of Houston, from New Orleans. A few minutes before midnight Jack Ruby called Wall from Dallas, allegedly. -- as both Wall and Ruby testified before the Warren Commission -- "to discuss A.G.V.A. problems". The next morning Ruby left his apartment and killed Oswald.
>
> In 1961, Wall took over the assets of a cabaret operation known as the Playbill Club. At that time he gave three references, one of which was Earle Cabell, the Mayor of Dallas. Cabell's brother is Charles Cabell, the former Deputy Director of the Central Intelligenc Agency under Allen Dulles.

Excerpt of a Garrison memo titled "An Analysis of Potential Witnesses Indicating Role of Military Industrial Complex in the Assassination of President Kennedy," dated September 1968.

Once again, propinquity in action.

Interestingly, in 2017, it emerged that Earle Cabell had signed a 1956 agreement with the CIA to possibly receive information about certain operational matters. This was all related to Cabell's work with two organizations: Crusade for Freedom and Radio Free Europe. Thank God that Garrison did not know about Earle's connections. It would have sent him into overdrive.

But there is another connection that worried Garrison, which he discussed at a conference with his investigators in September 1968. This is Garrison speaking, from a tape recording:

> **Garrison**: Well, anyway, Breck Wall in 1961 gives Earle Cabell as a reference. You can see the implications of that. Who's he working for now; he works at Las Vegas at the Thunderbird—the same one that Lewis McWillie works for—Breck Wall's name is on the outside about 6 times. He's the entertainment director.

Garrison was referring to Lewis McWillie, who ran casinos for the mob in Las Vegas and in Cuba. McWillie knew Ruby in the 1950s. He had last seen Ruby in 1961, and Ruby phoned him in 1963 to see if he could help with union problems.

But Garrison had his facts all wrong. McWillie was not the entertainment director—he was the assistant to the day shift casino boss. He started work at the Thunderbird in February of 1963 and left in August of 1964. *Bottoms Up* played at the Castaways in Las Vegas in 1964 and in

August left Vegas for a national tour. McWillie and Wall never overlapped at the Thunderbird.

Even if they did, would it have been insidious? Only to believers in the theory of propinquity.

Breck Wall almost got snared by Perry Russo, Garrison's key witness. Russo came out of the woodwork after David Ferrie died of a berry aneurysm in February 1967. He claimed to have known Ferrie in 1962 and 1963 and was brought to New Orleans for questioning. He was first interviewed under the influence of sodium pentothal, a so-called truth serum. He was then hypnotized on three separate occasions by Dr. Esmond Fatter, a local expert in hypnosis. What finally emerged was a recovered memory of a party at Ferrie's house where Clay Shaw and Lee Harvey Oswald [using the name Leon] discussed killing Kennedy.

Here is an excerpt of Russo's first session under hypnosis on March 1, 1967:

Dr. Fatter: I wonder, Perry, who is Brett Wall [*sic*]?

    Russo: A friend of Leon, he was supposed to help Leon.

Dr. Fatter: How, Perry?

    Russo: He didn't say, Dave [Ferrie] asked him about it.

Dr. Fatter: And I wonder—who is Jack Ruby?

    Russo: I don't know.

Dr. Fatter: I wonder if Brett Wall knew Jack Ruby.

    Russo: I don't know.

Dr. Fatter: And I wonder if Ferrie knew Brett Wall.

    Russo: I guess so, it sounded like a mutual acquaintance. Ferrie asked Leon if he would be there.

Dr. Fatter: I wonder if Ferrie asked Leon if he would be at Brett Wall's place in Houston.

    Russo: He just asked Leon if Brett Wall would be there. He said he supposed so.

Dr. Fatter: I wonder where Oswald was going to be in Houston, Perry?

    Russo: He didn't say.

Dr. Fatter: And I wonder who Larry Rost is?

    Russo: (No response)

Dr. Fatter: I wonder what is the Winterland Skating Rink in Houston.

Russo: I know one in New Orleans on St. Claude Street [a roller-skating rink].

Dr. Fatter: I wonder, Perry, where Leon was supposed to meet Brett Wall.

Russo: Dave didn't say.

Dr. Fatter: I wonder if it was just in Houston or some other place.

Russo: I don't know.

Dr. Fatter: I wonder what mutual friends Ferrie and Leon had—they were both friends with—I wonder if they had any other friends, Ferrie and Leon, like Brett Wall?

If Russo had Russo placed Breck Wall at the assassination party, Garrison might well have indicted Wall. Note that Russo himself did not bring up Wall, but Dr. Fatter did—clearly an improper suggestion.

Garrison never lost his interest in Breck Wall. Among Garrison's papers is an FBI report on David Ferrie, on which he wrote this note in 1977:

The notation on the upper right reads as follows:

8/3/77 Note: Within 1 hour after DF's [David Ferrie] check-in here, RUBY makes his last l/d [long-distance] call for the night, calling BRECK WALL who has already arrived in GALVESTON. Next A.M.—w/o any more l/d calls—RUBY goes to police HQ + kills Oswald.

But in Garrison's 1988 book, *On the Trail of the Assassins*, Breck Wall's name was removed from the story.

We also learned later that Ferrie continued on from Houston to Galveston, Texas, where he happened to be when Jack Ruby called there the night before he shot and killed Lee Oswald.

Breck Wall was lucky, and he escaped Garrison's lash. He went on to have a highly successful career, and *Bottoms Up* became the longest running comedy revue in Las Vegas. Wall died in 2010 at the age of seventy-five.

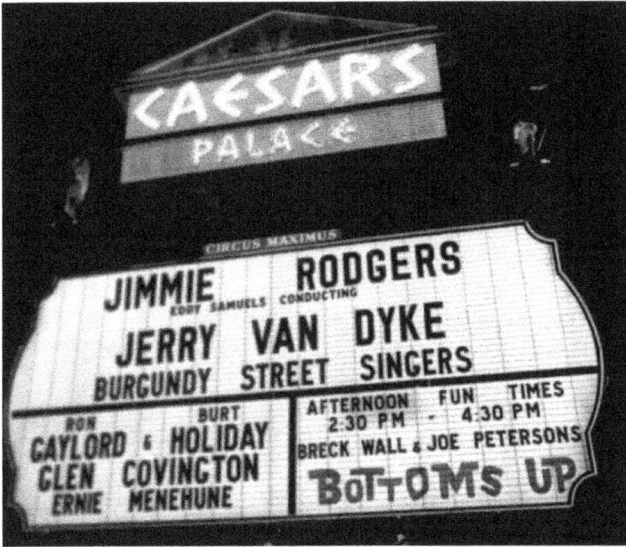

Photo taken November 24, 1969. Image taken by the Las Vegas News Bureau for the Nevada Power Company. Photo courtesy of the Las Vegas News Bureau Collection, LVCVA Archive.

3

THE LOST MAP OF DEALEY PLAZA

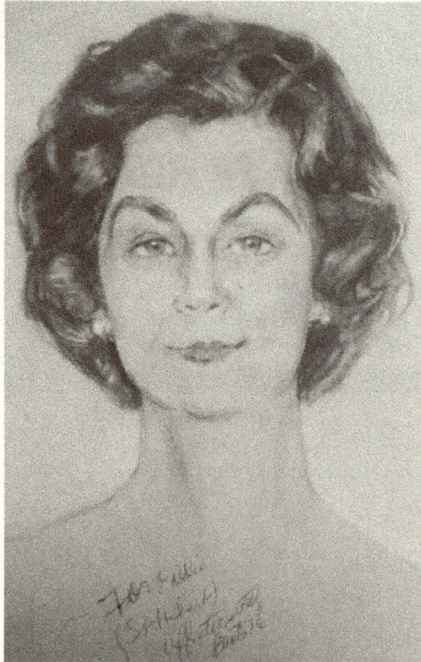

A portrait of Bootsie Gay that she sent to congressman F. Edward
Hébert.

On July 18, 1977, Jim Garrison sent a handwritten memo to the HSCA about Thomas Beckham, a "subject worthy of inquiry." He said Beckham was a protégé of Fred Crisman, whom Garrison believed was one of the three "tramps" arrested in Dallas after the assassination. During his investigation, Garrison had also come across a film, now vanished, that showed Beckham in front of the Texas School Book Depository (TSBD) on November 22. Garrison believed that Beckham's stay in a mental institution in 1963 was suspicious and wondered if perhaps he had been groomed to be an "alternative patsy in case of a last-minute problem with Lee Harvey Oswald."

The truth was that Thomas Beckham was a con man. In 1959, Beckham promoted a Ricky Nelson show in New Orleans when he was just sixteen. A Ricky Nelson did appear—not the famous one but someone with the same name. Beckham pocketed the money and ran. A few years later, he dressed as a priest to deceive people into donating money to a fake anti-Castro organization.

Garrison received an anonymous letter in May 1967 that discussed the details of the JFK assassination and that listed Thomas Beckham as an important witness. He subpoenaed Beckham to appear before the grand jury, and in February 1968 he testified for more than six hours. You can read the transcript online, and when I first read it, I couldn't stop laughing.

Beckham didn't even finish high school. He left in the seventh grade at the age of fourteen or fifteen. And he stumbled when asked about his priest's outfit:

Juror: No, the church that you did belong to. Was that the Old Orthodox Catholic Church of North America?

Beckham: I think it had Apololectic or Apolostetic or something to it.

Juror: Never mind about that …

Beckham: I don't know if that is the exact wording of the church, I don't …

Juror: Maybe this is not the exact wording, but is this the Old Orthodox Catholic Church of North America?

Beckham: I can't answer you.

Juror: Well, suppose you tell me the name of the church you belong to?

Beckham: I got the papers at home, I can show you the papers, but I don't have them with me.

Juror: Well, tell me what you recall that is on the paper?

Beckham: Let me see if I can recall what is on the paper. I don't know, it says that I am an ordained priest within the Holy APOLOTOTIC, or something like that.

Juror: Are you trying to tell me you don't know what church you are a priest in?

Beckham: No, because I wasn't even interested in that, I never even messed with it.

Juror: Were you wearing a habit?

Beckham: At that time, yes.

Juror: While you were wearing the habit what church did you think you belonged to?

Beckham: That's a good question. Ask Mr. Martin. I don't know myself.

A couple of HSCA investigators were intrigued by Garrison's memo, and they wanted to speak to Beckham. The only problem was that he was in the city jail in Mobile, Alabama, facing two counts of federal wire fraud. Beckham, under the name Eggleston Zimmerman, had promoted a benefit concert for the widows of two Mobile County sheriff's deputies killed in an ambush in 1975. Ernest Tubb and the Texas Troubadours were supposed to headline the event, but it was canceled, and Beckham made off with the money.

At the end of July 1977, Beckham was found not guilty. He took the stand during the trial and told the jury that he was a former CIA agent from 1961–1964 and that they provided him with different identifications to use in different cities. He also said that the CIA made him a Catholic priest in 1962 while he was living in New Orleans.

However, Bob Buras and L. J. Delsa of the HSCA still had to interview Beckham in his jail cell as he was awaiting transfer to authorities in Arkansas to face similar charges. Beckham had been practicing as a naturopathic physician in Pine Bluff, Arkansas. He was also marrying couples, claiming that he was an ordained bishop in a group called Essence Gospel of Peace. He also set up his own chamber of commerce and was selling raffle tickets.

Beckham was transferred to Arkansas, and after bail of $3,000 had been paid, left for Jackson, Mississippi. On August 9, 1977, Beckham sat down for a three-hour interview to determine whether he should be granted immunity from prosecution by the HSCA. They promised that should the HSCA not grant him immunity, anything he told them at this meeting would be privileged. Beckham was now ready to spill the beans.

He told them about a meeting in Algiers, Louisiana, with Sergio Arcacha Smith (an anti-Castro Cuban activist), G. Wray Gill, Vincent Marcello (Carlos's brother) and a few other people in which they discussed JFK's assassination. A second meeting took place with Jack Martin, David Ferrie, and Clay Shaw at the Town and Country Motel in New Orleans, where they talked about Cuba and JFK. Beckham said that Lee Harvey Oswald told him in September 1963 that he was going to be coming into some money.

Two weeks before the assassination, Beckham was told by David Ferrie to go to Gill's office, where they put maps, drawings, diagrams, and pictures of buildings and cars into an envelope for him to deliver to a Mr. Howard in Dallas. He also spoke of an "Organization" that was immensely powerful and that was employed by the CIA for high-level missions. A friend of Fred Crisman's told Beckham that Oswald and three others were involved in the assassination and that Crisman knew all the details.

Despite all this nonsense, the HSCA invited Thomas Beckham to be deposed. But that would have to wait until May 1978.

In the meantime, Buras and Delsa asked Jim Garrison if he had any information pertaining to any photos or diagrams in G. Wray Gill's office around the time of the assassination. Here is an excerpt from his reply:

```
In response to your request, I have found a series of memos -- which
I collected from various subject areas -- which indicate that one CLARA
FLOURNOY (better known as "BOOTSIE GAY") was in WRAY GILL'S office the
day following the assassination and allegedly observed several female
employees cleaning out DAVID FERRIE'S desk.  It was then that she saw
the diagram quite apparently referreing to the scene of the assassina-
tion in Dallas.  When she picked it up it was snatched from her by one
of GILL'S employees.
```

Buras and Delsa believed that the diagram supposedly found by Bootsie was the same one discussed by Thomas Beckham in his HSCA interview.

On Oct. 12, 1977 the investigators asked New Orleans Attorney Jim Garrison if he had any information pertaining to photos or diagram in G. Wray Gill's office around Nov. 22, 1963. On Oct. 20, 1977 Jim Garrison gave the investigators statements taken by his staff in between 1967 and 1969. (see memo Buras and Delsa with cover letter by Jim Garrison dated 10-20-77). New Orleans Police Captain Fred Soule took a statement from Clara Flournoy Gay on April 24, 1969 in which Gay states that she saw diagrams of Elm St. in the Office of George Wray Gill Sr. on Saturday Nov. 23, 1963. At the time of Clara Flournoy Gay's statement JIm Garrison and Fred Soule thought that the diagrams belonged to Daivd Ferrie, an investigator for Gill. Thomas Beckham's statement puts the diagrams in the possession of George Wray Gill Sr. As of the writing of this memothe investigators have not learned of any connection or association between Beck-Ham and Gay. Clara Flournoy Gay's statement was made and recorded seven years before Thomas Beckham's statement to this Committee.

Excerpt of report by L. J. Delsa and Bob Buras on the background of G. Wray Gill.

Clara Flournoy Gay (known as Bootsie Gay) was born in 1907 and was a poet. She was even listed in the *International Who's Who in Poetry* for 1974–1975:

> GAY, Clara Flournoy, b. 19 Dec. 1907. Owner of Art Gallery. Education: Centenary Coll., Shreveport, La. Positions held: Owner & Operator, Art Galleries, New Orleans, La., 1943-70. Memberships: La. State Poetry Soc., New Orleans, La.; The Out Door Int. Poets & Writers; The Round Table Club. Contbr. to: newspapers in New Orleans, Shreveport, Natchitoches, Ark.; La. Heritage; Reader's Digest. Recip., Int. Boswell Inst. Award, Rome, Italy. Address: 507 Rosebud Dr., Natchitoches, LA 71457, U.S.A.

While living in New Orleans in the mid-1960s, she worked at a painting supply company, and she ran a small gallery. Her lawyer was G. Wray Gill. Her name came up in an interview researcher Harold Weisberg conducted with witnesses at the Dixieland Hall:

BOOTSIE GAY according to this story was in G. WRAY GILL's office at the time FERRIE was first being "investigated" by the FBI. She is said to have said she saw GILL going over FERRIE's papers in his office. These included a chart of the assassination scene.

This rumor was not followed up. The next mention of Bootsie Gay was after the Clay Shaw trial in a March 28, 1969, memo to Jim Garrison about some new leads:

> Also, BOOTSIE GAY was supposed to have been in G. WRAY GILL's office when GILL was going through FERRIE's papers and saw a chart of the assassination scene among FERRIE's papers. JOHN DODT and BOOTSIE GAY, who are friends of SHAW, are known for their parties which cater to the "gay" crowd.

In April 1968, Captain Fred Soule, head of the New Orleans Vice Squad, interviewed Al Clark, who verified that he told Weisberg about Bootsie and that "she saw a chart that had belonged to DAVID FERRIE that indicated an assassination plot."

Two days later, Soule interviewed Bootsie Gay.

M E M O R A N D U M   Re : FERRIE

April 24, 1969

TO: JAMES L. ALCOCK, Exec. Assistant D. A.

FROM: CAPT. FREDERICK A. SOULE, SR., Investigator

RE: INTERVIEW WITH:
               CLARA FLOURNOY "BOOTSIE" GAY UNDER ITEM #2,
               AL CLARK INTERVIEW.

* * * * * * *   *

        In answer to a subpoena, Bootsie Gay came into
the office on this date at about 2:45 p.m. She stated to
Soule and Mr. James Alcock that she resides at 528 Dumaine
Street, and is employed at Max Hills Painting Suppliers
located at 629 St. Peter Street - telephone: 523-9302.

        She stated that just prior to the assassination
she was having G. WRAY GILL do some legal work of a civil
nature for her. She made several trips to GILL'S office
and observed DAVID FERRIE who had an office at GILL'S office,
and she understood that FERRIE was an investigator for GILL.

        The day following the John Kennedy assassination,
a Saturday, she (MRS. GAY), went to GILL'S office and
observed that two female employees were cleaning out FERRIE'S
desk. She saw a chart or a sketch, and what caught her eye
was the fact that this chart had ELM written on what appeared
to be a street. There was also a building and on the street
was a square with letters "VIP" written in this square.

        MRS. GAY stated that she remarked to the
receptionist that this should be turned over to the F.B.I.
The receptionist then picked it off the desk and threw it
in the trash can stating it was nothing.

        MRS. GAY stated that she then took the document
from the trash can stating that she would give it to the F.B.I.
The receptionist then grabbed the document from Mrs. Gay's
hand and again threw it in the trash can.

        MRS. GAY seemed to be about 60 years, reasonably
intelligent, slightly nervous and very cooperative. She
appears to be the type of individual that likes to see justice
prevail.

                          CAPT. FRED SOULE, SR.

Gay claimed she went to Gill's office on the Saturday following the assassination and that she saw a "chart of a sketch" with the word "ELM" written on "what appeared to be a street." The letters "VIP" were written on a square on the street. Bootsie wanted to turn the sketch over to the FBI, but a receptionist grabbed the document and threw it away. She took it out of the trash only to have it grabbed again and dropped in the garbage.

Bootsie Gay drew a facsimile of the sketch and gave it to Soule. Unfortunately, I cannot find that sketch anywhere in the Garrison files.

Soule then interviewed the two receptionists who worked in Gill's office. Alice Guidroz said she had never seen such a sketch. She also said that she was not working on that Saturday and that she was in Baton Rouge that day. Regina Franchevich also did not recall seeing such a document. Soule noted that "she appeared to be extremely nervous."

It does seem strange that Bootsie Gay would just walk into Gill's office on the Saturday after the assassination and go through Ferrie's desk. After all, she was just a client. Joan Mellen claims this occurred on the Tuesday after the assassination—after Bootsie had heard about Ferrie being the subject of attention by the FBI and the Secret Service.

My guess is that Bootsie had a good imagination. Perhaps she saw a diagram of Dealey Plaza that was in the newspaper.

Of course, conspiracy theorist James DiEugenio took Bootsie Gay's story as gospel:

> When she heard about Ferrie being questioned by Garrison's office, she called up Gill and noted the tumult on the other end of the phone. One secretary said words to the effect that Mr. Gill knew nothing about this. She then went to his office. Clara looked over at Ferrie's desk and she saw what looked like a diagram of Dealey Plaza: it was a drawing of a car from the perspective of an angle above, the car was surrounded by high buildings, reminiscent of Dealey Plaza.

Gee, Mr. DiEugenio is just a tad more certain about this than I think he should be, no?

Joan Mellen also mentions Bootsie Gay in her book, *A Farewell to Justice*, and adds her own dialogue:

Learning that Ferrie had been questioned by the district attorney in connection with the Kennedy assassination, Gay telephoned Gill's office to find the secretaries "in a turmoil." One told her, "Mr. Gill knew nothing about Ferrie—it was all new to him." Bootsie knew otherwise. She went to Gill's office only to find Gill employee Regina Franchevich packing up Ferrie's papers. If Ferrie walked into the office, we would all walk out, someone said.

Bootsie sat watching as Regina took a chart, it looked like a diagram, of an automobile from a high angle looking down, surrounded by buildings at what was clearly Dealey Plaza. When Franchevich tossed it into a wastebasket, Bootsie fished it out.

"This should be turned over to the FBI or the Secret Service," Bootsie said.

Franchevich angrily snatched the diagram back. "It's nothing," she said. She threw it back into the trash. Again Bootsie plucked it out. "I'll give it to the FBI," she said. Franchevich grabbed the paper, this time for good, if not before Bootsie Gay spotted on that diagram the words "Elm Street." Bootsie Gay later reconstructed the diagram for Jim Garrison. She drew a square, denoting a building. Inside a second square, she wrote "VIP," explaining that this square represented a vehicle. She had come forward, she explained, because she considered herself "a good citizen and a damn good and loyal American." David Ferrie, she now believed, "must have done something pretty evil."

As Bootsie Gay had left Gill's office that late November day, one of the secretaries imparted a word of advice. "Mrs. Gay, if I were you I wouldn't call Mr. Gill's house for a while. I'm sure his phones are tapped."

When I first read this passage, I knew I had to check Mellen's sources. She listed the Garrison memos mentioned above, and she also had a first-hand source. This was a letter that Bootsie Gay had written to F. Edward Hébert, a New Orleans congressman from 1941 to 1977. Mellen wrote that she found this letter in the Papers of Clara Flournoy Gay at the Tulane University Library in New Orleans.

The only problem was that we were in the midst of COVID-19 and most everything was shut down. I searched online and found that Tulane did not posses any of her papers. Mellen had made an error in her source—her letter was actually among the papers of F. Edward Hébert.

Fortunately, in April 2022, I visited New Orleans for a few days with my JFK buddies. On my first day, I went to Tulane University, where the relevant boxes from the Hébert papers were waiting for me.

She was clearly friends with Hébert, and there was a long series of correspondence between the two of them. She called him "Eddie" in her letters.

On April 22, 1963, Bootsie wrote Hébert a letter asking him to help David Ferrie in his attempt to get his job back from Eastern Airlines. She wrote that "He has been so good to me—he is a Saint on Earth." She added "Imagine trumped up charges that are lies brought on by a vicious emotional man." He wrote her back (addressing her as Bootsie), saying that "I am sure you realize that Eastern Air Lines is a private corporation and the matter of its hirings and firings is something which would not come under my jurisdiction as a member of Congress."

She also sent a note to Hébert saying that David Ferrie "Made two trips for me (I was without funds) paid his own expenses—did not charge for his time." She added that Ferrie "is a good man. He is honest."

Ferrie typed up two pages about his case with Eastern Airlines, and she included them with her letter to Hébert.

He replied on May 2, 1963, and said that "you know I would help you in any way I could," but he reiterated that Eastern Air Lines was a private company and that he could not interfere.

After the assassination, on December 29, 1963, Bootsie wrote a thirteen-page letter to Hébert. She told him that David Ferrie was "furious" after she told him that Hébert would not help. She left a note on his desk that read, "Talking religion is one thing but living it is another." She wrote that the stenographer in the office told her that Ferrie threw a fit when he read the note.

And then Bootsie read in the newspaper that Ferrie was being held for questioning by the FBI and the Secret Service:

but lo + behold a few weeks later I look in the paper—he had been arrested + the notice read the D.A.'s office was holding him for the F.B.I. + Secret Service. I nearly dropped my bridgework. I went to the phone +

before I could ask Alice Guidruz or the other lady who works for Gill "she asked me if I had heard about Dave Ferrie + I said I just saw paper."

Her reply was it was on T.V. + radio + their office was in a turmoil—+ I was furious that I had been not only introduced to him in their office but allowed to write you re him—I was told Mr. Gill knew nothing about him —it was all news to him. Now I have enough sense to know F.B.I. + Secret Service do not pick up people at random—There must have been smoke there—so I was called into the office where Mrs. Franchevich was packing all this man's personal papers etc—to send to him—he was told if he walked into the office all would walk out (the female help I mean) I told her she should turn over all his papers to the FBI or secret service (none of my business I guess) but I felt they should have let these men come to office + see if there was anything there of value to them—or whatever he was picked up for --

I have never found out why they wanted him. I knew better than to ask Gill so I asked Mr. Bernstein (his associate) what should I do—+ he said "Forget it" but I have found I can't + wish to get it out of my system. All I can say is please forgive me for any embarrassment I may have caused you but I swear on all that's Holy—I didn't mean to do anything but help someone—but never again.

There is nothing in her long letter about seeing a map on Ferrie's desk. Not a word. The story about Regina Franchevich picking up a chart is also not there. All she says is that Ferrie's personal papers should be turned over to the FBI or to the Secret Service.

An honest researcher would have noted that the contemporaneous record does not corroborate her later story about finding a map. Unfortunately, Joan Mellen knew this but decided not to tell her readers.

As for Thomas Beckham, well, he ended up embarrassing himself in his testimony before the HSCA:

Q: What is the extent of your formal education? In other words, did you graduate from high school?

    A: I went through the third grade.

    Q: Third grade. And where was that?

    A: That was Henry W. Allen.

Q: Henry W. Allen School?

A: Right. New Orleans, Louisiana.

Q: And you dropped out of school after the third grade?

A: That's right.

Q: Okay.

A: Of course, when you've spent three years in each grade, you're not that young when you drop out.

Beckham was then questioned about his university degrees:

Q: What degrees do you hold?

A: M.D. PhD, and—

Q: All right. Keep going.

A: A bunch of others. I hold a Maryland Medical License from the Maryland State Board of Medical Examiners.

Q: So then, you're a licensed physician for the State of Maryland?

A: That's right.

...

Q: What other degrees do you hold?

A: I hold an Ms.D., Doctor of Metaphysics.

Q: From where?

A: I hold—oh, boy, I don't know. There's so many on my wall, you'd have to take a look and see.

Q: Where are they hanging now, at your home?

A: Yeah. Medical degrees. United American Medical College, I even got one from there, which was based at Metairie, recently—if you are familiar with the man—which is also part of the Association. He has also Louisiana Association of Naturopathic Physicians.

Q: Are you a Naturopathic Physician?

A: I hold an M.D.J., right. I'm a member of the National Congress of Naturopathic Physicians, American Coordinated Medical Society, the Georgia Association of Naturopathic Physicians, Louisiana Association, Texas, Indiana, Kentucky.

He then told them he was an "ordained priest of about four different Catholic denominations." Everybody laughed when he told them he had "more degrees than a thermometer." At that point, the HSCA realized that Beckham was a complete fraud, and the questioning ended.

In 1969, Hébert, a staunch segregationist, published a bigoted poem by Bootsie Gay in the congressional record:

Oh! come to Louisiana.
Where corn and cotton grow.
And sugar cane stands proudly.
Against the man made row.

Oh! come to Louisiana.
Where pine trees touch the sky.
And willows line the bayou banks.
As pirogues pass them by.

Oh! come to Louisiana
Where magnolias caste a light.
On colored folk with banjos.
As they sing and dance all night.

Oh! let me live in Louisiana.
Until the day I die.
Then bury me on a hill top.
Beneath the Southern Sky.

Clara Flounoy Gay died in July 1980 at the age of seventy-two. Little did she know that she would be immortalized not for her poetry but by conspiracy theorists who believed her fanciful tale.

4

THE MAN WHO CHANNELED LEE HARVEY OSWALD

The Reverend Raymond Broshears, Raymond Broshears Papers,
1965–1984, courtesy of the Gay, Lesbian, Bisexual, Transgender
Historical Society.

R aymond Broshears was a fringe character in the Garrison saga who made up all sorts of stories about the assassination. For a while, he was taken seriously and was brought to New Orleans for questioning. Ultimately, Garrison's investigators figured out that he was a fabulist of the highest order, and he was sent back to California. In 1997, the Assassination Records Review Board (ARRB) released fifty-two pages from his Secret Service files that indicate that he was even crazier than we all thought.

It starts with Stan Bohrman, a newscaster for KPIX in San Francisco in the 1970s. He was controversial and brought a liberal voice to television. Before he worked at KPIX, he had a daytime talk show, Tempo II, on KHJ-TV in Los Angeles. His July 8, 1968, show was scheduled to feature the Reverend Elaine Chambers talking about psychic prophecies. Unfortunately, she could not make the show, and the Reverend Raymond Broshears and Jeff Mann, the "hippie minister" from Long Beach, were last-minute substitutes.

Reverend Broshears told Bohrman that he was a psychic and that he had a 97 percent success rate in his predictions. But Bohrman was prepared, and he confronted Broshears with his prediction that George Wallace would be elected president of the United States. Broshears objected, saying that he did not say that. Well, Bohrman asked, "Who said that?" Broshears replied, "The spirit said it."

Bohrman knew that Broshears had a bombshell allegation. In his monthly magazine, The Light of Understanding, Broshears claimed that he had channeled Lee Harvey Oswald at a séance. Bohrman read to the audience an excerpt of what Oswald had to say:

> I raised the rifle to aim at the target, and I suddenly realized that the target was the president of my country, my president. I couldn't go through with it. Then the motorcade came into sight. I dropped the rifle. I was wearing gloves, that accounts for the lack of fingerprints, and I started to run. And then Bill said, 'Shoot the so-and-so or you'll be shot.' I did not care. I just ran out of the book depository and then I knew that others had hit him. I ran, I ran for my life ...

Innocent

"I DID NOT KILL PRESIDENT JOHN F. KENNEDY."
by Lee Harvey Oswald, as taken from the
Akashic Records by the Right Reverend
Raymond Broshears, D.D. (Bishop Broshears
has spent time in New Orleans before the
"suicide" of David Ferrie, from the Spirit
World, Mr. Oswald has told Bishop Broshears
what really happened in Dallas, November 22.)

"I raised the rifle to aim at the target, and I
suddenly realized that the target was the President of my country, my president. I couldn't go
through with it. Then the motorcade came into
sight, I dropped the rifle, I was wearing
gloves, that accounts for the lack of finger-
prints, and started to run, then Bill said,
"shoot the ~~bastard~~ or you'll be shot", I did-
not care, I just ran out of the Book Depository, and I then knew that the others had hit

The Tragedy Of Our Time

him, I ran, I ran for my life, for that it
what it was. I knew they would be after me, so I thought I would wait
until dark, hide in a movie, yes, that's it in a movie, but then Tippett
spotted me, I had seen him at the meetings, he was one of us, he was going to kill me, I knew it, I tired to hide, but he seen me, I had to kill
him. But it was too late, for they were closing in all about me, the
police, and the "cell members", so I knew that my best chance was going
to jail and tell all. But then, that fat fool Jack, he knew all the
angles, he knew everyone, no one in the police paid him much attention,
and when I saw the guards parting, I knew that I had been "set up", for
they didn't want me to talk, Jack fired, it hurt for a second, then it
was over. But they think by killing me that it is over, that no one will
ever find out the truth, but they will. Remember, the gun dropped by me
in the Depository had not been fired, and the DPD and the FBI did not
even bother to check that part. But the guilty ones shall all be in the
light someday, Richard, Carlos, Kent, Terry, Clay, Bobby, Jerry, Don, and
you too Tom, someday you all shall be know. David told enough to enough
to "hang" you all.".........It was at this point contact with Oswald was
broken, but he said that he would return once more, of course we do not
know when. But I feel he has told enough now to erase many of the doubts
surrounding the entire affair.
One thing that was made clear, was that
"that man in New Orleans is a fool".

An excerpt from the May 1968 issue of Broshears's magazine, *The Light of Understanding*, Raymond Broshears Papers, 1965–1984, courtesy of the Gay, Lesbian, Bisexual, Transgender Historical Society.

Bohrman's skeptical tone annoyed Broshears who asked if he denied psychic phenomena:

No, I don't deny psychic phenomena, but I really don't think that you have talked to Lee Harvey Oswald. I really don't believe that you can prophesize correctly and knowledgeably all the things that you've said. I don't want to call you a charlatan because I have no basis in fact for calling you names. But I can't believe that you are telling the truth.

Bohrman went to the phones, and the first caller asked Broshears if he was ever a roommate with David Ferrie, which he confirmed. He also said that Ferrie admitted that he was involved in the assassination and that the assassins flew out of Dallas and crashed off Corpus Christi, Texas:

Broshears: No. The assassins crashed off Corpus Christi and were killed.

Bohrman: But who were the assassins? Who were the assassins if you know that they crashed off of the Corpus Christi?

Broshears: I'm not at liberty to say that.

Bohrman: But you know who they are?

Broshears: I am not at liberty to say that.

Bohrman: But you know who they are. You're not at liberty to say who they are, but you know who they are.

Broshears: I'm going to play Senator McCarthy, Joseph McCarthy. I take the Fifth Amendment.

Broshears told the audience that Ferrie was murdered:

Bohrman: So that David Ferrie was in fact involved with the-

Broshears: Yes, he was.

Bohrman: He was?

Broshears: Oh, there's no—yes, David admitted that, and he did not commit suicide.

Caller: He didn't?

Broshears: No.

Caller: Well, then what happened?

Broshears: He was murdered.

Bohrman: He was murdered?

Broshears: He was murdered.

Bohrman: So, Jim Garrison is correct in his analysis.

Broshears: Yes. Yes. But I'm not going to go like Mr. Garrison and say it was CIA because that's too far for me to believe.

David Ferrie wasn't murdered. On February 22, 1967, after a month of extremely poor health, he died of a berry aneurysm. Ferrie had a full forensic autopsy, and there was no doubt that he died of natural causes. In fact, the coroner found evidence of an earlier bleed. He was one of Garrison's prime suspects, and his death allowed Garrison to spin all sorts of tales—like perhaps that Ferrie had been a getaway pilot for the assassins.

So was Ferrie really associated with Broshears? Stay tuned.

The caller also asked Broshears if he had ever been arrested for threatening the life of President Johnson. Broshears was put on the spot and had to admit that, yes, he had once done so and had been arrested.

That same day, Broshears appeared at a meeting at the Los Altos Public Library, where he introduced the Rev. Robert Short, who talked about flying saucers. Short told the audience that aliens tune in to the people from Earth through the means of a resotron, a device that fits on the head and "translates earthlings' thoughts and language into super space intelligence."

So just who was Reverend Raymond Broshears?

Raymond Broshears was born as Earl Raymond Allen on February 14, 1935, in Centerville, Illinois. His mother remarried and changed his name when he was three years old. He completed the twelfth grade in Los Angeles, California, and he worked as a clown, a public relations man for an amusement company, an interior decorator, and an assistant manager of a restaurant in San Francisco. He claimed that he enlisted in the Navy in 1952, the Army in 1953 and 1954, and the Coast Guard in 1955. This sounds somewhat strange, but all we really know is that he was discharged from the Navy for medical reasons in 1955.

Eric Markowitz of *Newsweek* wrote that Broshears claimed he had received a "serious injury to the head causing what was then thought to be a minor brain dysfunction." A 1975 article in Broshears's own news-paper, *Crusader*, said that "He was beaten up in the Navy and injured in a fall and suffered brain damage, but it did not, according to VA officials, impair his thinking abilities."

In the late 1950s, Broshears supposedly graduated from Lee Bible College in Tennessee and then allegedly studied under Billy James Hargis, an anti-gay evangelical preacher. George Mendenall, a reporter for the *Bay Area Reporter*, wrote that Broshears was dropped by Hargis because of his homosexuality.

On November 10, 1964, Broshears was arrested by the Belleville Police Department in East St. Louis, Illinois, for contributing to the delinquency of a minor. A seventeen-year-old male stated that Broshears approached him on October 18, 1964, at a discount store to engage in "homosexual relations." Broshears told the police that a similar complaint was filed a year earlier, but he was not arrested. He also said that he had recently "been released from a hospital for homosexuals" and that he was "subject to epileptic fits." Broshears pleaded guilty and was sentenced to six months at the State Penal Farm at Vandalia.

On July 22, 1965, Broshears was admitted to a VA hospital in New Orleans. He was referred there by another VA clinic after he had taken an overdose of medication. A Secret Service report noted that Broshears was "said to be subject to seizures (form of epilepsy), for which he has allegedly been taking phenobarbital and dilantin."

On September 6, 1965, while confined to the psychiatric ward at the VA hospital, Broshears attempted to send a postcard to President Johnson. A nurse took it to the staff psychiatrist who censored all outgoing mail. He found the following notation:

"In recognition of theft, degrading of individual rights, and murder this certificate is awarded to Lyndon Baines Johnson by the Rev. Raymond C. Broshears at 1600 Pennsylvania Ave. Date September 8, 1965. Signed: Raymond Broshears High Avenger for President Kennedy".

The postcard also had a handwritten notation: "Mr. Johnson, you are to die at 3 p.m. E.D.T.!"

On September 13, 1965, Broshears was visited by Mr. Victor LeBeau, an attorney representing the Louisiana Civil Liberties Union. Broshears told him that he belonged to an organization known as NOW, which had thirty-five members, and "that the organization intended to work toward having President Johnson unseated by any means necessary including assassination."

Broshears also said that "the members of the organization feel that President Johnson had President Kennedy killed." He told LeBeau that one of the members of the group, Mac Bell, was an explosives expert and that "it would be possible for an individual with explosives attached to his body to kill the President if such individual would be willing to sacrifice his own life." LeBeau was so disturbed by Broshears's statements that he told the Secret Service that "he would make no attempt to have him [Broshears] released from the hospital on a writ."

Broshears also disclosed that he had a long-standing interest in the JFK assassination. A Secret Service report notes the following:

> Broshears stated that he and his associates in "NOW" think that President Johnson has intentions of becoming a dictator and that he "white washed" the killing of President Kennedy. He said they do not believe that Oswald killed President Kennedy and indicated that they had tested rifles similar to the one allegedly used by Oswald in the assassination of President Kennedy and had decided that several persons would have had to be involved in the shooting of President Kennedy.

On September 20, 1965, Dr. Richard Stone, chief of psychiatric services at the VA hospital in New Orleans, said that he considered Broshears "to be paranoid schizophrenic, and dangerous, with suicidal and homicidal tendencies." Stone also remarked that Broshears "had attacked other patients and also nursing assistants at the hospital; that he is a potential heckler and likes attention."

A week later, Broshears was diagnosed as "schizophrenic paranoid potentially dangerous to himself and others" and was committed to the New Orleans VA hospital. He was then transferred on October 25, 1965, to the VA hospital in Gulfport, Mississippi.

It was also noted in Broshears's file that he had a combat disability for "Schizophrenic Reaction, Paranoid Type," for which he received a 10 percent veteran's compensation of $20 per month.

The Secret Service records do not mention his sentence or when he was supposed to be released. Broshears told Stan Bohrman that he pleaded insanity. His lookout worksheet says that he was granted a weekend pass on January 7, 1966, and that he did not return.

```
                    L O O K O U T    W O R K S H E E T

NAME: BROSHEARS, Raymond aka Earl Raymond Allen Jr.        FILE NO:  CO-2-42,269    .

DESCRIPTION: W/M, dob: 2-14-35, 6', 180 hazel eyes,       DATE: 1-10-66            .
  brown hair, ruddy complexion, med. build, wears mustache &
  goatee.
LAST KNOW ADDRESS : VA Hospital, Biloxi, Mississippi & 411 N. 56th St., Centerville, Ill.

BRIEF FOR CARDS:    Attempted to send postcard to Pres. Johnson from hospital stating "Mr.
                    Johnson, you are going to die at 3 P.M., EDT.  Feels Johnson is respon-
                    sible for Kennedy's assassination.  Claims person could kill Pres. by
                    explosives strapped to self.  Has suicidal and homocidal tendecies.
                                      on 1-7-66
                    Was given weekend pass from hospital and has not returned.

(This brief will include a concise statement concerning the reason for our interest
any any information known of the subject's reputation for violence.)
WHP CONTROL CENTER TELEPHONED  : ( X ) Yes   ( ) No.

PREPARED BY: Relford W Jones          DATE: 1-10-66

CARDS PREPARED AND DISTRIBUTED BY                DATE: 1/10/66


APPROVED :
       SAIC OR ASAIC
```

Lookout Worksheet for Raymond Broshears.

It's not known exactly what happened next, but Broshears headed to California.

Broshears had to report to the Secret Service whenever he moved, and on January 5, 1968, Broshears told the them that he was relocating to Long Beach, California, from San Francisco. He also told them that he wished to be near Mexico because a friend of his had been indicted by Jim Garrison and that he was worried "of being called to testify inasmuch as he had made homosexual contacts in the past in New Orleans." Broshears was referring to Thomas Beckham, a con man we met in the previous chapter.

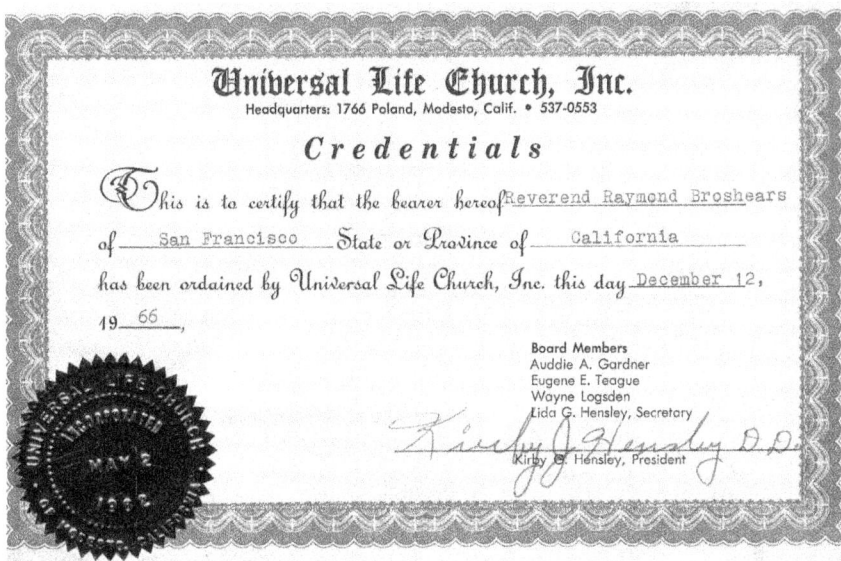

Universal Life Church, Inc.
Headquarters: 1766 Poland, Modesto, Calif. • 537-0553

Credentials

This is to certify that the bearer hereof Reverend Raymond Broshears

of ___San Francisco___ State or Province of ___California___

has been ordained by Universal Life Church, Inc. this day __December 12__,

19__66__,

Board Members
Auddie A. Gardner
Eugene E. Teague
Wayne Logsden
Lida G. Hensley, Secretary

Kirby J. Hensley D.D.
Kirby J. Hensley, President

Both Thomas Beckham and Raymond Broshears had credentials from the Universal Life Church. All you had to do was mail in an application, and they would send you your ordination papers, free of charge. Raymond Broshears Papers, 1965–1984, courtesy of the Gay, Lesbian, Bisexual, Transgender Historical Society.

On January 13, 1968, Broshears showed up at Secret Service offices in Los Angeles. He told them that he had moved from the San Francisco area because "they" were putting the "heat" on him. He said that people posing as FBI agents were trying to find him, but he knew they weren't real. He called the FBI, and they told him they were not trying to find him. He also told agents that "he knew that he was a 'lunatic' but meant no harm to anyone."

The Secret Service noted that "this mentally ill person is perhaps unique as he admits that he is mentally ill." Broshears said nothing to the Secret Service about David Ferrie and his knowledge of the JFK assassination.

Once in Long Beach, Broshears began to contact leftist groups at Long Beach State College. He aroused the suspicion of the managing editor of the student newspaper, David Snelling, who wrote a letter to Jim Garrison:

Broshear

LONG BEACH STATE COLLEGE

THE FORTY-NINER

Student Newspaper Published by the
Associated Students

California   Phone GEneral 4 8121

F U

February 22, 1968
Long Beach, California

Mr. James Garrison
U.S. District Attorney
New Orleans, Louisiana

Dear Sir;

I understand that you have information regarding
Rev. Raymond Broshears. He is also known as Rev. Ray,
Brother Ray, and Brother Broshears. Brother Ray confided in me that he was once a roommate of David Ferrie
and that he (Broshears) was indicted in your district
about three years ago in connection with a plot to ass-
asinate President Johnson.

Brother Ray has been attempting to gain favor with
the leftist groups on our campus at Cal-State Long Beach
and we would like to know who we are dealing with. Any
information you might have will be appreciated.

Sincerely Yours,

David P. Snelling
Managing Editor

Garrison gave this letter to Bill Turner, a former FBI man who was
helping his investigation and who was also writing for *Ramparts* magazine. Turner sent a memo to Steve Burton, a nineteen-year-old student
who was chairman of the LA-based Citizens Committee of Inquiry. He
told Burton that Broshears had called the *Berkeley Barb* several months
earlier and said he was being hounded by a Secret Service agent named
Newman. Broshears claimed there was a New Orleans group called
Action Now! comprising seven men who knew the facts of the assassination, or who were witnesses themselves, and that they were all dead.
Turner asked Burton to locate and interview Broshears.

Burton met with Snelling and with Dixon Gates, chairman of the
Department of Journalism at California State College at Long Beach. They
told him that Broshears confided that he had been a roommate of David
Ferrie's. Burton was also told that Broshears claimed he had lived in New

Orleans prior to 1965 and that he had an evangelical radio show. The two men said that Broshears had been trying to get in with groups like the Students for a Democratic Society (SDS), "although they have almost totally rejected him." Last, Broshears had claimed that Jim Garrison's men had been trying to find him for some time while posing as FBI agents.

Burton then called Broshears on the phone. Broshears said the reason he had moved to LA was because he had been harassed by Garrison. He wouldn't meet unless he was assured that Burton had no relationship with Garrison. Burton never informed Broshears that he was indeed working with Garrison.

On April 12, 1968, Burton interviewed Broshears, who told him the following:

- He was an intimate friend and roommate of David Ferrie's from late August 1965 until late 1966. Ferrie told him a lot about the JFK assassination.
- He said that he hated Jim Garrison because "Garrison murdered David [Ferrie]." Broshears claimed that Garrison's men were harassing Ferrie in 1965–1966 "because they had him pegged in an assassination plot." Garrison, he thought, drove Ferrie to suicide.
- Broshears admitted that he had been arrested for threatening President Johnson but said that when Johnson came to New Orleans in November 1965, he put himself in a hospital so that he would have an alibi.
- He eventually moved to San Francisco after New Orleans, and he was harassed by FBI agents. The local FBI office told him these men were Garrison's agents.
- Broshears claimed that Lee Harvey Oswald was a bisexual who had sex with David Ferrie. Ferrie told Broshears that Oswald was with the CIA.
- He said that the Minutemen, the John Birch Society, the CIA, and Lyndon Johnson were behind the assassination. Right after JFK was killed, a light plane with the assassins took off from an airport in Arlington, Texas, for Mexico City. It crashed at

Corpus Christi, killing the three people aboard. Another plane then took off from Austin.

Burton wrote Garrison and told him that "Broshears did not provide much information that was not already known, or that could not be easily found out." As Burton was leaving, Broshears said, "If you ever get serious about finding out who killed Kennedy, come back and see me. I can tell you who pulled the trigger."

Despite hearing some incredible fairy tales—for instance, that Lady Bird Johnson owned the Carousel Club (Jack Ruby's club in Dallas)—Burton concluded that "the mere fact that he knew of so many of the principal figures lends credence to his story, in my opinion."

In late April, Burton called Broshears and set up another interview. Broshears said that he just had a spiritual meeting at his home and that Lee Harvey Oswald spoke to the group in Russian "through Broshears' mouth." Broshears also informed Burton that his phone was about to be disconnected for failure to pay his bill.

The next day, Burton interviewed Broshears at his home. Broshears told him more details about the plot:

- Oswald did not fire a weapon on November 22. The gun with his palmprint was never used. Oswald was supposed to shoot JFK but chickened out. He was on the first floor of the TSBD when the shots were fired and ran out of the building. He met officer J. D. Tippit, who was supposed to kill Oswald but he killed Tippit instead. Then he went to the Texas Theater and phoned Jack Ruby.
- Oswald asked Ruby for help, and Ruby called the police. Ruby, Tippit, and three other police officers were involved. There were twenty-five officers in front of Ruby in the basement of the police department, and the whole line opened for Ruby as he walked down the ramp. While in jail, he was injected with live cancer cells. Ruby was in on a second plot to kill JFK if the first one failed.
- One hundred people were involved in the assassination. There were supposed to be three shooters, but Oswald chickened

out. One shooter fired from the sewer opening, and the other
from the grassy knoll.

- Two of the gunmen were killed at Corpus Christi. They had
planned to go to Houston, where David Ferrie would fly them
to Mexico and end up in South Africa.

Burton asked Broshears about Oswald and his work for the CIA.
He denied telling Burton any such thing and believed that he had
already said too much. Burton concluded that Broshears "knows
nothing and wants to feel important" and realized that a lot of things
he told him were "inconsistent with what he knows to be true." But
Burton was still impressed enough with Broshears to want to move
forward.

And then Broshears went on the Stan Bohrman show. The caller who
asked about David Ferrie was Steve Jaffe, another part-time staffer for
Jim Garrison. Burton called a few of his friends who worked at the KHJ
radio newsroom, and they reported back that Broshears said he was
planning to leave town.

Burton recommended that Broshears be subpoenaed immediately,
and he sent a tape recording of the Bohrman television show to Garrison's office. Jaffe then phoned Broshears, who told him that the séance
was a cover story designed to get out the news about the JFK assassination and for him to appear crazy and thus be out of danger.

On July 27, 1968, Mark Lane and Steve Jaffe visited Broshears at his
home. Broshears told them that Ferrie said that his job was to fly two of
the assassins out of the country from Houston. He was to fly to Central
or South America and then to Cape Town, South Africa. The assassins
never showed up. They were supposed to come to Houston in a small
aircraft, but they tried to make it over the Mexican border, and their
plane crashed and burned just off Corpus Christi. One of the assassins
was named Carlos.

Broshears said that "some people had been killed as a result of what
they knew about the assassination" and that if Robert Kennedy or
Jacqueline Kennedy ever spoke about the assassination, they would also
be killed.

In talking about Oswald, Broshears said that Ferrie had told him that "they murdered one of the best lays I've ever had. He didn't have anything to do with killing President Kennedy. He was set up."

As a result of his appearance on the Bohrman show, Broshears claimed he was told by a Secret Service agent that he would lose his pension if he appeared on another such television show. Another agent told him he would "end up in Alameda Bay" if he did not keep his mouth shut.

Broshears then gave Mark Lane a letter that requested Lane visit and consult with him if he were ever taken into custody or placed in an institution.

Church of God of Light

"A LIGHTHOUSE OF TRUTH"

LONG BEACH, CALIFORNIA

July 27, 1968

To:Mr. Mark Lane
    617 Dauphine Street
    New Orleans, La.

From:Rev. Raymond Broshears
     725 Orange Avenue
     Long Beach, CA 90813

     P.O. Box 1027
     Long Beach, CA 90301

Re:Visitation

        Sir;

        Should I at anytime become ill or I am jailed for any reason, at whatever location, I sincerely request that you, and your designated representative, please come to visit me, no matter how critical the illness or serious the situation,

                                        Reverend Raymond Broshears

Steve Jaffe re-interviewed Broshears on August 2, 1968. Jaffe showed him a photograph of Clay Shaw, and Broshears said he had known him in New Orleans and had met him in the company of David Ferrie in late August or early September of 1965. Ferrie introduced Shaw as "Clara," "Burt," or "Clay." Once, on the way to a restaurant, Shaw told Broshears that he liked "little boys," and Broshears told him to "go find one." Shaw then patted him on the rear. Broshears "rebuked" Shaw for this and told Shaw to cut it out. Shaw patted him once again at the restaurant, and Broshears slapped him.

Broshears said that he was with Shaw on two other occasions, including a time when Shaw drove up and handed Ferrie a large envelope. Shaw asked Broshears if he would fly south with him to avoid trouble with the government.

Jaffe also asked Broshears about the assassination, and now Broshears said there had been two assassins behind the fence. He also said there was a person by the name of "Bill" who worked in the TSBD and that he might have been one of the assassins firing from the rear.

Jaffe had heard enough in these interviews to write an article for the *LA Free Press*, a weekly counter-culture newspaper:

JFK ASSASSINATION
Broshears: Ferrie was involved

Headline from August 9, 1968, edition of the *LA Free Press*.

Jaffe repeated Broshears's story of the assassins flying out of Dallas and crashing off Corpus Christi and how David Ferrie had been murdered. Jaffe wrote that Broshears's admissions "have earned nothing but total torture and harassment for him ever since the television program." According to Jaffe, Broshears was evicted by his landlady, and he received anonymous phone calls asking him "how many presidents did you kill today, Reverend?" Jaffe concluded that "Broshears only fault or sin seems to be his persistent honesty."

It was now time to bring the good Reverend to New Orleans for questioning, and Raymond Broshears was subpoenaed. He was questioned twice in New Orleans, and he didn't shy away from telling Garrison's investigators all sorts of stories. Large parts of the interviews were just streams of consciousness—they just let Broshears talk away. Here are just a few of the many stories he told them:

- Jack Ruby was a "fat clown from Dallas, and he's a faggot, and he likes to eat pussy." He told Garrison that "a lot of them like to get it in the rear, while eating the pussy."
- Tippit, Oswald, and Ruby were in the same "cell." Three TSBD workers were part of the cell, which Oswald infiltrated for the FBI.
- Ferrie told Broshears that Oswald shot and killed Tippit. Garrison wrote in the margin of the write-up of the interview that this is "possible misinformation originating from Ferrie— but misinformation, in any case."
- Ferrie claimed that Clay Shaw "wanted to preserve the Anglo-Saxon Protestant White area and race, and that included his doing away with all black people."
- Clay Shaw had some pictures or film of a sixteen-year-old boy with Ferrie and was blackmailing him. This is interesting because Oliver Stone included this in his film *JFK*. Broshears also said that if they could find this film, they could break the case.
- Ferrie had some of Oswald's possessions, such as a hunter's cap with the initials LH. Ferrie said that these possessions were the only things keeping him alive.
- Broshears said that he met Kerry Thornley, who briefly served with Oswald in the Marines, in a gay bar and that he was gay. Broshears told Garrison's investigators that it was Thornley's body in the infamous Oswald backyard photographs. How did Thornley know? He told them that "Well, I had sex with Thornley, and I know his slender hips."

Here is one of the three backyard photographs of Lee Harvey
Oswald. Broshears told Garrison that the body is that of Kerry
Thornley, and Garrison wrote a memo about this for the HSCA.
Broshears told researcher Hal Verb that David Ferrie had the
original photograph with Thornley in the picture.

Thornley eventually heard about this and wrote a friend who was in
touch with Broshears:

🗐 NO HURRY

Dear FAB:

I understand you are or will be in contact with the Rev. Broshears.

As you probably know, this is the character who was going around saying
I posed for the body on the LIFE Magazine cover pix of Oswald & was also
claiming to know me in New Orleans.

If you ever get a chance I would like you to sound him out on this, asking
him questions as if you don't know me just to establish to your own satisfaction that he doesn't know what he is talking about -- and then try
to find out what his angle is. Publicity? Bread? Immunity?

PLEASE DON'T TRY + CONVERT HIM;
HE IS FAR MORE VALUABLE ON THE   EWIGE BLUMENKRAFT
OTHER SIDE AS A HOSTILE WITNESS.

1970 letter from Kerry Thornley to Louise Lacey. Thornley had been indicted by
Jim Garrison on a baseless perjury charge, which is why his handwritten notation
refers to Broshears as a potential hostile witness. Letter courtesy of Adam
Gorightly and the Discordian Archives.

Lacey replied with a choice paragraph about Broshears:

Yes, I've been in contact with Rev. Broshears. What a mind-cracking experience.
Jamison told me he had a MWO unit, so I called him, left a message to call Lady
L. (Fortunately.) He called back and gave me 30 minutes of tortured insanity
about his fear (the cops were going to bust him because he had the MWO machine,
though it was hidden in the back of a closet. It's against the law, it's against
the law and I don't break the law, he kept telling me.), his anti-communist
activities, etc. His head is so messed up that I can't think of a better hostile
witness you could have. I didn't sound him out on you, because there was no chance
to talk with him again; he immediately wrote Jamison about the communist Lady L
who had to be destroyed — although I said nothing during the conversation, just
goaded him a bit, laughing hysterically, though silently, all the time. I have
without a doubt established to my own satisfaction that he doesn't know what he is
talking about. His angle is mental illness.

August 1970 letter from Louise Lacey to Kerry Thornley. Her reference to a
"MWO unit" refers to a multiple wave oscillator, a device developed by Russian
scientist Georges Lakhovsky, who claimed it could cure diseases. Letter courtesy
of Adam Gorightly and the Discordian Archives.

I don't think it took Garrison investigators long to determine that
Broshears was worthless as a witness. JFK conspiracy theorist Harold
Weisberg wrote another researcher about the fun time that Broshears had
while in New Orleans:

He chased young boys through New Orleans, created a scene at
Barbara Reid's when he wanted to bring one in, got himself arrested in his
cavortings only to proclaim immunity because he was Garrison's star witness,
was finally eased out of town and went back east to announce he had given
14 hours of the most important testimony, and awarded almost everyone in the
office an honorary bishopric! Believe <u>him</u>?

When Broshears returned to Los Angeles, he was once again a guest
on the Stan Bohrman show. Bohrman asked him why he had said
nothing about knowing Clay Shaw on his first appearance. He replied
that at the time he did not trust Garrison and did not want to get
involved in the investigation. Broshears also claimed that he had asked
Bohrman not to ask him about Shaw because he did not want anyone to
know that he had met Shaw.

Broshears also wrote about his New Orleans experience in his church
newsletter:

the **LIGHT**
of Understanding

AUGUST 1968   SPECIAL # 11   VOL. 2

JIM GARRISON
A VOICE FOR TRUTH

Jim Garrison

Jim Garrison, District Attorney of New Orleans is leading fight for JUSTICE in a "fear-ridden" land. He is as John the Baptist, a voice crying in the wilderness, calling to the American conscience to awaken before it is too late. A President has been murdered, a U.S. Senator, and Civil Rights Leader have also been murdered, and the general American Public sets back and lets it all go by without blinking an eye. Mr. Garrison and his assistant James Alcock, and Andy Sciambra are all working to bring to light the most vile plot against America by "so-called" American patriots. CIA moves rapidly to impede progress case as does FBI and Secret Service. The INVISIBLE GOVERNMENT scores once more. Are you going to stand by and see "chains applied to you" and do nothing? Write your Congressman, take action (non-violent), do not let your freedom die without having at least raised your voice. For his actions, the ESTABLISHMENT PRESS, has called Garrison every known evil thing there is. The PRESS is the EVIL ONE. For they do the bidding of the CIA. Inside is a view of New Orleans and Mr. Garrison by Rev. Raymond Broshears of Long Beach, California. He has witnessed first hand the intrigue and dangers that go with telling the truth. SUPPORT TRUTH. SUPPORT JIM GARRISON. SUPPORT FREEDOM. SUPPORT JIM G.

Now Broshears had seen the light and wrote that Garrison "was not the bad boogie man he has been portrayed to be." He also wrote that he had run into some "old flames who didn't seem too pleased to see me." Interestingly, what shocked Broshears the most was that "the government had removed all trace of my having ever being [sic] in that city. But they 'slipped' up, and a couple of cards were found in various agencies, that gave light to the fact that I was indeed in Orleans and that I had indeed been involved in the 'underground' there."

In late September, Broshears and Jaffe spoke at a meeting of the Long Beach Town Hall on the JFK assassination. Jaffe told the audience about the 36–38 witnesses who have died or been killed under "mysterious circumstances." Television host Stan Bohrman also spoke and told the crowd that he had just left his job in a protest against censorship.

In December, in an interview with the *Berkeley Barb*, Broshears now claimed his life was at risk:

EXCLUSIVE DEC. 13-19 BERKELEY BARB
LIFE AT STAKE

He said that he was hiding "for his life" in the Bay Area because a man that Garrison was investigating threatened him. Broshears claimed that this man was connected with the CIA and that this "agent" warned that "none of the witnesses [in the Garrison investigation] will live to come to trial." Broshears also claimed that Garrison would be assassinated by two "Spanish gentlemen" sent to New Orleans to kill him.

The trial of Clay Shaw started in early February 1969. Raymond Broshears was not called to testify for the prosecution.

In March 1969, Broshears met FBI Special Agent Irving Dean to discuss a matter about a military deserter. Dean then went on a road trip, and when he returned found that Broshears had called him. He called him back twice but could not get Broshears. Two days later, Broshears called him and wanted to know why his phone calls had not been returned. Dean explained that he had been out of town and asked Broshears what he wanted to talk about. Broshears told him, "If that's the way you feel, forget it," and hung up.

Broshears then wrote to the FBI complaining that an agent was "uncooperative and rude." He was invited to discuss the matter in person but said this would solve nothing "since Special Agents of the FBI were rude." They gave him the address of HQ in Washington to address a complaint.

The FBI report noted the following about Broshears:

> During the course of another investigation, in August, 1968, it was determined that BROSHEARS has received treatment at the following Veteran Administration Hospitals: St. Louis and Jefferson Barracks, Missouri; Gulfport and Biloxi, Mississippi; Topeka, Kansas; New Orleans, Louisiana; Los Angeles, California; Palo Alto, California and Long Beach, California. Hospital records at Palo Alto reflected that all hospitals treating BROSHEARS had diagnosed him as a schizophrenic reaction, paranoid, incompetent. He is described as having a history of fraudulent enlistments in the military - manipulative behavior - difficulty with authority, assaultiveness, suicidal attempts, strong and poorly controlled hostility, guilty and anxiety, homosexuality, chronic brain syndrome associated with convulsive disorder, probably secondary brain trauma.

Broshears did write to Hoover:

Orthodox

EPISCOPAL CHURCH of GOD

Rectory-office: 811 Geary St. #21(
San Francisco, CA 94109

Church of God
P. O. Box 1523
San Francisco
California 94101

April 9, 1969

Director
Federal Bureau of Investigation
9th & Pennsylvannia Avenues
Washington, District of Columbia 20535

30 APR 14 1969

Sir;

    This letter is in regards to a complaint about the "lack of co-operation", and the "rude manners" of Special Agent Dean of your San Francisco Office.

    I have many times in the past co-operated with the Bureau regarding U.S. Service personnel (desertions), and have most willing to help. But, this man Dean, I seriously wonder if he is doing your Bureau any real good by his lack of co-operation and rude speaking, for after all, we receive such manners from people within groups such as Progressive Labor, SDS, TWLF, etc., as we have from Mr. Dean.

    In the program which we have in the "central area" of San Francisco, we oft times have to deal with Service personnel, and have been in the past of assistance we feel to the Bureau, and have asked nothing in return. But, by asking your men to be of civil-tongue is too much?

    Recently a man who was "gone" from the service for nine months, whom we talked into returning after receiving certain assurances which were never lived up to, your Bureau was unable to find in your "locator" that the man was even a deserter, even tho we gave the Bureau the Service number and the ship from which he had deserted. This is poor work, or at least I would never permit such work in the Church.

    In trying to relate to Mr. Dean recently, a Progressive Labor Party projected program that is designed to undermine our country through it's servicemen, Mr. Dean was most rude. Now, the "G.I. COFFEE HOUSE" is open, called the Cabaret, at 260 Valencia Street. Had Mr. Dean been willing to listen perhaps they would have never been able to open.

    In closing, I wish to say, that all of our ministers currently co-operating in the Street-Night Ministry Program are still most willing to help should we be able, your Bureau at any time that we can.

MCT-36   62-112857

In Understanding, I am

Raymond Broshears, D.D.
Evangelist and Director
Street Ministry Program, SF area

ENCLOSURE

Broshears then formed the Helping Hands Community Center, which helped youth in the Tenderloin, a district with a lot of seedy bars, gay hustlers, drag queens, and transsexuals. He also started the San Francisco chapter of the Gay Activists Alliance, which organized "brunches and other activities to aid the Tenderloin's large population of indigent elderly."

In June 1972, Broshears organized San Francisco's first gay pride parade. About fifteen thousand people attended, but Broshears was involved in an ugly incident with some lesbians. One woman carried a sign that said, "Off Prick Power," and Broshears tried to take the sign away, thinking it was obscene. It all turned into a big brouhaha, and Broshears was no longer to be involved in San Francisco gay pride parades.

Gay sunshine in San Francisco

Reverend attacks lesbians

Headline in the *LA Free Press* on July 7, 1972.

In March 1973, Broshears called the FBI with another one of his complaints:

```
                                          3/8/73


AIRTEL                    AIR MAIL - REGISTERED


TO:      ACTING DIRECTOR, FBI (62-112857)
FROM:    SAC, SAN FRANCISCO (100-66706)
SUBJECT: REVEREND RAYMOND BROSHEARS
         INFORMATION CONCERNING


         A telephonic complaint was received 3/8/73 from
captioned Subject who said he represented the Gay Alliance
in San Francisco. His remarks were directed toward
newspaper accounts on 3/7/73 of Acting Director GRAY'S
testimony, specifically concerning support of Sheriff
HONGISTO (San Francisco County) by gay activists. BROSHEARS
was most uncomplimentary and abusive in his comments. He
demanded a copy of this report or an official release by
this office as to whether we were investigating homosexuals.
He became paranoiac by insinuating that the Federal Govern-
ment intended to arrest and shoot all homosexuals. He
rambled on about LEE HARVEY OSWALD, SIRHAN SIRHAN, and a
host of others who had been described as homosexuals. When
he was repeatedly advised that we would have no comment,
he finally asked what would coerce a release by this office,
a demonstration? He promised to organize a group demonstration
Monday, 3/12/73, in front of the Federal Building, 450 Golden
Gate Avenue, San Francisco. True to his part tendencies to
seek publicity, he requested that we bring cameras and lots
of film. No time was specified for this demonstration.
```

In July 1973, Broshears held a press conference and announced the creation of the Lavender Panthers, a vigilante organization to help patrol the Tenderloin, the same area that housed his Helping Hands outreach center. Gangs had been beating up gay people, and Broshears decided to take matters into his own hands.

Gay Vigilantes to Fight Back

Headline in the *San Francisco Examiner*, July 7, 1973

Broshears urged gay people to carry aerosol cans of red paint to spray on attackers. "Of course, the assailant will lose his eyesight, but he will remember he attacked a lavender person."

The Lavender Panthers lasted until the spring of 1974. A few teenagers were beaten by some Panthers, and many people complained to the police. They told Broshears that he had to pack it in, and on May 22, 1974, he disbanded the group.

Broshears's paranoia was still on the rise. Markowitz quoted one of his close fiends who said Broshears thought the CIA and the FBI were poisoning him.

In 1975, JFK conspiracy theorist Dick Russell interviewed Broshears, who insisted that he would refuse to testify before Congress. I guess he changed his mind, because on May 18, 1977, two investigators from the HSCA interviewed Broshears at his home. Now Broshears told them that he had met David Ferrie in 1961 1962, 1963, or 1965, and that he had talked to Ferrie on the phone in 1967.

But he also had a bombshell that he hadn't even told to Jim Garrison.

Broshears now claimed that he had met Lee Harvey Oswald at the home of David Ferrie. And he believed that he also saw Oswald at the offices of Guy Banister, a former FBI man who ran a detective agency in the early 1960s in New Orleans. Broshears said Oswald was a "nice looking young man" who was nervous and sweated profusely. He was also quiet and didn't say much.

Broshears had much to say to the HSCA:

- He now said that he had never met Clay Shaw, despite telling Garrison's investigators that he had met Shaw three times.

- David Ferrie told him that his life was in danger. Someone Ferrie had once worked for wanted him dead; Garrison wanted to kill him, as did the FBI.
- When Broshears was in New Orleans in 1968 to be interviewed, his hotel room was ransacked, and two bullets were fired through the window. Broshears then called James Alcock, Garrison's second in command, who hid Broshears in two separate places and then got him out of New Orleans safely.
- After the attack, Broshears decided not to tell Garrison's investigators anything because he was scared, although his two interview transcripts are each twenty pages single-spaced.
- Lou Sciambra, an assistant district attorney for Garrison, worked for the CIA and had David Ferrie killed. But there was no Lou Sciambra—this was a mashup of Garrison's chief investigator, Lou Ivon, and Andrew Sciambra, an assistant district attorney.
- David Ferrie never had an autopsy.
- Ferrie told the details about the assassination to four people: Broshears, Garrison, a woman, and a minister with the Old Catholic Church.
- One of the people involved in the assassination was named Garcia, who was Cuban.

It was clear to HSCA investigators that Raymond Broshears was just not believable. You will not find his name in their final report nor in any of their volumes of evidence.

On January 10, 1982, Raymond Broshears suffered a cerebral stroke and died in his apartment.

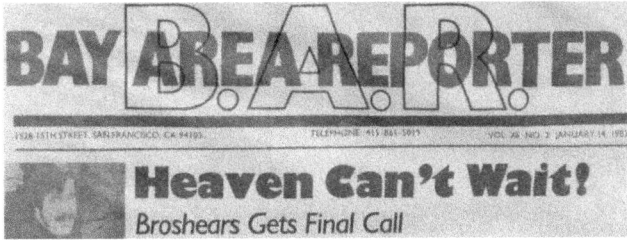

Front page of the *Bay Area Reporter* for January 14, 1982.

The *Bay Area Reporter* quoted a variety of people who had known or worked with Raymond Broshears. Ben Gardiner, president of Stonewall Democrats, said "He did some good things—but the bad more than canceled them out. I am glad he is dead. It is safer now." Randy Johnson, an activist friend, said "He did ten things, and maybe nine were rotten—but one was good. He meant well. He did all the right things in the wrong way. There are better ways of dealing with people you do not like." And Elliott Blackstone, a former police officer and friend, said "Ray loved people, but he didn't know how to say that. I could never understand his bitterness."

You would think that the Raymond Broshears's association with the JFK assassination would have ended with his death. What serious researcher could believe his ridiculous stories? But that is not the case— Broshears is mentioned in at least seventeen JFK conspiracy books as a witness that proves Clay Shaw knew David Ferrie.

Jim Garrison wrote a full two pages about Broshears in his 1988 book *On the Trail of the Assassins*:

> Broshears saw Ferrie and Shaw together another time on the corner of Dauphine Street and another French Quarter cross-street that Broshears could not remember. Ferrie brought him to the corner and indicated that they were waiting for Shaw to come by. Shaw drove up, again in an imposing black car, and handed Ferrie a large brown envelope. Then, glancing in Broshears' direction, Shaw informed Ferrie that the F.B.I. was looking for Broshears. After Shaw drove off, Ferrie opened the envelope, which contained cash, and gave Broshears some of the money inside.

Joan Mellen, in her book *A Farewell to Justice*, mentions Broshears a total of thirteen times.

> Lee Harvey Oswald and David Ferrie figured prominently in Shaw's sexual pursuits. The Reverend Raymond Broshears of the Universal Life Church told Jim Garrison that one day Ferrie introduced Shaw to him as "Clara" at Dixie's Bar of Music. Ferrie had confided that Oswald did not kill President Kennedy. His own assignment had been to fly two of the assassins from "south of Houston on down through Central and South America." Shaw was close to Kent Courtney, Ferrie had told him, corroborating other witnesses. Shaw knew arms dealer, Richard Lauchli. Ferrie had also introduced Broshears to Kerry Thornley, with whom Broshears had sex. "I had sex with Thornley, and I know his slender hips," Broshears bragged.

James DiEugenio, in his book *Destiny Betrayed*, lists Broshears as one of his witnesses who saw Shaw and Ferrie together: "Raymond Broshears who had a drink with Shaw and Ferrie, and later joined them for dinner."

Crossfire, the book by Jim Marrs that helped form the basis of Oliver Stone's film *JFK*, also mentions Broshears:

> Raymond Broshears, a longtime friend of Ferrie's, had seen Ferrie and Shaw together on several occasions. Furthermore, Broshears told Garrison how Ferrie once became intoxicated and detailed how he had driven to Houston the day of Kennedy's death to meet two members of the assassination team from Dallas. The pair was to have arrived in Houston in an airplane piloted by one of them, a Cuban exile known only as "Carlos." Ferrie was to have taken Carlos and his fellow assassin out of Houston. Ferrie told Broshears that something had gone wrong. The two men never showed up.

Dick Russell, author of *The Man Who Knew Too Much*, went to San Francisco to interview Broshears, who was extremely happy to tell him all sorts of stories. One of the assassins was named Garcia, whereas Broshears had previously said one was Carlos. And then there was this whopper:

What did Ferrie tell you about Oswald? I asked. Another pause. "Oh, lots of things, some of it very personal. But he certainly knew Lee Harvey Oswald when he was chicken [a gay phrase that means a teenage boy.] And knew him later. I myself met a person who was introduced to me as Leon Oswald. A very fleeting passing meeting, I had sex with him. He looked a helluva lot like him, but it's highly unlikely this was the same Lee Oswald.

The notion that there was another Oswald, named Leon Oswald, was also picked up by James DiEugenio in *Destiny Betrayed*:

Richard Case Nagell [whom you will soon meet in Chapter Seven] also said he knew a Leon Oswald in that summer of 1963. Nagell said that this Leon Oswald was meant as a Second Oswald and was working with the anti-Castro Cubans, he was not at all pro-Castro. Raymond Broshears, a friend of Ferrie's, also spoke about a Leon Oswald. He described him as resembling Oswald.

And in Oliver Stone's film *JFK*, Kevin Bacon played Willie O'Keefe, a gay prostitute who attended a JFK assassination planning session. Stone based this character on four people, one of whom was Raymond Broshears, because he believed Broshears had met Clay Shaw through David Ferrie.

Jeffrey Caulfield's 2015 book, *General Walker and the Murder of President Kennedy*, takes the cake. He included nine pages on Raymond Broshears and bought about every single story the good Reverend told.

So did Raymond Broshears know David Ferrie? Was he really David Ferrie's roommate?

He said he came to New Orleans in July 1965. But he told the Secret Service that he attended an event in St. Louis on July 18, and we know that he was in a New Orleans VA hospital on July 22. Broshears said he met Ferrie in August of 1965 and that they were roommates, but he never specified when. He didn't leave the VA hospital until early 1966, and then he moved to California.

Broshears also told Garrison that he had never been in Ferrie's apartment, but then he told the HSCA that he had been in Ferrie's apartment on two occasions—in 1963 when he met Lee Harvey Oswald and in 1965 when he had a conversation with Ferrie.

To make it all even more confusing, when JFK conspiracy theorist Dick Russell interviewed Broshears in 1975, he asked him if he had roomed with Ferrie in 1963. And Broshears answered, "On and off, yes."

Researcher Stephen Roy, author of an unpublished biography of David Ferrie, phoned Broshears in the late 1970s and noted that Broshears did not know the layout of Ferrie's apartment:

> In connection with my Ferrie biography, Broshears was one of the first persons I contacted in the late 70s by telephone. Some of the things he said initially seemed in conflict with other documented information (example: that Ferrie flew for Eastern Air Lines when Broshears roomed with him in the 1965 period), so I decided to slip in a few "test questions". I made a reference to the layout of Ferrie's apartment, and he replied with incorrect information. I asked a follow-up, and he avoided answering. I pressed a bit harder, and he again seemed completely unfamiliar with Ferrie's apartment ("When you came up the back stairs, the door opened into the kitchen, wasn't it?" "Yeah, the kitchen."). I then pressed a bit about the general layout of streets in the neighborhood and New Orleans, and he seemed completely unfamiliar with the city. I came away from the call thinking he had never even been to New Orleans.
>
> In subsequent interviews with acknowledged friends of Ferrie, I could find nobody who even recalled him.
>
> This feeling was strengthened when the HSCA and other interviews with Broshears became available in the early 90s. I think it is very unlikely that Broshears was ever Ferrie's roommate.

How could anybody take Broshears seriously as a witness?

I went back and asked Steve Jaffe, the man who insisted that Broshears be brought to New Orleans for questioning, what he now thought about the Reverend's credibility:

Broshears was, in my opinion, a credible witness but other than having lived with Ferrie and seen and heard things that were about what preceded the assassination, I don't know how much of what he had to offer was of material significance.

Raymond Broshears deserves his place in gay and lesbian history. Unfortunately, Reverend Ray will be increasingly known for his loopy statements on the JFK assassination. Even so, I am sure he'd be delighted that he's finally getting the attention he felt he deserved.

5

HE COULD HAVE BEEN A CONTENDER

A rthur Strout almost made the big time. He was just a twenty-six-year-old dishwasher in Boston, but he had dreams of being right in the center of Jim Garrison's JFK investigation.

In March of 1967, he told the *Boston Traveler* that he had met Lee Harvey Oswald and Jack Ruby on four occasions in the Carousel (Ruby's club) about one month before the JFK assassination. He also had knowledge of a photograph "taken in the nightclub, which showed me sitting with Oswald, Ruby, Russo and two other men." He was referring to Perry Russo, Garrison's star witness.

Strout claimed that in February of 1966, he was visiting his sister in Amarillo, Texas, and that he went to a pawnshop with David Ferrie, who then sold the pawnshop a .22 pistol that was used as a decoy in the assassination. He then contacted the Garrison investigation and told them that he had "explosive information" about the assassination.

Here is an excerpt from a March 13, 1967, phone call between Strout and Garrison investigator Lynn Loisel:

> **Strout**: I can tell you a few things about Mr. Russo himself. I can also tell you about Mr. Bertram, Clay Shaw, whatever want to call him.
>
> **Loisel**: You know him? You know him when you see him?

Strout: I know him personally.

Loisel: You know for a fact that he and Ferrie knew each other? You know that for sure?

Strout: Yes, I do.

Loisel: You know Ferrie himself?

Strout: Yes, I do.

Loisel: All right. Wait. You say you pawned one of the cross rifle guns?

Strout: One of the cross pistol guns.

Loisel: It was a pistol used?

Strout: Right. That was a cross fire gun. That was to draw attention.

Loisel: Where was that pawned at, you said?

Strout: Huh?

Loisel: Where was that pawned at?

Strout: I don't know the name of the place. I can show you the place. Like I told the detective tonight, the FBI from here in Boston, I can show you the place. I can't remember the name of it. It was on Amarillo Boulevard, Route 66 or whatever it usually was called. But Amarillo Boulevard. My sister was living out there. They're still living out there. He's overseas right now in Guam. And he took me down when pawned the gun.

Loisel: All right. Now, were you in the room when they talked about killing the man?

Strout: When they talked about the assassination itself?

Loisel: Right.

Strout: Yes, I was. I was there.

So Strout was there when they discussed the assassination, and he knew Clay Shaw, Perry Russo, and David Ferrie.

But Lynn Loisel was not going to be fooled and so asked some pertinent questions:

Loisel: All right. Let me ask you this. Do you know where Shaw lives? Have you ever been to his house?

Strout: Like I told the detective tonight, yes. I've been there twice.

Loisel: All right.

Strout: Ask him does he still got the yellow tablecloth on the table. I know all about it.

Loisel: All right. Can you name one or two other friends of Shaw's that you know that maybe we don't know?

Strout: I can name them. I can name them, but like I told the detective tonight, I can name a couple other people that's involved in it. I can also disrupt Mr. Russo's testimony, what he's saying, because what he's saying is on the wrong line of what you're believing. Now, he's supposed to be your witness, okay. But I also told when I called up two months ago, I told them about Mr. Russo. I knew Mr. Russo. Mr. Russo is not what you're thinking he is. He's your informant, your witness. He ain't. I know and I'll verify it right in the court. I'll come right down there in the court and I'll verify it.

Loisel: We need people like you.

They need people like Strout? The only thing he knew about Clay Shaw was that he had a yellow tablecloth.

Strout continues with his nonsense:

Strout: Now, look, I know where the gun is pawned. I can take you there. I also know that Mr. Russo is not ... He might be an informant on your side. I know that Clay Bertram is associated with him. I know that Mr. Ferris was. I know that Leon Oswald was. I know that Mr. Russo was. And Mr. Russo was in with it. So, whatever you want to say, I'll say something. I'm willing to come right there right now. All you got to do is call the FBI here in Boston, and they said they'd be willing to get me down there. I'll go ahead in the court with you, and I'll testify against him. He can't say nothing against me because he knows that I know.

Loisel: All right. Let me ask you this. How many guns were used in the assassination? Do you know?

Strout: All together?

Loisel: Yeah, all together.

Strout: There was three of them.

Loisel: There were three guns.

Strout: I got one of them.

Loisel: You have one of them?

Strout: I got one of them.

Loisel: Is that the one that's pawned?

Strout: Right.

Loisel: Uh-huh. All right. Let me ask you this. Did Ruby know Oswald?

Strout: Jack Ruby?

Loisel: Yeah.

Strout: Yes.

Loisel: He knew him.

Strout: It was me and Ruby and Leon Oswald and Mr. Shaw were all together down in Dallas down at Ruby's nightclub down there when we was down there. That's the first time I ever met him. I didn't have no money. Now, I hate to explain it this way over the phone now because it's not right. Like I told the FBI just now, it ain't right. But it was … how do I say it? I don't know. Queer situation.

Loisel: Right, that's right.

Strout: I didn't have no money. I got so much money from Mr. Shaw.

Loisel: Okay. Thanks for that. Now let me ask you something. Did Tippit know Oswald? Did Tippit know Jack Ruby? Tippit the policeman?

Strout: The one that got killed?

Loisel: Right.

Strout: Yes. He knew Oswald and Ruby both. He knows Mr. Shaw.

Loisel: He knows Shaw too?

Strout: He knew Shaw too.

Throughout the conversation, Strout gets some of the names wrong. He refers to a Mr. Bertram instead of Bertrand, which was supposedly the alias of Clay Shaw. He also said Ferris instead of Ferrie.

Loisel decided to test Strout one more time:

Loisel: All right. Now look, Arthur, when you went into Shaw's house, what is the first room you entered? That's all I want to know.

Strout: When I went into his house?

Loisel: Yeah.

Strout: Let me think now, what the rooms up front-

Loisel: You remember what the outside of his house looks like?

Strout: When I first went to his house, I think I went into the kitchen first.

Loisel: Into the kitchen?

Strout: I think so. That was the first place I went into.

Loisel: Is that a big house?

Strout: Where he lives?

Loisel:Yeah.

Strout: Yeah, it was an apartment.

Loisel: Can you just give me a little description of it?

Strout: I can't give you that much because I was drunk the night I went in there anyways. Both times I went in there I was drinking. The only thing that I can tell you is that Mr. Bertram, you call him Shaw. I don't call him that. I know him by Bertram. We made out all right. I made all right on Monday. That was the whole thing.

Loisel: He gave you money?

Strout: Oh yeah. Oh yeah.

Loisel: Look, did you ever see what kind of car that Bertrand had?

Strout: What kind of what?

Loisel: Automobile.

Strout: No, I didn't.

Strout clearly fails Loisel's test. He could not give a description of Shaw's house because he was drunk both times he was there.

Despite this, Loisel still felt he should come to New Orleans to be questioned, and he told Strout that they have bought a plane ticket for him to fly to New Orleans that night.

The only thing that arrived in New Orleans was Strout's luggage. Investigators from Garrison's office were at the airport to meet Strout, but he was not on the plane. Strout then called Garrison's office and said he had run into some weather problems.

Right from the start there were serious doubts about Strout's credibility. The sheriff from his home town in Maine, Robert Bonnefant, told a local newspaper that "If he said anything, I would not believe him." He said Strout had a series of minor offenses since he was fourteen years old. The *Boston Traveler* contacted Strout's sister, who confirmed that while he did visit her for about three days one year earlier, he did not leave the house.

Strout's father told the *Traveler* that "there is no photograph. There never was one. Arthur would say he was with John Wilkes Booth at Lincoln's assassination if he thought he could get publicity out of it." He also said that his son was "given to exaggeration and likes to seek attention."

It turns out that Strout was drunk when he originally called Garrison's office. He admitted that "there is no photograph ... and I was never in Dallas." Strout got as far as Baltimore and then flew back to Boston. He said that "I've changed my mind about the whole thing and have nothing to testify about."

Strout also probably had some mental issues:

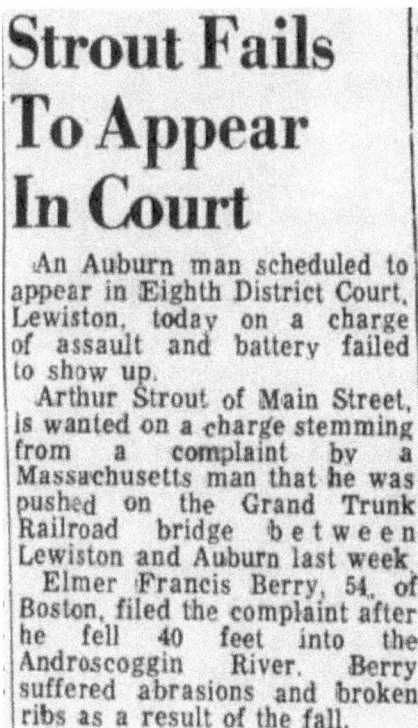

Strout Fails To Appear In Court

An Auburn man scheduled to appear in Eighth District Court, Lewiston, today on a charge of assault and battery failed to show up.

Arthur Strout of Main Street, is wanted on a charge stemming from a complaint by a Massachusetts man that he was pushed on the Grand Trunk Railroad bridge between Lewiston and Auburn last week.

Elmer Francis Berry, 54, of Boston, filed the complaint after he fell 40 feet into the Androscoggin River. Berry suffered abrasions and broken ribs as a result of the fall.

Lewiston Evening Journal, April 24, 1967

There was another "witness" who was drunk when he called Garrison's office. At the end of March 1967, the Reverend Clyde Johnson was drinking with his wife's cousin, and he thought it would be fun to call up Garrison and tell him about a plot to kill JFK. His story was that in September of 1963, he met with Oswald, Ruby, and Clay Shaw in a hotel room in Baton Rouge. Shaw, using the pseudonym of Alton Bernard, gave cash to Oswald and Ruby.

Garrison believed the story and during jury selection in the Clay Shaw trial listed his story as one of the six overt acts that the state would seek to prove:

> Clay L. Shaw, traveling from New Orleans to Baton Rouge, Louisiana, in the fall of 1963, and there meeting Lee Harvey Oswald and Jack Ruby at the Capital House and delivering to Lee Harvey Oswald and Jack Ruby a sum of money.

A few days before the trial, Johnson told the press that "I'm the ace-in-the-hole in Garrison's case." But he was then arrested for not paying a $162 bill at the Roosevelt Hotel, which he had expected Garrison to pick up, and was criminally charged. During jury selection, Shaw's trial attorney, Irvin Dymond, received several phone calls from Johnson "wanting to testify for us." Dymond said he was "loaded every time he called. And —the wee small hours of the morning—every time."

There was a reason why Johnson's nickname was Slidin' Clyde—people viewed him as shifty. Garrison ultimately removed this "overt act" from the Clay Shaw trial.

At least Mr. Strout turned back. Had he continued to New Orleans, Garrison might have bought his claptrap and had him testify against Clay Shaw. He could have then been immortalized in Oliver Stone's *JFK*.

He could have been a somebody.

6

DID ROSE CHERAMI PREDICT THE JFK ASSASSINATION?

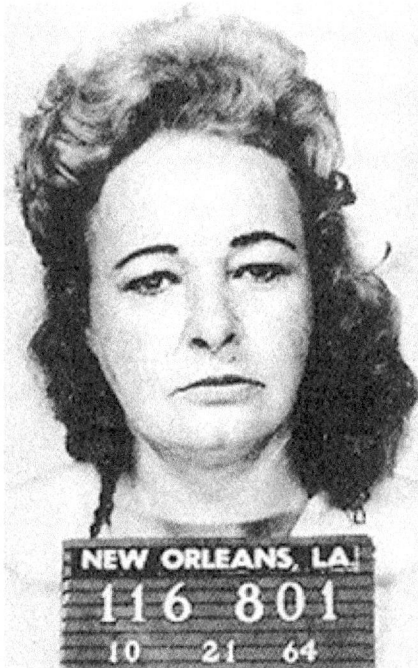

Mug shot of Rose Cherami in 1964. She had been arrested on
10/19/1964 for being drunk, resisting arrest, and disturbing the
peace.

H ere is one of the opening scenes in Oliver Stone's JFK, just after the prologue:

LOUISIANA HIGHWAY—DAY (1963) A moving car carrying two Cuban males disgorges a rumpled, screaming woman, Rose Cheramie [*sic*], a whore in her thirties, lying there bleeding in the dirt. The car drives off.

ROSE: You fucking assholes. You come back here. Don't leave me here.

HOSPITAL—DAY (1963) We see Rose, badly cut but quite lucid, trying to reason with a policeman, Lt. Fruge, and a doctor—in a remote black-and-white documentary.

ROSE: … They've gone to Dallas. Friday, they're going to kill … Kennedy. Call somebody. Stop them. These are serious fucking guys.

DOCTOR (to the police officer): She's high as a kite on something. Been that way since they brought her in.

ROSE: Help. Please …

When I first saw *JFK* back in 1992, I did not know anything about the Rose Cherami story. It's since become a staple of conspiracy books, and it's taken as gospel that she had foreknowledge of the JFK assassination.

But is this story true? What really happened back in 1963?

Rose Cherami was born in Dallas, Texas, as Melba Christine Young-blood on October 14, 1923. When she was twelve, she was admitted to the hospital with kidney trouble and then had an "encephalitic complication" accompanied with a high fever, somnolence, headaches, and other serious symptoms. This lasted for twenty-three days. She recovered physically, but her mother told her doctors that she "began changing completely in her personality. She has become irresponsible, high-tempered, childish, stubborn, disobedient, destructive and losing all respect for her parents." Her mother said that she had been "incorrigible since the age of 12."

A few months later, Cherami ran away from home and went to Houston. Her parents picked her up and returned her to Dallas and put her in psychiatric care. She was placed in a different school with mediocre results. She failed some grades but did manage to complete the ninth grade. She then ran away and started working at various jobs, and the longest time she held a job was six months.

She married for the first time in 1944 and was divorced two years later. She married again in 1952 to Edward Joseph Marcades but only lived with him for three or four months. Her son Michael was born in 1953. They were divorced in May 1955. Michael lived with Rose until the age of four, and then his grandparents took care of him.

Her rap sheets detail fifty-one arrests until her death in 1965.

Rose's first arrest was on February 14, 1941, in San Antonio, Texas, for vagrancy. Four months later, she was arrested in Amarillo for car theft. In October 1942, Cherami was given a two-year prison sentence for larceny and was sent to the infamous Angola prison in Louisiana.

In September 1947, Cherami was arrested in New Orleans for being drunk. She then tried to commit suicide in jail and said she would make another attempt.

Suicide Try Girl Moved To Hospital

Melba Youngblood, the 23-year-old blonde who attempted Tuesday to take her life in a cell at the Third Precinct, has been transferred to the City's Mental Hospital, police said.

Miss Youngblood told The Item she arrived in New Orleans Tuesday about 11 a. m. and had been jilted by the man she was to marry, and started a round of drinking.

New Orleans States-Item, September 19, 1947

Less than a week later, Cherami was involved in an auto theft:

Charge Blonde In Auto Theft

More trouble came yesterday for Melba Youngblood, 23-year-old strawberry blonde, who last week attempted suicide by hanging in the Third Precinct police station following her arrest in the French Quarter.

She was brought before U. S. Commissioner Carter on an FBI charge that she drove a stolen automobile from Houston, Tex., to New Orleans, Sept. 14. The car is the property of Marvin B. Grace.

The woman seemed unperturbed

New Orleans States-Item, September 25, 1947

In February 1956, Cherami was taken to John Sealy Hospital in Galveston, Texas, after having been found beating her head against a sidewalk. Cherami "related a history about her illnesses, which changed during each interview, and with special fabrications and confabulations, wanting to appear as an innocent girl, and so forth."

The note from the hospital said that "during the past few years, the mother has a very poor contact with the patient, but she does know that Melba has been in psychopathic hospitals, jails, prostitution houses, night clubs, et cetera. Last year Melba was in the state hospital in Louisiana at which time she received electroshock treatment." During her stay, Cherami "developed some spells with convulsive disorder characteristics. She stated that she has had spells of unconsciousness before and received treatment in Louisiana for them." Cherami discharged herself after thirteen days in the hospital. She was told to continue taking anticonvulsive medication "because we felt that she has some diffuse abnormality suggestive of convulsive disorder."

At the end of February 1956, Cherami was arrested in Houston for "public intoxication, cursing and disturbing the peace." She was committed for ninety days to the Austin State Hospital. The diagnosis was "sociopathic personality disturbance" and alcoholism. She was discharged on April 17, 1956.

In May 1957, Cherami received a ten-day sentence for public intoxication in Tucson, Arizona. While in custody, she told police that she had information about the murder of Franklin Doan Jr., a twenty-eight-year-old bank teller who was found shot in the head on May 6, 1957. Several investigators wasted four days checking out her story. She directed police to a truck stop where she said the killer had discarded his gun. An intensive search found nothing. She also named two people who were involved in the murder, but when they determined that Cherami was not even in town when Doan was killed, they charged her with furnishing false information.

Cherami tried to escape after serving seven days while being questioned about the Doan case. She was caught after a three-block chase. When her sentence was completed, Cherami slipped out of the city jail's booking area, walked across the street to the police department annex, and talked a detective into ordering a taxi. She promised police that she'd be back with the murderer and the murder weapon. The taxi was traced to a truck stop where one witness saw her boarding a car going north.

Doan Case Blonde
Walks Out On Cops

Headline from *Tucson Daily Citizen*, May 25, 1957

Two days later, Cherami was arrested in New Mexico driving a stolen car from Arizona. She had caught a ride with Otis Sutton of Ft. Worth. She convinced him that a tire was low on air, and when he got out of the car, she drove away.

Elusive Texas Blonde Finally Nabbed
In New Mexico After 80 MPH Chase

Headline in the *Albuquerque Journal*, May 29, 1957.

Cherami tried to evade arrest by engaging in an eighty-mph car chase, which was only brought to a halt when the police fired bullets through her rear tire. She told the police that she was not guilty of car theft because the owner of the car made improper advances on her. Authorities in Arizona decided not to have her extradited because they "feel they have had enough trouble with the woman."

Judge Hatch Holds Woman Incompetent

ALBUQUERQUE (UP) — Federal Judge Carl A. Hatch ruled Friday that Mrs. Melba Marcades, 28, of Houston, Tex., is "mentally incompetent" to be tried on charges of driving a stolen car across state lines.

Judge Hatch ordered the Houston woman placed in custody of federal authorities for treatment and observation until such time she is mentally capable to be tried. She also is charged with attempting to escape from the Bernalillo county jail.

Mrs. Marcades was charged with driving a stolen car from Safford, Ariz., to Deming, N. M., and with attempting to escape from a cell at the county jail by crawling through a transom.

Carlsbad Current-Argus, June 23, 1957

Rose Cherami was sent to the Saint Elizabeth's Hospital in Washington, DC, on September 20, 1957, as "mentally incompetent." The hospital record notes that "she had a history of numerous previous hospitalizations and asocial and antisocial conduct since the age of eight." Her stay at the hospital was "very disturbed" and "extremely stormy." On February 4, 1958, Cherami walked out of the hospital and became intoxicated and was returned, "disturbed and combative." She left again on March 11, 1958, and was returned on March 20. She blamed her "other self" for her behavior.

The U.S. attorney's office dropped the charges against her.

On May 25, 1958, she fell while mopping the floor. She was sent for examination to rule out a fracture of her pelvis. While there she had a series of "grand mal" seizures, which were attributed to the amytal she had been prescribed. She was then on good behavior for two months and was "allowed to have privileges to attend entertainments with the group." On October 17, 1958, she was granted ground privileges. About a week later, she left the grounds with a friend who encouraged her to drink. She came back the same day intoxicated. She was recommended for discharge on January 9, 1959, to return to court for a trial. She was considered competent to stand trial, but by this time, the charges against her had been dismissed, and she left the hospital on the morning of January 31, 1959. By late afternoon she was intoxicated and in a disturbed state and was taken to the DC General Hospital.

In the fall of 1960, Cherami was living in New Orleans with a fire marshal. He told her he was going to marry her, but she found out he was already married. She was living in the Senator Hotel, and he came to visit her. They fought, and he left and then came back extremely drunk. He passed out on her bed, and Cherami claimed that he set fire to the bedspread and the curtains accidentally. She called two seamen to help. But Cherami was arrested for starting the fire.

While in jail she started another fire in the First District police station. She was arrested for being drunk and attacking a policeman. She took off all her clothes in jail and set them afire. She then told officers that she was going to kill herself and began beating her head against the cell wall.

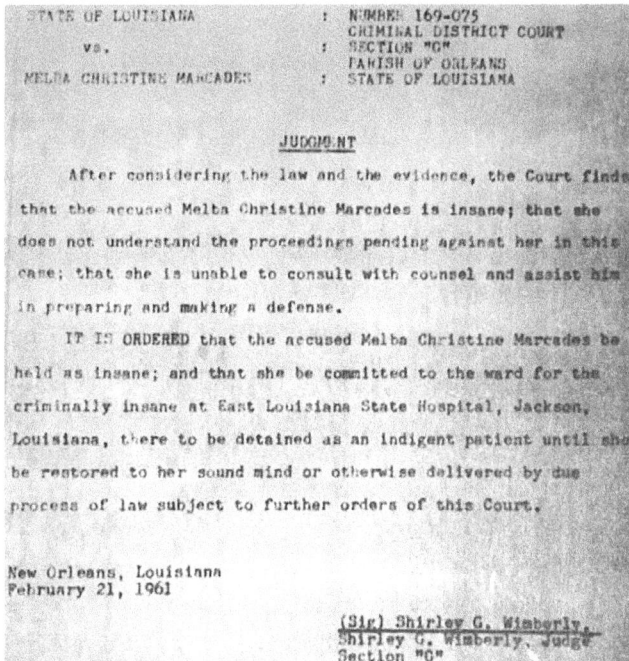

STATE OF LOUISIANA : NUMBER 169-075
CRIMINAL DISTRICT COURT
vs. : SECTION "C"
PARISH OF ORLEANS
MELBA CHRISTINE MARCADES : STATE OF LOUISIANA

JUDGMENT

After considering the law and the evidence, the Court finds that the accused Melba Christine Marcades is insane; that she does not understand the proceedings pending against her in this case; that she is unable to consult with counsel and assist him in preparing and making a defense.

IT IS ORDERED that the accused Melba Christine Marcades be held as insane; and that she be committed to the ward for the criminally insane at East Louisiana State Hospital, Jackson, Louisiana, there to be detained as an indigent patient until she be restored to her sound mind or otherwise delivered by due process of law subject to further orders of this Court.

New Orleans, Louisiana
February 21, 1961

(Sig) Shirley G. Wimberly,
Shirley G. Wimberly, Judge
Section "C"

Judgment of the court in New Orleans.

Melba Christine Marcades was admitted to the East State Louisiana Hospital on March 23, 1961, "on a commitment from Orleans parish." She "admitted to seeing visions but denied hearing voices."

PERMISSION FOR ELECTRIC SHOCK THERAPY

Date _____

I, Mrs. I. J. Youngblood _____, do hereby give permission to the East Louisiana State Hospital to administer Electric Shock Therapy if indicated for treatment to my _daughter, Melba Christine Marcades w/f / .5664_ _____. I hereby relieve the East Louisiana State Hospital and the attending physician of all responsibility in case of unforeseen accident or complications.

WITNESS:

(Name)

Permission form for Rose Cherami to receive electric shock therapy.

On June 1, 1961, she was diagnosed with "schizophrenic reaction, chronic undifferentiated type," and they noted that "this patient is presently legally insane and is unable to differentiate right from wrong and is unable to understand the consequences of her acts." Further hospitalization was recommended.

In April 1963, Cherami was stopped by the Oklahoma Highway Patrol for drunk driving. She was then committed to Central State Hospital for psychiatric evaluation.

And that brings us up to November 1963, when she was brought to the East Louisiana State Hospital.

There are no contemporaneous accounts of what Rose Cherami said at the hospital, and her charts say nothing about the assassination. No one called the FBI or the Warren Commission to alert them about the possibility she had inside information. As you will see, there is one U.S. Customs report from 1963, and it does not support the Cherami story.

This story was dormant until February 1967, when Garrison's investigation was publicly announced. Mr. A. H. Magruder called up Garrison's office and provided a statement about what he had heard back in Christmas of 1963. He had just returned from a hunting trip with Dr. Victor Weiss, who was then clinical director of the East Louisiana State

Hospital in Jackson. Weiss told him that prior to the JFK assassination, state police had picked up a woman on highway 190 near Eunice, Louisiana, who had been thrown out of a car. The police thought she was psycho, and they brought her to the hospital where she was examined by Dr. Weiss.

Magruder said that Weiss determined that Cherami was having withdrawal symptoms. She told him she was a "dope runner" for Jack Ruby. She claimed she was forced to pick up a shipment of dope in Florida to take to Dallas. Her young child was being held by some people to ensure she brought the heroin. Along the way she got into a fight with one of her male companions, and he threw her out of the car.

According to Magruder, Cherami told Weiss that JFK and "other Texas officials" were going to be killed in Dallas. Weiss paid little attention to her ramblings until the JFK assassination and said that the FBI came two days later to pick her up. Magruder gave Garrison investigator Frank Meloche Dr. Weiss's contact information.

Garrison put Meloche on the case, and he seconded Lt. Francis Fruge from the Louisiana State Police and Anne Dischler, an investigator for the State Sovereignty Commission, to help with the investigation. Their mission was to find Rose Cherami.

Dischler called Cherami's mother, who told her that she had died in 1965. Dischler also called Dr. Weiss, who told her that Dr. Don Bowers was the one who had talked to Cherami. She then called Bowers, who denied talking to her. Right from the start there was confusion over what Cherami said, when she said it, and who she said it to.

So here is what really happened in November 1963.

On November 20, 1963, at about 10:00 p.m., Lt. Francis Fruge was called to the emergency ward of Moosa Memorial Hospital in Eunice, Louisiana. Rose Cherami had been struck by a car on Highway 190 and had been brought to the hospital by Frank Odom, the man who had hit her. Fruge was called because Cherami was high on drugs, and he brought her to the local jail to sober up.

While in jail, Cherami stripped off her clothes and cut her ankles. Fruge recognized she was suffering from drug withdrawal and called the assistant coroner of St. Landry Parish, Dr. DeRouen, who administered a sedative and agreed to have her committed. Fruge then called for an ambulance to take her to the East Louisiana State Hospital, and she was put in a straitjacket for the two-hour trip. Along the way, Fruge said he asked her routine questions to keep her mind occupied.

So what did Cherami tell Fruge?

In April 1967, Fruge wrote a report for Jim Garrison that claimed she said that "she once worked for JACK RUBY as a stripper, which was verified, and that RUBY and LEE HARVEY OSWALD were definitely associated and known to be, as she stated, "bed partners." She further referred to RUBY as "PINKEY."

APRIL 4, 1967

Officer ANDREWS----

We wish to further state that fingerprint identification shows that deceased subject, MELBA CHRISTINE MARCADES, is the same person as subject ROSE CHERAMIE, who was in custody, by us, from November 21, 1963, through November 28, 1963, at which time she stated that she once worked for JACK RUBY as a stripper, which was verified, and that RUBY and LEE HARVEY OSWOLD were definitely associated and known to be, as she stated "bed partners". She further referred to RUBY as alias "PINKEY".

Other statements made by subject, relative to your inquiry, are hear-say, but are available, upon your request.

LT. F. L. FRUGE', LA. STATE POLICE

Excerpt from Fruge's report to Jim Garrison.

Of course, this was all nonsense. There is no evidence that Cherami ever worked for Jack Ruby, and there is no evidence that Ruby and Oswald knew each other, nor that they were "bed partners."

Cherami could hardly have stripped for Jack Ruby. Her arrest record shows that she moved around quite a bit, and she wasn't in Dallas all that much. In 1962, she was arrested at least five times in like Washington, DC, Missouri, Colorado, and Houston. In 1963, she was picked up nine times, all of which except one were in Oklahoma. So when could she have worked for Jack Ruby? Fruge's report for Garrison claimed that it was "verified" that she worked as a stripper. But in his HSCA testimony, Fruge said that "this might have been checked later." Doesn't sound like verification to me. And would Jack Ruby have hired a forty-year-old drug-addicted prostitute as a stripper?

There is no evidence these statements were made before the assassination, and they all refer to Jack Ruby. Note the last line: "Other statements made by subject, relative to your inquiry, are hear-say, but are available, upon your request."

In 1978, Fruge's story changed.

Fruge told the HSCA that Cherami was passing through town from Miami on her way to Dallas and Houston. Along the way to the hospital, she said "We're going to kill President Kennedy when he comes to Dallas in a few days."

A few weeks later in his HSCA deposition, Fruge said she was coming from Florida to Dallas with two men who were Italians. They stopped into a lounge to get some drinks, and they got into an argument and were thrown out. She started to hitchhike and was then hit by a car. On the way to the ESLH, Fruge said that she said, "She was going to, number one, pick up some money, pick up her baby, and to kill Kennedy."

I doubt Cherami said anything about the assassination to Fruge before it happened. The *Eunice News* ran a story on Fruge on July 18, 1967, and all he said was that Cherami told him that Oswald and Ruby had been close friends for years. He said he got into the case because she was involved in dope smuggling. George Rennar, an assassination researcher based in the Pacific Northwest, interviewed Bill Boxley, a Garrison investigator, in 1971. Boxley had met with Fruge in 1967, and they discussed Cherami but only about a drug pickup.

In addition, notes taken by Anne Dischler indicate that Cherami was brought to the ELSH in an ambulance accompanied by a relief man from Eunice Police Department. She said he was the dogcatcher who had an uncle who was working the narcotics ward at Jackson. I doubt Fruge even made the trip.

And this all makes sense. Fruge worked on narcotics for the

Louisiana State Police. When he picked her up on November 27, he was interested in her knowledge of a drug deal. And he felt it important enough to get his superiors involved and got permission to fly her to Houston. Had he really been convinced she had inside knowledge of the assassination, he would have gotten the FBI involved, no?

Here is what Fruge says happened next:

Right after the assassination, he called the hospital and told them to call him "as soon as she gets the monkey off her back." He was called on the Monday, and he went to the hospital to talk to Cherami. She told him, "They had to go to Dallas. The president was going to be killed; they were going to kill him." They were supposed to go to a house in Dallas, pick up her baby, and about eight thousand dollars. From there they were to drive to Houston and meet a seaman who was coming into Galveston on a boat. She was supposed to pay him the money and receive eight kilos of heroin. From there they were supposed to go to Mexico.

Fruge then called his immediate supervisor at the Louisiana State Police: Colonel Morgan. They then called Nathan Durham, who the chief customs agent in Port Arthur, Texas. Fruge gave him the name of the seaman and the boat, and Durham called back in thirty minutes and verified that the boat was due to dock and that the seaman's name was on the manifest. Colonel Burbank, who might have been Morgan's supervisor, told them to go to Texas and meet Durham.

The next morning, Fruge and Colonel Morgan flew to Port Arthur with Rose Cherami. On the way to Houston, Cherami picked up a newspaper and saw a headline about Ruby and Oswald. Fruge said "she popped out laughing," and said, "Them two queer son-of-a-bitches. They've been shacking up for years." She told Fruge she used to strip for Ruby at the Pink Door. Of course, Ruby never owned a club with that name.

Colonel Morgan then called Captain Fritz of the Dallas Police and asked if he had any interest in Cherami's information. He said no.

The customs agents called the Rice Hotel and verified the reservations. But the seaman never showed up. Fruge said they put a tail on him when he left the boat, but they lost him along the way. They then put

Cherami back on the street in Houston, and they all came back to Louisiana.

That's the story according to Francis Fruge. Fortunately, we have a report written on December 10, 1963, by Frederick Turner, a customs agent.

On November 26, 1963, they received a call from Captain Ben Morgan saying that they had a woman in custody who was "involved in a large narcotics smuggling operation." She was supposed to be in Houston on November 28, receive $29,000 from Pete Vallone, who was the operator of the Stage Door Lounge. The next day, she would be contacted by a Spanish or Puerto Rican seaman called "Luther" who was due to arrive in Galveston on a ship called the *Mary Etta*. She would use the money to pay for a large quantity of narcotics and then deliver them to Leo Parker in Dallas.

They then checked with customs agent Harold King in Houston about the arrival of the *Mary Etta*, and he said the only boats scheduled were the *SS Mar Negro*, arriving on the twenty-ninth· and the *SS Maturata*, arriving on the twenty-sixth. On the afternoon of the twenty-seventh, Fruge, Morgan, and Cherami arrived in Port Arthur. Cherami told a "long and detailed story about her involvement in the narcotics smuggling traffic." That evening, they all went to Houston.

Meetings were held with other customs agents who "partially" substantiated parts of Cherami's story. It was true that the Vallone family was involved in "narcotics, white slavery and other criminal activity."

At 2:00 a.m. on November 29, one of the agents determined that Cherami had been arrested in Houston on October 29, 1963, for being drunk and using abusive language, "at which time she had told of being involved in the narcotics traffic which was found to be untrue." They noted that "records revealed that the informer, under many aliases, has an extensive police record since 1941; has served time for felonies or being insane or criminally insane in several different States' prisons or mental institutions." The day after her arrest in Houston, Cherami failed to appear, and two one-thousand-dollar bonds had been forfeited. Because of this information, the agents discontinued their investigation and closed the file.

That is quite a different story from the one told by Fruge.

It wasn't the first time that Cherami had told this story. A 1965 FBI memo quoted from a May 1963 memo when Cherami was interviewed by agents in Oklahoma City:

> She was interviewed at the Carter County Jail, Ardmere, Oklahoma, and told a story of arriving in Ardmore enroute to Dallas, Texas, to deliver approximately $2,600 worth of heroin to a party known as Bob Parker, Oak Cliff, Texas. She was then to proceed to Galveston, Texas, to pick up a load of narcotics from a seaman on board a ship destined for Galveston in the next two days. MARCADES gave detailed descriptions as to individuals, names, places, and amounts of narcotics distributed. Based on her information, investigation was conducted by narcotics bureau through the States of Oklahoma and Texas and her information was found to be erroneous in all regards. Checks with the Oklahoma City Police Department reveals that MARCADES is well known to that department as a mental case who has previously been confined to a mental institution in Norman, Oklahoma, on at least 3 different occasions.

That November 1965 memo also notes that Cherami "has been previously interviewed by Special Agents of the Federal Bureau of Investigation on numerous occasions, and she has furnished false information concerning her involvement in prostitution and narcotics matters."

So did Cherami just repeat the May 1963 story in November to get out of the Eastern Louisiana State Hospital?

In 1978, the HSCA investigated the Cherami story. They interviewed Dr. Weiss, who told them that he interviewed Cherami *after* the assassination. "Weiss formed the opinion after interviewing Cherami that she was not psychotic, but that contrary to what has been published, she did not have any specific details of a particular assassination plot against Kennedy but had only stated that 'the word in the underworld' was that Kennedy would be assassinated." He suggested that the HSCA contact Dr. Don Bowers, who had attended to Cherami before the assassination.

For some reason, the HSCA did not speak to Dr. Bowers. However, in 2003 Dr. Bowers sent a letter to the JFK Lancer conference in Dallas. He said that he had never seen Rose Cherami at the hospital and only found out about the allegations on a hunting trip with Weiss on November 24. He called Weiss to ask about his comments to the HSCA, but Weiss refused to discuss it.

This confusion makes it hard to take the Cherami story seriously. There is no direct testimony that Cherami said anything about the JFK assassination before it happened. I should add that Francis Fruge's honesty came into question when author Patricia Lambert interviewed Anne Dischler in 1994. She told Lambert that she had had an affair with Fruge back in 1967 and that he had confessed to manufacturing evidence in a prior murder case. He also stole money from Dischler.

On August 3, 1965, Cherami, identifying herself as Rozella Clinkscales, contacted the Montgomery Resident Agency of the FBI claiming that she and seven other girls had been brought there by the mob for prostitution. She wanted an agent to come and protect her from the "syndicate." Two special agents picked up Clinkscales and brought her to the agency.

Her breath smelled of alcohol, and she said she was a "junkie" with a $40 a day habit. She then named several people who were responsible for her being in Montgomery. Cherami also gave an itinerary of places they were supposed to "tour" after they left Montgomery. She read the names from a little black book which she refused to show to agents. She had to go along with the mob because they were "holding her six-year-old boy, MIKE" in New Orleans, until she made $3,000 for them. Cherami refused to name those holding her son and walked out when the agents probed further.

It's interesting that she also told Fruge back in 1963 that mobsters were also holding her son. Why not reuse a good story?

Two hours after she left the FBI office, she called again and claimed that she had been given a "hotshot" by the mob because she went to the FBI. Two agents went back out to talk to her and saw that she was trying to persuade the druggist to give her an ounce of paregoric (a mixture of opium powder and ethanol) to "counteract" the "hotshot." She did not appear to be high, and it was apparent that she just wanted the drug. They took her to the hospital, where she refused treatment and assaulted a nurse. She was then taken to the Montgomery police station for investigation. After her release from jail, she was escorted to the edge of town where she was last seen hitchhiking.

Just one month later, Rose Cherami was dead. And the circumstances of her death have become another staple of the conspiracy community.

Penn Jones was the first conspiracy theorist to promote the supposed mysterious deaths of witnesses, and he wrote a series of books (*Forgive My Grief*) on that theme. *Argosy* magazine, in March 1977, published a major article that started with Rose Cherami:

*The appalling death rate stemming from the tragedy in Dallas
is much more than a coincidence.*

THE BIZARRE DEATHS FOLLOWING JFK'S MURDER!

By David Martindale

No one knows why Rose Cherami was lying on the road that night. Few people would have taken notice of her death, except that Rose Cherami is one one of dozens of individuals who have died mysteriously since the assassination of President Kennedy. Penn Jones, Jr., the feisty former editor of the *Midlothian Mirror* in Texas, was the first person to call attention to these strange deaths, and today his list includes well over fifty names.

Many conspiracy books (*Crossfire* by Jim Marrs, *High Treason* by Robert Groden and Harrison Livingstone, and *Cover-Up* by Gary Shaw) and Oliver Stone's *JFK* have claimed that Rose Cherami was killed in a hit-and-run. Jim Garrison also claimed she was the victim of a hit-and-run driver despite the fact that he had a copy of Francis Fruge's report from April 4, 1967:

APRIL 4, 1967
STATE OF LOUISIANA
PARISH OF ST. LANDRY
CITY OF EUNICE

Officer J. A. ANDREWS, Texas Highway Patrol, was interviewed
by us, relative to the death of one HELEN CHRISTINE MARCADES,
alias ROSE CHERAMIE, w/fm, d.o.b. 11-14-23, LSP #256-375, FBI
#234-7922.

Officer ANDREWS stated that subject died of injuries received
from an automobile accident on Hwy. #155, 1.7 miles East of
Big Sandy, Upshur County, Texas, at 3:00 p.m., on Sept. 4, 1965.
Subject died at the hospital in Gladewater, Gregg County, Texas.
The inquest was held by Justice of the Peace ROSS DELAY, Prec. #3,
Gregg County, Texas.

The accident was reported to Officer ANDREWS by the operator of
the car, after he had taken the subject to the hospital. ANDREWS
stated that the operator related that the victim was apparrently
lying on the roadway with her head and upper part of her body
resting on the traffic lane, and although he had attempted to
avoid running over her, he ran over the top part of her skull,
causing fatal injuries. An investigation of the physical evidence
at the scene of the accident was unable to contradict this statement. Officer ANDREWS stated that due to the unusual circumstances,
mainly time, location, injuries received and lack of prominent
physical evidence, he attempted to establish a relationship between
the operator of the vehicle and the victim to determine if any foul
play was involved. This resulted negative.

It should be noted that Hwy. #155 is a Farm to Market Road, running
parallel to US Hwys. #271 and #80. It is our opinion, from experience, that if a subject was hitch-hiking, as this report wants to
indicate, that this does not run true to form. It is our opinion
that the subject would have been on one of the US Highways.
ANDREWS stated that although he had some doubt as to the authenti-
city of the information received, due to the fact that the relatives
of the victim did not pursue the investigation, he closed it as
accidental death.

There was no hit-and-run. Cherami was run over by twenty-two-year-old Jerry Don Moore. He saw Cherami lying in the road and thought the right tire of his car hit her. He then took her to Gladewater hospital.

And Joan Mellen, in her book *A Farewell to Justice*, writes:

> Rose Cheramie's death certificate reads "bullet hole in head," although hospital records mention no bullet hole. Her death was ruled, "accidental." Fruge could uncover no record of the driver who killed Rose at the address he had provided. Jim Garrison requested that Rose Cherami's body be exhumed, but Texas authorities refused to comply.

Rose Cherami's son, Dr. Michael Marcades, has come out with a book about his mother: *Rose Cherami: Gathering Fallen Petals*. He also believes that she was shot. Conspiracy theorist Gary Shaw wrote the introduction:

> Rose died at age 41, her death sinisterly shrouded in mystery. Many believe she had to be silenced because she knew too much and therefore was a threat to the real killers of our President.

And:

> She could actually identify some of the people who were participants in the President's murder. To an astute and honest person, her death was no accident—Rose was murdered!

Here is Rose Cherami's death certificate:

As you can see, the death certificate does not state "bullet hole in head." It states the cause of death was a "Traumatic Head wound with Subdural subarachnoid & Petechial Hemorrhage to the brain caused by being struck by auto." You can also see that there was a nine-hour interval between being struck and death.

Cherami's death was covered by the *Tyler Morning Telegraph* of September 6, 1965. Gregg County Medical Examiner Dr. E. L. Jones told the paper that she died of a massive cerebral hemorrhage. "The physician continued that the bleeding was caused by a severe brain concussion. He said that the visual and tactile examination of the skull revealed no fractures."

Michael Marcades's book contains some additional documents from the Gladewater Municipal Hospital. Here are the comments from the hospital report:

When she was seen in our ER she was comatose and unresponsive. She had a deep punctate stellate laceration over the right side of the forehead and a deep long laceration extending completely around the left posterior

scalp, extending down to the underlying cranium. The left external audi-
tory canal was filled with blood and the left side of the face was swollen
and contused in appearance. The pupils were large and unresponsive to
light. There was blood in the nose and mouth. She was swollen and
contused over the entire left side of the face. The neck was supple, but
each time the head was turned to the right side the pt. apparently had
occlusion of her airway, because she would become cyanotic and begin to
vomit.

The reason the death certificate says she was DOA was because she
was comatose and unresponsive when she arrived in the ER. The doctors
sutured her scalp lacerations and dressed the wounds. She was then
transferred to her room, albeit in extremely poor condition.

Some conspiracy theorists focus on the phrase "deep punctate stellate
type laceration" as proof that she was shot. But even Dr. Cyril Wecht,
conspiracy theorists' favorite forensic pathologist, wrote that "there is
nothing to suggest a gunshot wound or any other kind of penetrating
injury."

The idea that Rose Cherami was murdered because of her knowledge
of the assassination plot was always ridiculous. She was a drug-addled
prostitute who would be the last person conspirators would confide in.
Her itinerary didn't make any sense. Driving from Florida to Dallas to
assassinate JFK, then going to Houston for a dope deal, and then to
Mexico. Quite a busy week. Why would conspirators let her live almost
two years after the assassination? And why did the conspirators toss her
out of the car while she was still alive? Why did Rose Cherami say
nothing about the assassination for two years after her November 1963
hospitalization?

In 2017, researcher Anthony Summers, author of the one of the most
popular JFK assassination conspiracy books, sent out an email saying
that while "Francis Fruge appeared forthright during his conversations
with me—he too may have fabricated or at least garbled. I think the
Cherami episode should now be consigned to the junkpile—as a red
herring that one could well do without."

Rose Cherami's grave just outside New Orleans. Photo by Fred Litwin.

I agree. But it's too delicious a story for conspiracy theorists to let go.

THE MAN WHO NEEDED HELP

Richard Case Nagell in prison in 1966.

On Friday, September 20, 1963, a decorated Korean war veteran, Richard Case Nagell, walked into the State National Bank in El Paso, Texas, and approached a teller asking for some traveler's checks.

He was sent to Patsy Gordon, the supervisor of tellers, and he asked for $100 in $10 bills.

'Lady, This Is A Real Gun'

Veteran Tries Daring Bank Robbery

The El Paso Times, September 21, 1963

He then leaned over the counter and said, "Lady, this is a real gun." Mrs. Gordon then ran out of the teller's cage. Nagell also ran and, on his way out, fired two shots into the ceiling. He was arrested by police officer Jim Bundren as he tried to get away in his car. He ordered Nagell out of his car and found a gun in his front pants pocket.

In the Robbery and Homicide office, Nagell told Detective Sgt. Bob Barron, "You punk cop, if I have a chance to hit you, I will."

That evening Nagell promised city jailors that he would "take a shotgun to every one of you so-and-so's." The next day, he pleaded not guilty to charges of bank robbery and said that that he did not want a lawyer to represent him. He then tried cutting his wrists using a tin can converted to an ash tray.

In February 1964, Nagell was judged competent to stand trial and in May was found guilty of attempted bank robbery. The next month he was sentenced to ten years in prison and was sent to Leavenworth Federal Penitentiary in Kansas.

So what was really going on? Was this really a bank robbery? And just who was Richard Case Nagell?

Richard Case Nagell was born on August 5, 1930, in Greenwich, New York. His father died when he was two years old, and he was separated from his mother and siblings at the age of four. He lived in various foster homes until he was eleven and then in an orphanage until he graduated from high school.

Nagell joined the U.S. Army on August 5, 1948, at the age of eighteen. He was honorably discharged on August 1, 1951, as a sergeant at Fort Benning, Georgia. He then accepted a commission in the U.S. Army's Reserve Corps and was commissioned a second lieutenant. Nagell served in the Korean War in 1952–1953 and was awarded the Korean Service Medal with one Silver Star, the National Defense Service Medal, the Bronze Star Medal, the Purple Heart with two Oak Leaf Clusters, and numerous other badges and citations.

An Officer Efficiency Report (OER) for the period of April 3, 1953, to June 11, 1953, said:

> Lt. Nagell assumed command of Company "C" when the unit was in a very low state of combat readiness. Almost immediately, Lt. Nagell's forceful, energetic display of leadership changed the entire complexion of this company from one of a defeatist attitude to an inspired combat effective unit. Lt. Nagell lacks somewhat in diplomacy and tact, however, this is completely overshadowed by his loyalty and devotion to his command, and to his commander. This officer has almost completed his second tour in Korea and has been on approximately 175 patrols. He is the type of officer that can be given any type of combat mission with the expectation that the job will be done in a superior manner. He is thorough and complete in the performance of all his duties to include minor details. This officer was wounded in action and evacuated as his company successfully recaptured and held a portion of OP Harry on the night of June 10–11 June 1953. He is fearless and a tower of strength in combat. He held his company together as an efficient fighting force in the face of heavy losses and aggressive assaults by the enemy.

The endorsing officer wrote that "this is one of the finest combat officers I have ever known. As a very successful company commander in combat I recommend him for promotion to Captain, and state that I would make every effort possible to get him back in my regiment."

In June 1953, Nagell was transferred from the infantry to military intelligence for training in the Counter Intelligence Corps (CIC). On July 4, 1953, Nagell was recommended for promotion to captain:

> Lt. Nagell as a company commander has demonstrated in combat outstanding characteristics of leadership and common sense. In the opinion of the undersigned he is outstandingly qualified, both physically and morally, for promotion to the grade of Captain.

Nagell was wounded in action twice. He received a flesh wound to the head in December 1952 and a brain concussion on June 11, 1953, when he was hit by fragments from a mortar. He was evacuated from Korea while unconscious and was hospitalized in Tokyo.

Nagell was the sole survivor of a plane crash on November 28, 1954, in which he suffered facial disfigurement and brain damage.

FIVE DEAD IN BOMBER CRASH HERE

Five Die, 1 Alive In B-25 Crash Near Airport

The bodies of five men were found today in the wreckage of a B-25 bomber which crashed against an Anne Arundel county hillside 2 miles from Friendship Airport last night as it attempted to make a landing on the rain-swept field.

A sixth man, found alive at the scene by rescuers, who chopped their way through dense undergrowth to reach the wreckage, was reported in critical condition. He was identified as an army officer, one of three passengers aboard the plane on a flight from Tulsa, Okla., to Andrews Air Force Base outside Washington.

Baltimore Evening Sun, November 29, 1954

The B-25, en route from Los Angeles to Washington, had been diverted from Andrews Air Force Base, which was closed because of dangerous weather. It crashed two miles from Friendship Airport as it attempted to make a landing in heavy rain. Nagell had a "severe cut of the face, head injuries, exposure and shock." Both jaw bones were fractured, he suffered a fracture and permanent depression of his left temporal skull bone, and he had a fracture through the base of the brain and a severe brain concussion. The blow to his skull injured the underside of his brain and some of the cranial nerves. Nagell also had partial paralysis of the left side of his face and some double vision.

Nagell laid in the wreckage for most of the night and was unable to crawl out. He was conscious when found but was in deep shock groaning for water. A state policeman gave him a tracheostomy to help him breathe. He was taken to the Bolling Air Force Base hospital, which gave him a fifty-fifty chance to live and put him on the "serious" list. Nagell was semi-comatose for a month and remained in critical condition until December 24, 1954. On January 3, 1955, he was transferred to Walter Reed Hospital because of the severity of his head wounds. It took six months for him to recover.

On January 7, 1955, Nagell was examined at Walter Reed by Dr. Edwin Weinstein, a research neurologist and psychiatrist. An electroencephalogram was performed, which showed abnormalities with questionable focal brain damage. But Weinstein did not treat Nagell; he only studied his case for an article and a book. His opinion was that Nagell had a severe brain injury, but his findings were not made part of the clinical record.

In March, Nagell was examined by another doctor, who found him depressed. Nagell was suspicious of the questions and told him that he wished he had died in the crash. By April 1955, Nagell's hostility had disappeared, and he was appearing more normal.

A medical board recommended in May that Nagell be returned to full military duty. It concluded that his concussion from 1953 had been cured but made no mention of his brain injury from the plane crash. They said he exhibited a passive-aggressive reaction, and he was then released from Walter Reed Hospital and returned to duty, becoming a student at the Counter Intelligence Corps Center at Ft. Holabird, Maryland. Nagell graduated in August 1955:

```
                           HEADQUARTERS
U. S. ARMY COMMAND RECONNAISSANCE ACTIVITY, FAR EAST
                           APO  613


                                            22 March 1957


                  C-E-R-T-I-F-I-C-A-T-E


    This is to certify that RICHARD C. NAGELL, Captain, 02028346,
was granted a Top-Secret security clearance on 22 September 1955.



                              ROBERT W. BURGHER
                              Major, Arty
                              Adjutant
```

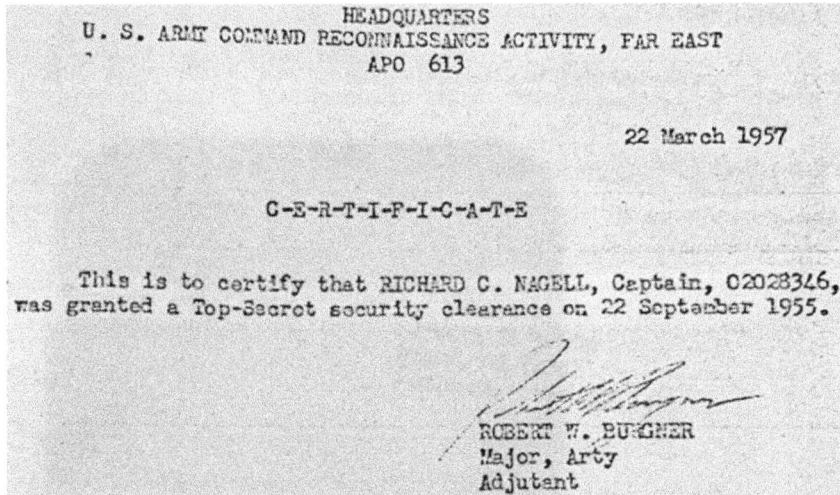

He went on assignment in Los Angeles, and beginning in April 1956 was transferred to Asia. From April 1956 to February 1957, Nagell was stationed in Korea, where he worked as an adviser to the army of the Republic of Korea. Nagell was then transferred to Japan, where he translated documents and investigated leftist organizations.

Nagell had increasing difficulties at work. His superiors noticed that the accident had affected his personality. Comments in his efficiency reports included "lacks self-confidence and is excessively sensitive," "somewhat discontent," "tendency to resent constructive or critical comment regarding his work and becomes agitated," "most obnoxious attitude," and "apt to lose his temper."

A series of confrontations ensued.

In March 1957, Nagell made "derogatory allegations" against several officers. An FBI report noted that Nagell "charged personal injustices, incompetence, corruption, mismanagement, mal-administration and lack of opportunity to present fully all matters relative to his complaints. He also alleged that Efficiency/Progress Reports submitted by him concerning other military personnel had been altered and changed by superior officers."

The investigating officer noted that Nagell made these allegations in "a highly agitated state of mind" and wrote:

Capt. Nagell was seriously injured in an airplane crash approximately three years ago and has a permanent facial scar and damage to facial nerves requiring intermittent medical treatment. This accident has apparently affected his personality as he is not completely compatible to his associates as is normally expected. This could easily direct an opinion from others of personality conflict or complex.

I do feel that his physical condition and assignment to a remote and unfavorable area in Korea influenced and affected Capt. Nagell and brought about these allegations. I do not feel that he was sufficiently recovered form his injuries for such an assignment although he performed well for most of his tour.

Nagell's efficiency report from March 1957.

In January 1958, Nagell received an official reprimand for having a woman in his room at the bachelor officer's quarters (BOQ). The woman was his fiancée, a Japanese national. His OER for the period talked about a "persecution complex" and stated that Nagell showed lack of "judgment, discretion and common sense and failure to observe basic concepts of conduct expected of an officer." Because of this incident and his impending marriage to a foreign national, Nagell was removed from counterintelligence duties.

Because of his removal, Nagell accused his commanding officer of bias. A superior officer wrote the adjutant general and said, "I am acquainted with the allegations made by Captain Nagell and consider them as malicious, unfounded, and further indication of his unsuitability as an officer in the United States Army." The subsequent investigation found no basis for Nagell's accusations.

On February 13, 1958, he was ordered to have a psychiatric evaluation. Dr. Carl McGahee examined him for five days at the neuropsychiatric ward at the U.S. Army hospital in Tokyo. Nagell told him there was no problem that merited attention. McGahee did not find any evidence of a mental disorder and recommended that Nagell be returned to duty on February 18, 1958.

Nagell's OER for February 1958 recommended that he be discharged from the U. S. Army because of "certain trends of character and conduct brought sharply into focus during recent months." This was based upon his various charges against senior officers and his "misdirected aggressiveness." Here is an excerpt from that report:

> Captain Nagell describes himself as the kind of person who, when he observes something wrong, must take aggressive action to correct it. His aggressiveness would be a fine quality if properly directed and if consistently applied under all circumstances and not merely to suit his own whims, convictions, and convenience. As it is, Captain Nagell is intelligent but immature, aggressive but motivated by selfish vindictiveness, very proud of his rank and record but not aways carrying out his personal responsibilities of his rank and position. He is not well versed in the military, he is not willing to accept the decision of senior officers, and has clearly established that he believes discipline, proper channels, and conduct conducive to good order are fine as long as they do not interfere with his own personal opinions, convictions, or convenience. In short, if every officer were to conduct himself in the same manner as Nagell, good order and discipline would be dissipated.

The endorsing officer wrote that "Captain Nagell lacks maturity, judgment, and common sense; apparently he has been unable to adjust himself to the requirements expected of a captain in the United States Army."

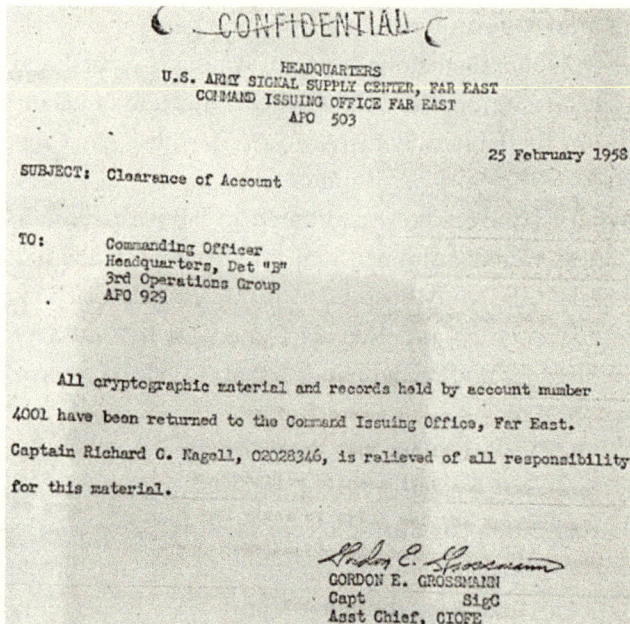

In March 1958, Nagell was relieved of counterintelligence duties. He then accused an officer of allowing unauthorized access to classified information to a Japanese national. The investigation determined that "Nagell's motive for reporting to DA considered to be a panicky gesture calculated to mitigate seriousness of having a female in his BOQ in violation of standing orders and retaliatory against his reprimand." The report deemed Nagell to be a "fault finder and trouble maker."

Nagell's top-secret clearance was revoked on April 4, 1958. He returned to the United States in July 1958 and took command of an infantry basic training company at Fort Dix, New Jersey.

On October 5, 1958, he submitted his resignation from the Army. He stated he was resigning because his current assignment precluded the efficient performance of his duties and affected his wife's welfare. He also cited his charges against his commanding officer in Japan. On

October 14, 1958, he sent a letter withdrawing his resignation, writing that his charges of bias should be investigated.

His review for the period of November 1958 to January 1959 was positive and said that he "has demonstrated considerable initiative, excellent judgment, and sound knowledge of military subjects." It concluded that Nagell had "accomplished highly effective results."

This all changed in his review for April 9, 1959, to August 16, 1959, which described his "tactlessness, temper, obnoxious attitude and inability to get along with people." His endorsing officer wrote:

> He is an intelligent officer but demonstrates very little initiative in the performance of his duties. Captain Nagell is tall in stature and appears to be physically capable of carrying out his duties which are expected of an officer of his grade and branch in the field in time of war. His behavior pattern has made it obvious that he does not know how to get along with people. If he controlled his temper and made a radical change in his most obnoxious attitude, he would undoubtedly be of great value to the service. Captain Nagell performs his duties in an excellent manner.

On August 31, 1959, Nagell once again submitted his resignation, citing his wish to "further my civilian education." He also asked that he be considered for disability because of his "service-connected injuries."

Nagell's separation physicals in September 1958 and August 1959 did not include an examination by a psychiatrist or a neurologist. He was honorably discharged on October 29, 1959. His half sister said he still complained of head injuries, and he had a twitch in one eye and loss of mobility in the other eye.

A Korean colleague, Colonel Ned Glenn, said that Nagell was not stable mentally and that this was due to brain damage suffered in the plane crash. Glen noted that Nagell had had a brilliant war record, which was why he was assigned to Army intelligence "in spite of what should have been an obvious psychological defect."

Nagell's first attempt at a civilian job was to apply to be a policeman. His physical examination on December 14, 1959, disqualified him for that job. The reason is not part of the record, although Nagell told the Veterans Administration in 1960 that it was because of a tic in his left eye.

On December 13, 1959, Nagell began employment with the California Department of Employment in the fraud section. He was transferred to the Alcoholic Beverage Control Board on April 1, 1961.

On January 29, 1960, Nagell applied to the VA for disability. He described his 1954 injury as "concussion of the brain." In March, he was examined by several specialists, including Dr. A. Trevisano, a neuropsychiatrist. His report said that Nagell "shows no deterioration nor psychotic or psychoneurotic manifestations. He states that he has not been aware of any personality changes. He is competent."

On May 30, 1960, Nagell wrote to U.S. Senator Thomas Kuchel seeking his help in getting a "a complete and adequate physical examination." He complained that the cursory nature of the physical exam upon separation was the reason it failed to disclose "disabling neurological damage." The adjutant general replied to Kuchel and said that Nagell should submit evidence to the Army Board for the Correction of Military Records.

On July 8, 1960, the VA awarded Nagell a 64 percent (60 percent compensable) wartime disability rating. His disability check was $158 per month.

On May 18, 1962, he was admitted to the VA hospital in Los Angeles because of "homicidal and suicidal tendencies." He did not tell Dr. Harvey Weintraub about his previous head injuries but did tell him that he had "fantasies of killing his wife and/or himself." The doctor diagnosed Nagell with "acute anxiety reaction with depressive features in a markedly aggressive character, passive dependent type." Nagell discharged himself in three days.

Two weeks later, Nagell tried to break down the door to his wife's apartment. The police were called, and he was arrested for being drunk, which he denied. Nagell was then suspended from his job on June 8, 1962, and then fired on June 27 for refusing to answer questions. He later told a psychologist that he was fired for telling the press that the LA vice squad was shaking down too many businesses. On other occasions, he told people that he had been dismissed for committing bribery.

On July 16, 1962, he was admitted to the same VA hospital for a gunshot wound in his right chest. At various times, he either said the gunshot was self-inflicted or that his wife shot him. He later told the FBI that he was returning from Oxnard and noticed he was being followed by another car. He stopped on the highway near Malibu, and two men from the other car, dressed in business suits, jumped into his car and asked Nagell where his gun was. He told them it was in the glove compartment and gave them the key. While they were opening the compartment, Nagell took out his gun. They struggled, and four shots were fired with one hitting Nagell in the chest. He never said who the men were.

He was released from the hospital a week later. Detectives from the LAPD came to the hospital to question him. Nagell did not like their attitude and refused to answer their questions. His car was impounded but returned ten days later. A court later concluded that Nagell likely shot himself.

On August 24, 1962, Nagell entered Mexico and on September 28, 1962, walked into the American embassy in Mexico City. He talked about his dismissal from the Alcohol Control Board and claimed that he was owed $800 in retirement contributions and $300 for unused leave. He had been "let down" by the U.S. government in helping him collect this money. He also said that he was "bitter, disgusted, disillusioned and disaffected" and that if he did go to some other country, it would cost the United States millions. He was "through being a good citizen" and had gotten a "dirty deal all around." Nagell added that he thought he had been approached for recruiting but refused to say by whom. The embassy noted that Nagell was "very tense, nervous, agitated and antagonistic throughout this interview."

Nagell went back to the American embassy in October and wanted to know what had been done in his case and was told to go to the protection and welfare section for assistance. They told him they could not help him in the collection of the debt. He then went to the passport and citizenship section and asked them what the penalty was for going to an Eastern Bloc country. They told him it was a violation of U.S. law.

Nagell also gave them a letter he had sent to the State of California Personnel Board in August. He had written that he was withdrawing his appeal of his dismissal because of his poor financial position. The stigma attached to his dismissal made it impossible for him to obtain employment. He also wrote that he was dismissed because of vindictiveness on the part of certain executives once it became known that he was going to disclose corruption.

Nagell left Mexico at the end of October and then wrote to the military, requesting reenlistment. They replied that the chances of his application would not be good.

On November 16, 1962, Nagell appeared at the FBI office in New York City. He wanted to expose the Alcohol Bureau and was willing to provide testimony that would result in the prosecution of many Los Angeles hoodlums and their attorneys, who acted as go-betweens in securing alcohol licenses through payoffs. Nagell left a typewritten document about his allegations, and they noted that he appeared "overwrought and obsessed with a desire to expose the ABC [Alcohol Control Board]."

Two weeks later, Nagell again contacted the FBI office in New York. He did not believe he had been given a fair chance to be heard when the LA County Superior Court granted his wife a divorce. Nagell thought the trial would take place in December and that his wife's attorney brought the case while he was still in Mexico.

On December 15, 1962, he phoned the FBI office in Jacksonville, Florida, from the cocktail lounge of the Townhouse Restaurant. Two FBI agents drove out and spoke to him in their car. He told them that while in a bar in Washington, DC, he had been approached by a person he thought was either a "Soviet Espionage Agent" or an FBI agent who wanted to give him an intelligence assignment. The more he thought about it, the more he was certain this person worked for the Russians. In September, he had been invited to a reception at the Soviet embassy. He then called the CIA, using the pseudonym of either Joe Cramer or Kramer, to ask if he should go through with this assignment. He was to meet someone at the Townhouse Restaurant and, "in order to be recognized, he was to place three nickels on the bar in line with a dime placed directly over the nickel." The CIA told him this was a domestic matter and to contact the FBI. Nagell said he went to the bar and was then told to go to a bar in Miami, wearing a red sweater, where he would be contacted about his assignment.

The FBI noted that during this interview Nagell was "in an inebriated condition and was very vague in answering questions." He was unable to identify any of the individuals in question and could also not furnish any physical descriptions. He "also gave the impression to the interviewing agents of being mentally unbalanced." Nagell then told them that "he believes in connection with his contacts that he is actually working for the Soviets." He was unable to give the FBI any information other than that he was to go to Miami and wait to be contacted by a Soviet agent. Two days later, they tried to reinterview him, but he had checked out of his motel and had left no forwarding address.

On December 20, 1962, Nagell complained of headaches and lapses of memory and was admitted to the Veterans Administration hospital in Bay Pines, Florida. He was examined by Dr. James Martin, acting chief of the psychology service. Nagell was quite honest and told Dr. Martin about his previous injuries. Martin's report notes that "at one time, the patient became tearful" and that "following the accident, patient noted that his efficiency began slipping, and that he had tendencies to become suspicious and irritable." Nagle also said that "it was difficult for him to learn, concentrate, or remember. He denies seizures but alleges amnesiac episodes. He states that sometimes his 'mind goes blank' when talking with someone."

Dr. Martin's impression was that "the patient's history, behavior, and test performance strongly resemble that seen in epileptic individuals. The possibility remains that this is a beginning of a paranoid break with reality, possibly a paranoid schizophrenia, although the patient certainly shows no clinical signs of psychosis at the present time." Martin recommended neuro-psychiatric studies to rule out epilepsy.

One week later, Nagell was given an electroencephalographic examination. The results were "borderline abnormal." In early January, Nagell was referred to Dr. P. C. Clark, chief of the psychiatric service because they believed he should not "be sent out of the hospital with no one to care for him ... this man has indicated suicidal tendency most recent 1/12/63."

Dr. Clark examined Nagell on January 14, 1963. His diagnosis was "chronic brain syndrome associated with brain trauma, cerebral concussion in 1953 & 1954, with behavioral reaction-passive aggressive type with paranoid traits." Nagell was then sent to staff psychiatrist Dr. M. L.

Schwartz. Nagell told him that his "trouble is physiologic" and "all due to my head injury."

Schwartz concluded that "since his insight and judgment were unpredictable at times and although no psychotic behavior was noted, it was felt he could leave the hospital," and Nagell was discharged on January 22, 1963.

That same month Nagell wrote to President Kennedy complaining that the Army's response to Senator Kuchel avoided the issue of his physical examination:

> In 1954, I was the sole survivor of a B-25 bomber crash in which I sustained a serious head injury. Sine then I have never been the same—mentally or physically—although the Army returned me to military intelligence. I was aware of my condition but pride made me try to 'hang on.' Eventually, many of my superiors and co-workers could see that there was something wrong. I know my subsequent military efficiency reports and other records, some of which are buried under the wraps of security classifications, substantiate this. My condition became worse as the years went by.

Nagell's letter was forwarded to the Army, and he received the same suggestion as before: go to the Army Board to correct his record.

On January 24, 1963, he contacted the FBI office in Miami identifying himself as Joe Kramer. Two agents interviewed him in his 1957 Ford hardtop. Nagell asked that if he were given a pistol with a silencer and possibly some microfilm by his sources—Cuban, Russian, or both—if he could be permitted to return these items to his contact "so he could be of further use to the United States government or anyone else."

Nagell said that the individual with the gun would soon contact him and that he would then contact the FBI. He was not certain about the microfilm but thought the gun might be used to kill someone. He tore off the corner of a ten-dollar bill, gave it to the agents, and said it could be used "as identification in contacting him when he would later call the FBI for a meeting." He instructed that it be "shown to a bartender in a bar that he would name and then a waiter could let him know that a friend wanted to see him." The FBI said this was all unnecessary. He also told them he had been fired from the Alcohol Control board under false charges of accepting bribes. Because of his disgust of the United States, he left for Mexico. In August or September 1962, he met a man from Maryland in Mexico City who introduced him to Soviet agents. Nagell refused to give "descriptions, names or other details. When questioned on specific points he became mysteriously evasive." Nagell said he would phone them the next day, but that was the last they heard of him.

On February 3, 1963, he applied to the Army Board, asking that he be given a complete physical and neurological examination so he could receive full disability. He told them that after his hospitalization "I could not physically perform my assigned Infantry duties in an efficient manner and repeated requests for reassignment to less arduous duties met with negative replies." He added that he had "been turned down for many jobs because of my wartime wounds and injuries. The last time that I was employed was on June 8, 1962."

On April 19, 1963, Nagell contacted the LA office of the FBI and informed them he had just been in court with his wife. He had gotten a divorce the previous October and complained that his wife had not complied with the court regarding visitation. Nagell had no money for an attorney and had represented himself, and the judge instructed him to get a lawyer. He told the FBI that he was unemployed and has no money. Nagell became emotional and demanded that the FBI investigate the judge. He then threatened that if he did not soon get a job, he would "blow the lid off" the LA Police Department, the LA Sheriff's office, and the California Alcohol Beverage Control Board.

On June 4, 1963, he appeared at the VA outpatient clinic in LA and was referred to the neurological clinic for treatment. He was diagnosed with "depression" and was "tearful, nervous, rigid. Would only utter words 'Got to see my kids.'"

Ten days later, the Army replied negatively to Nagell's request. They wrote that "the available records do not indicate a basis for additional neurosurgical or neurological examination or medical board action."

And then that fateful day in September when Nagell shot up the bank.

After the bank incident, patrolmen Bundren and Westfall brought Nagell to the El Paso office of the FBI. Because the bank was federally insured, it came under their jurisdiction. Nagell said that he had fired two shots in the bank "to keep anyone from following me." He then said that "all of my problems have been solved for a long time, and now I won't have to go to Cuba." When asked what this meant, Nagell only said that "I can see this is going to be a frame which is to be expected in our capitalistic system."

They asked Nagell his motive, and he "stated that he was unhappy with the American judicial system, because he had attempted, through judicial procedures, to get to see his two children, a girl 3½ and boy 2½, in custody of his divorced wife, and the California court had not executed an order in keeping with his request."

The next day, Nagell told the FBI that the night before he had used a piece of tin to cut his wrists and that he had lost about a pint of blood. He did not think he was crazy but "felt that he needed psychiatric attention and advice because of the fact that he was highly emotional and at times could not remember what he was saying or where he was for short periods." He said he was too upset to even consider getting a job and that he had gone into the bank "so that they would take him back at the hospital." He had been suffering from headaches for several days and was out of the pills prescribed by the VA hospital.

Nagell waived a hearing and said that he did not want to be represented by an attorney. Bond was set for $25,000, and Nagell was sent to the El Paso County jail.

The government quickly realized that it was possible that Nagell was insane and filed a motion to determine his mental competency. They noted that he had been released from the Bay Pines facility on January 20, 1963, with a diagnosis of "chronic brain syndrome associated with brain trauma with behavioral reaction characterized by passive-aggressive and paranoid features." The jail physician also recommended that Nagell be examined by a psychiatrist "due to unusual behavior on the part of the defendant."

The district court judge directed that he be examined by a psychiatrist. On October 11, Dr. R. J. Bennett reported that on two occasions he had tried to examine Nagell, but Nagell was "unwilling to give any information." The court then ordered him to be taken to the Medical

Center for Federal Prisoners in Springfield, Missouri, for thirty days and for them to make a finding as to his mental competency.

The court first appointed James Hammond of the El Paso bar to represent Nagell. On November 4, Nagell told the court he did not desire his services because Hammond had disclosed some confidential information. Nagell told the court he would only agree to be examined by a psychiatrist from a VA hospital because if anything was wrong with him, it occurred during the Korean War. The judge told him that this was impossible because a VA hospital would not have the facilities to ensure his detention.

The court then appointed John Langford to represent Nagell. At a hearing on December 4, Nagell told the court he was not happy with Langford and launched into a long diatribe about being denied a speedy trial. He told the court that he did not try to hold up the bank but would not disclose his motive for going into the bank. He filed a writ of habeas corpus claiming that he was being held prisoner illegally. He then asked the judge to dismiss his court-appointed attorney, and his request was granted. He also agreed to be examined by a psychiatrist from the VA.

On December 19, 1963, Nagell told the FBI "for the record" that he had met Lee Harvey Oswald in Mexico City and in Texas and that his association was strictly social. He refused to comment further. On January 3, 1964, Nagell, upon his request, met with a Secret Service agent and an FBI agent and told them that he had known the Oswalds socially, "that Oswald had the same type marital difficulties as he did," and that he "knew nothing about Oswald killing the President." Nagell thought the Secret Service investigation would show that he knew the Oswalds and he felt that if he admitted he knew them that "he would not be associated with Oswald's crime." He added that Marina Oswald could identify his photograph. Nagell became agitated during the interview, and toward the end a tic in his face was "very noticeable."

Marina Oswald was then shown a photograph of Nagell, and she said that she had never seen him before. She did not know anybody by the name of Nagell or his other aliases.

On January 3, 1964, the FBI interviewed George Stanga, a prisoner who was incarcerated with Nagell. Nagell had told him that after he left the military, he had drifted from job to job "and had become more and more mentally confused as to his religious and economic allegiances." He said he had joined the Communist Party and that he only went to El Paso because he believed that everything was against him in Los Angeles and "that he should attempt to leave the United States for a Communist country in Europe."

He said he had arranged to meet a Communist Party contact in El Paso who would have a visa and a passport for him to go to Czechoslovakia. During his drive from Los Angeles to El Paso, Nagell stopped at the side of the road three times to attempt suicide with his pistol. He tried again in his hotel room but did not have the nerve "to pull the trigger." He then figured the best way to commit suicide was to have a shootout with a policeman. So he decided to go into the bank because he knew a policeman would be there.

Nagell also told Stanga that he had several rolls of microfilm hidden in a gas mask at his sister's house in New York City, which contained the names, meeting places and activities of the Communist Party.

On January 4, 1964, he submitted a signed statement to the FBI, which addressed his motive:

In September 1962, while I was in Mexico City a representative of a foreign government proposed to me that I participate in an act: Such act being a criminal offense and inimical to the best interests of the United States. At that time I refused such proposal. In May, 1963, another representative of the same foreign government made the same proposal to me. At that time I agreed to such a proposal.

In Sept. 1963, I was informed by an American, known to me as an agent of the same foreign government, that arrangements for my participation in the aforementioned act were completed. At this time I refused the aforesaid proposal.

Approximately one week later I was instructed by this same person to either participate as previously agreed or derogatory information pertaining to me would be disclosed to the Federal Bureau of Investigation. Thereupon I agreed to follow the instructions of this person, although I did not intend to do so. This existing situation actuated my conduct of September 20, 1963, for which I was arrested and am presently charged.

I did not actually attempt to rob any bank. I thought that my arrest would provide an immediate, though temporary solution to the problem with which I was confronted.

I am not guilty as charged.

Later that month, Nagell's mother heard about the charges against her son and called the FBI. She had last seen him in August, at which time he told her that he wanted nothing to do with his relatives. She also said that Nagell had had a brilliant career until the plane crash and that he "underwent a complete personality change" after his recuperation.

At the next hearing on January 24, Nagell denied that he had ever been treated by a psychiatrist. He claimed that he had been questioned by the FBI regarding subversive activities and that he had been asked questions by the Secret Service about Lee Harvey Oswald. He said he did not want a psychiatric examination and that his military records would prove that he had no psychosis.

The U.S. attorney then filed a motion, which was granted, to have Nagell committed for psychiatric treatment. Nagell was sent to the Medical Center for Federal Prisoners (MCFP) in Springfield, Missouri, for thirty days. He told the court he would not cooperate with the psychiatrists.

While being moved from the courthouse, Nagell he in an elevator that the FBI had not attempted to prevent JFK's assassination and that the FBI had questioned him about Lee Harvey Oswald.

Suspect Says Agents Asked Him About Oswald, Activities Link

El Paso Times, January 27, 1964

On February 3, the FBI spoke to Nagell's wife, Mitsuko. She said she had filed for divorce on April 19, 1962, but it was still not finalized. She claimed that "Nagell stayed out late nights, beat her, never gave her any money, and did not like his children." She also said that in her opinion, "there is something mentally wrong with Nagell" and that he would "fly into violent rages without apparent reason." The couple was always in financial difficulty, and since their separation Nagell had only sent her a total of $180.

That same day, Nagell was admitted to the MCFP for evaluation, but he refused to cooperate. He was examined on February 14 by three members of the MCFP's neuropsychiatric staff. Dr. Gustave Weiland agreed with a diagnosis of mental illness, undetermined "by a man who is utilizing passive aggressive tactics." Nonetheless, he concluded that there should an adjudication of competence.

On March 6, the chief medical officer at Springfield reported that Nagell was "opposed to psychiatric examination and will not cooperate in this area or any examination that may be performed on him." He also reported that he felt Nagell was competent to stand trial.

On March 20, 1964, Nagell wrote a letter to J. Lee Rankin, the general counsel of the Warren Commission. He wanted to know if they had been advised that he had informed the FBI in September 1963 that an attempt would made to kill JFK. He also wondered if they had been advised that the day before JFK went to Dallas, he had requested the FBI contact the Secret Service to again inform them of what was going to happen.

> Has the commission been advised that I informed the Federal Bureau of Investigation in September 1963 that an attempt might be made to assassinate President Kennedy? Was the Commission advised that the day before Mr. Kennedy visited Dallas, I initiated a request through jail authority to the F.B.I., asking them to contact the Secret Service Division in order to inform such agency of the same information, when it became apparent to me that the F.B.I. believed my revelation to be mendacious?

On March 24, Nagell told the court that he had been without counsel since December 9 and requested that the court appoint counsel. The court then appointed Gus Rallis and Richard B. Perrenot and gave them additional time to prepare. Nagell told the court on April 10 that "I think that I am being railroaded because I am a communist and because I have been accused of being an espionage agent."

One week later, Nagell wrote to the FBI saying that in September 1963, he had sent a registered letter to the FBI, under the name Jack

Kramer, warning them that JFK would be assassinated. Of course, the FBI never received such a letter.

April 16, 1964

Director
Federal Bureau of Investigation
U. S. Department of Justice
Washington 25, D. C.

Dear Mr. Hoover:

This letter is being sent to you, at my insistence, through the facilities of my counsel, Mr. Gus Rallis, in order to insure that it is brought to your personal attention.

I wish it to be understood that Mr. Rallis was appointed by the U. S. District Court, El Paso, Texas, to represent me at my forthcoming trial on a charge of violating Section 2113 (a), Title 18, U.S.C., and is not cognizant of any details pertaining to the matter discussed herein, although such matter is most relevant to my defense against the aforesaid charge.

My purpose in writing this letter is to advise you that since it is apparent the Federal Bureau of Investigation is determined to have me convicted of this deceptive charge by witholding pertinent information from the U. S. Attorney, you, as director of the F.B.I., will not be able to relinguish at least partial responsibility for the death of President Kennedy.

My responsibility concerning the then prospective action of Lee H. Oswald (Albert Hidel) terminated with the dispatch of the registered letter from Joseph Kramer to the F.B.I. in September 1963.

Since the information disclosed in that letter was judged to be mendacious by the F.B.I., as is quite evident, then with whom the responsibility lies for what subsequently happened in Dallas is rather obvious.

Certainly, F.B.I. files in Washington, D.C. (or Miami, Florida, Mexico City, etc.) reflect who "Joseph Kramer" is. And, such information received from a known Communist who allegedly had been effective enough to penetrate several U.S. military intelligence

agencies, should not have been ignored. In this respect, the
efficacy of the F.B.I. is the responsibility of its director,
regardless of the actions or judgement of his subordinates.

In any event, I shall not acquiesce to sit idle and maintain
silence while the F.B.I. railroads me into prison on a phony charge,
simply because it cannot have me convicted of other matters.

Very truly,

Richard C. Nagell
El Paso County Jail
El Paso, Texas

Nagell's letter to the FBI.

A few days later, Mr. Perrenot was allowed to withdraw from the case
because of prolonged disagreements with Nagell, and the court-
appointed Joseph Calamia. Later that day, Calamia told the court that
Nagell was refusing to cooperate in obtaining complete psychiatric
reports and that he could not go to trial without such reports. Nagell told
the court that he had been found to be competent to stand trial and that
that was the end of it. The court allowed his attorneys to withdraw and
told Nagell to prepare his own defense. The next day, Nagell changed his
mind, and Calamia and Rallis were back.

During the trial, Nagell interrupted witnesses on the stand, called
them liars, and jumped and shouted that he was not insane. Dr. Manuel
Hernandez testified that Nagell had been "suffering a serious mental or
emotional illness" on September 20, 1963. He thought Nagell was "a
schizoid personality with rather strong paranoid features" and
concluded that Nagell's mental state would not have rendered him
unable to distinguish between right and wrong.

Dr. R. J. Bennett said that he had not been able to examine Nagell but
thought he was suffering from a paranoid condition. He believed that on
September 20, Nagell could distinguish between right and wrong. Dr.
Martin Schwartz, a VA staff psychiatrist in Highland Park, Illinois, had
observed Nagell for one week during his stay in Bay Pines, Florida, and
he agreed with Dr. Bennett. Dr. Gustave Weilland, staff psychiatrist at
Springfield, also agreed that Nagell could tell the difference between
right and wrong.

Nothing was said about any organic brain damage.

Nagell was convicted on May 6, 1964.

Calamia made a motion for a new trial after Nagell told him his complete medical history and after an FBI agent interviewed Dr. Weinstein, the doctor who had examined Nagell at Walter Reed in 1954. The government had not disclosed anything about his assessment. Dr. Weinstein then examined Nagell in the El Paso jail.

He reported that unless a psychiatrist had an accurate account of what had happened to Nagell, they "would be confused by the manifestations in this case." He emphasized Nagell's denial of illness and "his attempt to conceal information." Weinstein testified that Nagell had suffered a fracture through the base of his brain, which injured the underside of the brain and some of the cranial nerves coming off the brain.

Here is what Weinstein said about the bank incident:

I would say that this was a symptom or a manifestation of disturbed brain function and during this period his judgment and perception of reality was seriously disturbed so that he could not accurately differentiate right from wrong, that, in his opinion, Nagell was disassociated with reality at the time of the incident.

Weinstein believed that the bank incident was "an alternative to suicide." He criticized the 1955 conclusion that Nagell's concussion had been cured. He said this was inaccurate and was partly due to Nagell's deceptions and denials of behavioral changes. An accurate diagnosis would not have returned Nagell to active duty.

Government psychiatrists, after hearing Weinstein, changed their testimony. Dr. Hernandez said Dr. Weinstein was one of the foremost authorities on brain injuries and that he knew of no one better. He now said that Nagell was not able to distinguish between right and wrong on Sept. 20, 1963. Dr. Hornisher agreed with Weinstein and did not believe Nagell could distinguish between right and wrong. Dr. Martin Schwartz conceded that Nagell had a mental disorder but did not know how serious it was.

Despite this testimony, the court on May 9, 1964, denied the motion for a new trial.

On June 9, 1964, Nagell was sentenced in El Paso to serve the maximum term of ten years. One week later, Nagell attempted suicide by swallowing six or seven tranquilizers. He was taken to La Tuna Federal Correctional Institution for emergency treatment, where he fully recovered. He was then taken to the U.S. Public Health Service hospital in Ft. Worth for psychiatric treatment.

Bank Holdup Man Tries Suicide

El Paso Times, June 17, 1964

Nagell was examined by Dr. Jo Anne Holzman. Her clinical record of June 19 notes:

> He states that he has periods of 'loss of memory, can't speak, loss of balance.' He states that he had battle fatigue twice … On describing an incident of taking a hill … he breaks into tears and cannot continue. He states that he fell back five times, that he lost almost all of his men and that he became somewhat angry with the company commander for not ordering them back … the patient states that he really wanted to die in the recent suicide attempt but with his court appeal now pending, he now feels that things are more hopeful and does not consider suicide at this time. However, he goes on to state that he does get depressive episodes and fears that he might again consider suicide.

Nagell was kept on suicide watch for eleven days. He was then sent to the maximum-security ward for further observation. The final psychiatric diagnosis was "acute brain syndrome, secondary to drug intoxication improved, and sociopathic personality, dissocial type, unimproved." He was then returned to prison.

Nagell was next examined by H. R. Passaro, a psychologist, on August 17, 1965. He said that Nagell's attitude had changed considerably and that he was "cooperative and quite free to express himself." He believed he would need psychiatric counseling after his release.

On January 4, 1966, the Fifth Circuit Court reversed the district's court refusal to grant a new trial. Judge Coleman wrote:

> Every doctor who testified at the trial was of the opinion that Nagell could distinguish between right and wrong on September 20, 1963. As a result of the newly discovered evidence, which the defendant concealed as the result of a damaged brain and a diseased mind, three doctors, one of them an outstanding national authority on brain damage, are now prepared to testify that in their opinion he did not then know the difference between right and wrong. This puts an entirely different face on the matter. Of course, we do not decide the merits of the case, but we believe another jury should have an opportunity to decide the guilt or innocence of this man in light of this new evidence.

On April 7, 1966, Nagell was ordered recommitted to the MCFP for psychiatric observation and examination. But Nagell refused to be removed from his cell to be transferred. He used towels to secure his jail door and threatened to slash his throat with a razor if anybody tried to remove him. Jail Captain O'Rourke told the press that Nagell spent most of his time sitting or pacing in his cell and that his conversation took a paranoid turn "in which he considers he has nothing but enemies."

This continued for a week, after which Nagell walked out and "surrendered to authorities" so that he could be transferred.

Nagell was interviewed on May 31 by Dr. Robert Murney, a clinical psychologist. Nagell told him that he "never intended to rob a bank in the first place, that he had only been seeking a desperate way of obtaining help. He went on to explain that several requests for admission to a VA hospital had been turned down and that in desperation he involved himself in the act to call attention to his need."

Murney did not uncover any evidence of "an active psychotic process" or any evidence of "cortical brain damage." However, his findings "point to significant functional emotional problems which appear to be of long standing, and which definitely interfere, particularly under conditions of stress, with this man's ability to function at a level commensurate with his intellectual capacities. In my opinion, this patient has both neurotic and characterological problems which I would infer at time have reached psychotic proportions." Murney concluded that "nothing will be gained for society or for Mr. Nagell by continued incarceration in a penal institution."

On June 13, 1966, Nagell was examined by Dr. Joseph Alderete, chief of psychiatric services, and Dr. George Parlato, a regular psychiatric consultant to the MCFP. Their report noted that Nagell "emphasized … his whole purpose of entering the bank in El Paso was for the purpose of obtaining psychiatric help and treatment and not for the purpose of actually robbing the bank." They concluded that Nagell was competent to stand trial but said that he was not mentally competent at the time of the bank incident. They also concluded that Nagell was "a lifelong paranoid personality under slowly building conditions of stress" and that he "went into an actual psychosis (paranoid state) and subsequently went into remission, and is now again a paranoid personality." The recommendation was continued outpatient psychotherapy for a year.

Dr. Alderete and Dr. Weinstein testified at Nagell's second trial in September 1966.

Weinstein reiterated his view that Nagell suffered a brain injury in the plane crash and that "a diagnosis of plaintiff as suffering from a life-long personality disorder would be incorrect." He testified that an EEG would only show abnormality if performed in the initial stages of the injury and if the electrodes were placed within the brain. He also said that it would be hard to accurately diagnose Nagell's case unless a doctor knew his full history.

Nagell's brain injury exaggerated his "pre-accident tendency to regard illness as imperfection and consulting a doctor as a confession of weakness. This trait … became exaggerated to the point of psychosis after the injury." He used the term "anosognosia," also known as Anton's disease, which is a tendency to deny mental illness. He detected this when he saw Nagell in 1955. Weinstein said before Nagell's accident, this trait was not abnormal but after the accident had become "exaggerated to the point of psychosis."

A good example of this was the fact that throughout his initial trial,

Nagell continually protested that he had no mental illness even though this was against his own interest.

Weinstein said that Nagell also had confabulations—inventing fictitious stories:

> Nagell started to use these untrue delusional formations with no awareness at the time that these were false, and these came out particularly when he was admitted to the Veterans Hospital in Bay Pines, Florida, around Christmas in 1962.

He mentioned three stories that Nagell made up:

- Nagell said he received a telegram from California saying that his two children had been killed.
- Nagell said he had been hit on the head with a blackjack in New York City and robbed of eight hundred dollars.
- He told a psychologist in Bay Pines that he was born in Montana, but he was actually born in New York.

Dr. Alderete testified that Nagell was not in a psychotic state when he examined him but was at the time of the bank shooting. Since he was not a neurologist, he could not confirm nor deny that Nagell had suffered a brain injury.

Two other psychiatrists-neurologists now said that Nagell was not able to determine right from wrong when he entered the bank.

One of the lighter moments of the trial came when Calamia made a motion that the court instruct witnesses not to refer to what took place in the bank as a robbery or an attempted robbery and that "one witness not refer to the fact that he was called a 'capitalistic s.o.b.' by Nagell" as it would be prejudicial.

Calamia complained that statements like that would be like "throwing a skunk in the jury box. You can 'strike' it, but the smell is still there." The judge overruled Calamia's motion saying that he had no way of knowing "who is going to throw skunks in the jury box."

——EL PASO HERALD-POST, Tuesday, September 20, 1966

Holdup Suspect Has 'Brain Injuries'

El Paso Herald-Post, September 20, 1966

The jury started deliberating on Thursday, September 22 and twice sent out notes to Judge W. D. Suttle saying they were deadlocked. On the afternoon of September 26, the jury returned a verdict of guilty, and Nagell was again sentenced to ten years in prison.

Nagell needed help, and he asked his sister on October 16, 1966, to contact Mark Lane, a lawyer who had recently published *Rush to Judgment*, a critique of the Warren Report:

> I request you follow the first of my instructions. Please contact the lawyer concerned (Mark Lane) and show him the material I listed, in the order listed, including, first, the remaining two pages of my proposed testimony. Show him a copy of this letter and copies of any other letters which will assist in explaining my situation and predicament.

On January 3, 1967, Nagell wrote Senator Richard Russell, a former member of the Warren Commission, and said that "Oswald and his activities came under my scrutiny during 1962 and 1963" and that Oswald was involved in a conspiracy to murder JFK in September 1963. Nagell claimed he was then given instructions to "initiate certain actions against Mr. Oswald" and then to leave the country. Nagell did neither and claimed he wrote a letter to J. Edgar Hoover warning about the conspiracy.

Later that month, New Orleans DA Jim Garrison's investigation into the JFK assassination was made public. Nagell was keeping tabs, and he wrote his sister in March asking her to contact Garrison and to get him a copy of the letter he had written to Russell. Garrison also received a letter from a Nagell acquaintance informing him that he wanted to get in touch.

Nagell received a one-sentence perfunctory reply from Russell:

United States Senate
COMMITTEE ON ARMED SERVICES

January 20, 1967

Mr. Richard C. Nagell
Register No. 83286-L
P. O. Box 1000
Leavenworth, Kansas 66048

Dear Mr. Nagell:

Permit me to acknowledge and thank you for
your letter and the information it contains.

With every good wish, I am

Sincerely,

Nagell sent this reply on April 1:

April 1, 1967

Hon. Richard B. Russell
United States Senate
Washington, D. C. 20515

Dear Senator Russell:

Thank you for your tactful response to my letter dated January 3. It
suggests you have neither jumped to conclusions about the information furnished
nor rendered any harsh judgement on me personally, notwithstanding the implications involved. If this is the case I am grateful. I feel if the authorities
had exercised similar tact in dealing with me from the very beginning, the
overall situation would be quite different today.

One purpose in communicating with you at this time is to advise that I am
no longer certain the letter I dispatched to the Director, Federal Bureau of
Investigation, in September 1963 was sent via postal registry, or, for that
matter, even mailed. I am not in a position to elaborate on this aside from
saying the reference made in my previous letter was made in good conscience.

I think you should also be apprised that all information resulting from
my surveillance of Mr. Oswald's activities, including his involvement in a
conspiracy to murder President Kennedy, was passed on to Soviet officials
without delay. In fact, my last report concerning him was dispatched the
evening before my arrest.

Regarding the inquiry currently underway in New Orleans, I can only point
out that my knowledge of Mr. Oswald's contacts and associations during the
summer of 1963 indicate that he had no relationship with the persons identified
as Messrs. Clay L. Shaw, David W. Ferrie and Perry R. Russo.

In closing, I would like to assure you that while I am quite aware of the
stigma attached to me as a result of my defense of insanity and my present
location, I am not now, nor have I ever been, incompetent or otherwise devoid
of my mental faculties.

Sincerely,

Richard C. Nagell
FMB 16600-8
Springfield, Mo. 65802

Now Nagell tells Russell that he is no longer certain that the letter he wrote to Hoover in September 1963 was even mailed.

New Orleans Assistant District Attorney William Martin flew out on April 10 to Springfield, Missouri, to interview Nagell and met with him for four hours over two days. Right at the start of the interview, Nagell told Martin that he would not provide any material or evidence. He said that "he had been a Marxist for many years and that he had no particular loyalty to the United States."

Martin reported that Nagell talked of three plots to kill JFK:

[T]here had actually been three separate plots to assassinate President Kennedy. The first was a plan to kill President Kennedy by bombing (a concealed bomb in the speaker's platform or the speaker's podium) on the occasion of December or January of 1962 when the President traveled to Miami, Florida to address the group of Cuban prisoners who had taken part in the Bay of Pigs invasion and who had just been released and returned to the States. A second and similar plan to kill the President was to have taken place in June of 1963 when the President traveled to Los Angeles for an important speaking engagement. The subject stated that the first and second plots (above mentioned) had never really become serious and that the plans never did reach more than just the talking stage. The third and final plot, which did in fact end with the assassination of President Kennedy, was an offshoot of the other two plans and was planned and put into effect by the same group of people.

At the start of Martin's second interview, Nagell asked Martin about Garrison's theory of the assassination. Martin replied that the assassination was meant to trigger an invasion of Cuba. This interested Nagell, and he told Martin that he had worked "for the other side" under the specific control of the Soviet embassy in Mexico City. He claimed he had been able to "infiltrate the assassination plot" and that he made a "tape recording of four voices in conversation concerning the plot." The tape was primarily in Spanish and was currently in a small trunk left with a friend. The contents of the trunk could only be released to a person bearing a handwritten letter from Nagell.

Nagell insisted that his friend's name not be written in Martin's report, but he was willing to whisper the name. He was worried that his report might fall into the hands of the FBI or the CIA and that if that should happen, the FBI would kick in his friend's door and harass him into turning over the tape.

Martin's "job one" was to get a letter from Nagell so that he could get the tape.

Toward the end of April, Martin flew back to Springfield and met with Nagell. Nagell told Martin the tape would show "conclusive proof of a plot to kill President Kennedy." He said there are four voices on the tape, including Nagell's, and that he was only acting as an interpreter at the meeting. Initially, he said the tape was made in late August 1963 but later said it was late September. Of course, this was impossible since Nagell was in jail. Martin pointed out the contradiction, and Nagell replied that he wasn't thinking clearly. Nagell then said his friend would give Martin the recording without an introductory letter.

The next day Martin met with Robert Nicholas, the chief of classification and parole at the medical center. He wanted to arrange further privileged meetings with Nagell to make him feel more comfortable. Nicholas asked Martin what grounds he "was going to use to appeal the subject's case to a higher court." He clearly thought Martin was there to help Nagell legally.

Nagell then passed by the office and saw the two of them speaking:

The subject continued by saying that he had overheard Mr. Nicholas and myself speaking and that he had changed his mind about confiding in me and hat he did not want to associate with me any manner and did not want to speak to me at all. Mr. Nicholas and I both attempted to calm the subject down. He was visibly shaken, pale, and moving his hands about in an extremely nervous manner. After a few minutes I was able to convince Mr. Nagell that he should sit down with me in private at least long enough to tell me what was on his mind and what had upset him so much. Mr. Nagell and I were seated in a private room adjoining Mr. Nicholas' office and he proceeded to tell me that he had overheard me speaking to Mr. Nicholas in a "friendly" manner and that he had become extremely agitated, excited and lacking in confidence since I had become "friendly" with Mr. Nicholas.

Nagell stalked out. Nicholas called Nagell's physician to have a talk with Nagell. He returned after twenty minutes and said that Nagell did not want Martin to represent him "in any manner" and for him to "just forget the whole thing." The doctor also told Martin that in a few days, Nagell might have an "equally strong and opposite reaction" and might be anxious to see him again.

Martin then immediately wrote Nicholas a letter to give to Nagell to help put his mind at rest. He said all past conversations would be held in confidence and that he would not pursue anything related to Nagell. Nagell refused to accept the letter.

UNITED STATES DEPARTMENT OF JUSTICE
BUREAU OF PRISONS
MEDICAL CENTER FOR FEDERAL PRISONERS
SPRINGFIELD, MISSOURI 65802

April 28, 1967

Mr. William R. Martin
Counselor at Law
International Trade Mart
New Orleans, Louisiana

Re: NAGELL, Richard C.
Reg. No. A-16606-H

Dear Mr. Martin:

I regret that I must return your letter pertaining to Mr. Nagell
in that he has refused to accept it. It appears that his reaction
is completely out of proportion since he has also requested his
caseworker to remove all persons on his official correspondence
list except magazines and newspapers.

Your dedication to this man is remarkable.

Sincerely,

R. S. Nicholas, Chief
Classification & Parole

But Nagell wrote Martin in May saying that he was preparing a writ of habeas corpus along with a supporting memo. Five days later, he sent another letter asking Martin to arrange a visit so he could hand over his handwritten petition and memo to be typed up. He added that he had "terminated correspondence with his sister because I don't want her dragged into this mess."

On June 7, 1967, Nagell gave Martin a letter of introduction to a Mr.

Frederick H. John that asked him to hand over one of the tapes kept in a cigar box. He also asked that other tapes, his passport, and all "embarrassing material" be disposed of. Martin took the letter and found Mr. John. Alas, the material was no longer there—it had been the subject of a burglary. Martin wrote Nagell to inform him what had happened.

WILLIAM R. MARTIN
COUNSELOR AT LAW
INTERNATIONAL TRADE MART
NEW ORLEANS, LOUISIANA

Mr. Richard Case Nagell   20 June 1967
U. S. Penitentiary
Leavenworth, Kansas

Dear Mr. Nagell:

After my most recent visit with you at the Springfield Medical Center, I traveled briefly to interview the witness you had indicated as being valuable to your appeal and to obtain from him evidence that he might have had.

Fortunately enough, I was able to locate the witness with absolutely no trouble and managed to spend several hours in amiable conversation. I was much impressed by this individual; by his dignity, bearing and loyalty. I am satisfied in my own mind that he would have helped in every possible manner in the legal battle that lies ahead.

Unfortunately, however, the physical evidence that I had hoped to obtain was not available. Apparently it was the subject of a burglary sometime in 1964 and was the only item of interest to the burglar, who did not disturb, as far as can be determined, any other items of value...so I am told. In any case, I was interested in nothing else.

Of course I will continue the preparation of our case with all diligence, but I wanted you to know that this particular effort had been in vain.

WILLIAM R. MARTIN

WRM/lm

P.S. In as much as I am not certain of your present address, I would appreciate acknowledgement of this letter.

Nagell replied that since the physical evidence was no longer available, there was no point continuing "the preparation of my case." Martin agreed. Nagell wrote back in July saying that had procedures been followed at the outset, the tape would have been in his possession and that it had not disappeared in 1964, nor was it the "subject of burglary by the opposition."

Nagell also wrote his sister about the tape:

> In this regard, I can state with good foundation that if it was stolen, it was not taken in 1964. In the same vein, I can also say that while the item involved may indeed no longer be available, it is not in the custody of the opposition either.

He also told Martin that a friend had retained an attorney for him and that he longer needed his services. Martin forwarded several documents, including the typed-up writ of habeas corpus to Nagell's sister. Their correspondence continued for several months, but no tapes ever emerged.

Nagell's habeas corpus memo ran forty typewritten pages covering thirty-six allegations, mostly complaints about court-appointed counsels and his insistence that he was competent. Nagell repeated his claim that he had sent a letter to the FBI in Washington prior to his arrest "about Lee Oswald." He also claimed he sent a letter to the chief of the Secret Service advising that there had been a conspiracy to kil JFK "and other government officials" and that he never received a reply.

In late September, Tom Bethell, a member of Garrison's staff, wrote a letter to conspiracy author Richard Popkin about the Nagell lead, then a topic of discussion among the DA's staff:

```
I recently read through the X file, and I must say I am at
a loss to understand why you evidently think there might be
something important to this. When one bears in mind that he
was in custody before Oswald went to Mexico, that he is in
the everything-to-gain and nothin-to-lose position of all
other prisoners (almost daily we get mail from prisoners all
over the country with offers to identify Bertrand, etc.),
and that he alleges possession of a tape recording of people
planning the assassination which, even if it were located,
would be of almost no value in view of the ease with which
such a tape could be forged, this all amounts, in my view,
to a very tenuous lead.
```

X was a Garrison code term for Nagell, which makes him the original Mr. X.

Bethell also wrote in his diary entry for September 22, 1967, that he had just "reviewed the Nagell file and consider[ed] it a complete waste of Bill Martin's time and office money."

The Nagell story appeared in print for the first time in Bill Turner's lengthy article on the Garrison investigation in *Ramparts* magazine in January 1968. Turner wrote that Nagell staged the bank incident "as an alibi when the assassination took place." According to this version of the story, JFK had to be assassinated because he was moving toward rapprochement with Cuba. Anti-Castro Cubans approached Oswald in New Orleans and "appealed to his ego in setting him up as a patsy." The CIA got wind of the plans and sent agents into the field, Nagell among them, to find out the truth. Nagell was then instructed to kill the patsy after the assassination. He "got cold feet and bailed out." Nagell would later claim the article was "completely erroneous" and that he never needed an alibi since he was on his way out of the country.

And that was quite typical. Nagell was always taking exception to what people wrote about him. You could never be sure what his exact story was since it always changed and everybody had their own interpretation of what he was or was not saying.

On April 3, 1968, the Fifth Circuit reversed Nagell's conviction and issued an acquittal. The court said "the trial court instructed the jury that it might infer intent from Nagell's conduct in the bank. Viewing the totality of Nagell's conduct, and in light of the strong evidence of his insanity at the time," the court found that the jury received improper instructions. Because it was not possible to infer that Nagell's intent was to rob the bank, the evidence did not sustain a conviction, and there was no good reason for a new trial.

The court described the expert testimony as follows:

Here the record is replete with expert testimony regarding Nagell's mental condition: "Mentally disturbed," the particular characterization being "chronic traumatic encephalopathy"—a disease of the brain caused by trauma. Its symptoms: paranoia, suicidal preoccupations, "confabulations", tendency toward projection, impaired judgment, lack of contact and reality.

Nagell was released from prison on April 29, 1968, and he then went to New York City to visit his sister.

On or about May 14, Nagell met with Jim Garrison for three hours in Central Park. Here is some dialogue from that meeting taken from Garrison's book *On the Trail of the Assassins*:

> **Nagell**: I am not going to identify the organization I worked for in 1963. You simply will have to draw your own conclusions about that. Nor will I say exactly what I was working on. I am bound by some laws in this area, and I've already had enough problems from the government without having any new ones.
>
> **Garrison**: Were you with the Company?
>
> **Nagell**: (shaking his head) I cannot answer that question.
>
> **Garrison**: Then just what information can you give me?"
>
> **Nagell**: I am already on record about my learning that the assassination was scheduled and about my effort to contact the Bureau and warn them about it. As far as I am concerned, I have a right to go into that because I have already done so before. I just thought that you should know firsthand what I have to say. Is this of any interest to you?
>
> **Garrison**: (nods)

Garrison then asked him a few questions:

> **Garrison**: Had you actually been in physical association with Lee Oswald? Right there with him?
>
> **Nagell**: Yes.
>
> **Garrison**: And with other men connected with Oswald?
>
> **Nagell**: Yes.
>
> **Garrison**: Where did this occur?
>
> **Nagell**: In New Orleans and in Texas.

Garrison asked him the names of the other men involved, and Nagell said Guy Banister, Clay Shaw, and David Ferrie. Wouldn't you know it— Nagell named three of the people that Garrison was investigating.

The next day, Garrison claimed, he spent six hours talking to Nagell in a hotel lobby. Garrison told his colleagues that Nagell said he was a

KGB man—initially a U.S. intelligence officer in the Army who was "married to the Soviet apparatus." He then became a "CIA operator" who was sent to see "what was happening with the group around Oswald." Garrison said that Nagell was "concerned about being able to get out of the country" and that it was the Soviets who were trying to extricate him. Nagell told Garrison he knew Oswald in Mexico, Texas, and in Japan where Oswald had served in the Marines in the late 1950s. The assassination plan, according to Nagell, was initially scheduled for Washington, and Oswald had some sort of decoy assignment.

Soon after this meeting, Nagell claimed that he was almost hit by a car driven without lights. He felt this was an attempt by the CIA to kill him and he decided to go to Europe.

On June 4, 1968, Nagell appeared at the American consulate in Zurich, Switzerland. He told them a confusing story about working for a "secret U.S. government agency" on a mission to Geneva, where he was to meet some Japanese people, and he wanted assistance to get money he claimed had been deposited in a New York bank. The next day, he came back and was "quite incoherent" and appeared "psychotic possibly dangerous." He told them that Jim Garrison had warned him that he was in danger of being killed, and therefore he wanted the CIA to know he was in Zurich.

On June 11, Nagell boarded a train in Zurich headed to West Berlin. At about 3:00 a.m., it arrived at the border crossing with East Germany, and the authorities found that Nagell did not possess a transit visa. He told them that he intended to go to East Berlin to visit the embassies of the People's Republic of China, North Korea, or Cuba to apply for political asylum.

Nagell was charged with espionage on June 14.

DER GENERALSTAATSANWALT
DER DEUTSCHEN DEMOKRATISCHEN REPUBLIK

Stadtbezirksgericht   Berlin, 14. Juni 1968
Berlin-Mitte
zu Hd. d. Gen. K. Krautter

B e r l i n

Gemäß § 141 StPO beantrage ich, gegen

                N A G E L L , Richard Case
                geboren am 5. 8. 1930 in New York/Greenwich
                Wohnanschrift unbekannt

Haftbefehl zu erlassen.
Der Beschuldigte NAGELL ist dringend verdächtig, fortgesetzt
handelnd es unternommen zu haben, als langjähriger Mitarbeiter
der amerikanischen Geheimdienste CIA und CIC Spionagetätigkeit gegen die DDR und andere mit ihr befreundete sozialistische
Staaten betrieben zu haben, indem er geheimzuhaltende Infor-
mationen sammelte und auslieferte.
Der Beschuldigte befand sich zum Zeitpunkt seiner Festnahme
im Besitz persönlicher Unterlagen und Aufzeichnungen, die
über seine Spionagetätigkeit für die genannten Geheimdienste
Aufschluß geben.

Strafbar gemäß § 14 StEG
Der Erlaß des Haftbefehls ist erforderlich, da der Beschuldigte keinen festen Wohnsitz hat und der Spionagetätigkeit
für amerikanische Geheimdienste dringend verdächtig ist.
Darüber hinaus bestehen ernsthafte Zweifel an der Personen-
indentität des Beschuldigten, so daß auch ein Personenfest-
stellungsverfahren erforderlich erscheint.

                                        i.A.
                                              Staatsanwalt

Arrest warrant for Richard Case Nagell. It accuses him of being an employee of
the CIA and of carrying out espionage activities against East Germany and other
socialist states.

Nagell was interrogated in July and August, and he spun a variety of
tales about his military intelligence service and his supposed employ-

ment by the CIA. He said he had been in contact with the CIA during his time in prison and since his release and that they were the ones who had ordered him to go to Switzerland. He told the East Germans that he thought the CIA was afraid that Garrison would call him as a witness because he might say something about what he knew about the assassination. The CIA, he claimed, was very afraid of Garrison.

Nagell told the East Germans that he feared being assassinated by the CIA and knew of five intelligence comrades who had died mysteriously. One jumped out of a hotel room, another was hit by a car, and three died from a heart attack. Nagell said they were all young people in good health.

He told the East Germans about two operations he was involved in that were designed to provoke the Soviet Union. The first was in Tokyo in 1958, in which a Soviet diplomat was to be kidnapped. The other was in 1962, in which Nagell would "defect" to the Soviet Union in order to determine how they treated such people. He said both operations failed.

Nagell didn't tell the Germans much about the JFK assassination. He said that in 1962 the CIA had commissioned him to investigate the Fair Play for Cuba Committee, and that had led him to Lee Harvey Oswald. Nagell said he learned from Oswald information about the planned assassination, which he passed on to the CIA. He then received the order to kill Oswald, presumably from the KGB. He now said that he shot up the bank because he feared he would be prosecuted because of his knowledge of the assassination plan. Somehow the CIA had him sentenced to an extraordinarily long prison sentence.

He also claimed that the CIA had given him a capsule laced with poison to kill himself.

At one point he said he wanted to go to China and "be of use to the international socialist movement." He claimed he had worked intermittently for the PRC from 1956 to 1962. He said he was not paid by the Chinese and complained he never even received a thank you.

On June 14 and June 15, Nagell refused to talk and on June 18, he shouted obscenities and insults. He refused to leave his cell from June 19 to June 26, and he then smashed a table. On July 1, he started destroying his cell, and by the third he had destroyed all the furnishings (bed, table, lighting fixtures, and toilet bowl) in his cell as well as the radiator. He then tried to smash the cell door. At 9:00 p.m. on July 3, Nagell was given a new cell. The Stasi files indicate that Nagell had permission to smoke, to read English materials, and to receive special meals. In addition, "the prison management was instructed not to use violence against" Nagell.

On July 4 Nagell submitted a handwritten appeal of his arrest and detention to the investigating judge. He wrote that his involvement with American intelligence agencies were "made known by me, quite voluntarily, to representatives of your government prior to my setting foot on German soil." He claimed he was brought to East Berlin on June 14 with a promise that he would be allowed to visit the Cuban embassy.

Nagell's interrogators noted "after he became increasingly involved in contradictions and found himself faced with the need to provide concrete and detailed information, he fundamentally refused to make any statements and became violent." A psychiatrist was then brought in to examine him.

A twenty-six-page report was issued on October 16, 1968. During Nagell's psychiatric examination on October 10, "he was conspicuously incontinent of emotions, cried frequently and stated suicidal intentions." Nagell told the psychiatrist that "I admit that I am a paranoid personality. But that's not a bad thing, because every person has a certain personality. It only becomes serious when you get into a paranoid state."

The report noted that during his first psych examination in July, "Nagell showed himself to be a typical American in terms of outward appearance, posture, hairstyle, demeanor, overall behavior, expressive movements, facial expressions, gestures, voice, manner of speaking, etc."

They found this examination to be "unsatisfactory" and found there was some "dissimulation" on Nagell's part.

The factors that made N.'s insanity unrecognizable for a long time in the preliminary proceedings are essentially his efforts not to appear mentally disturbed and the fact of his extraordinary good intelligence under the impression of which changes in his nature in the form of emotional and volitional disorders, in particular irritability and loss of inhibition, are often only extremely difficult to see, especially when there are still attempts at dissimulation on the part of the person concerned, or the behavior shown fits into the range of forms of prison reactions, as was the case here.

But they soon realized Nagell was disturbed:

After this exploration, however, the mental picture soon changed again and N. showed symptoms of neurasthenia, defiance, protests and sometimes even paranoid reactions (signs of being persecuted and observed, of alleged disadvantage, references to pseudologisms, signs of querulousness), all of which, however, cannot be interpreted as understandable reactions of detention.

In addition, there were now clear symptoms of a change in character as observed after severe craniocerebral injuries, e.g., a neurasthenic-apathetic-depressive syndrome, hypomaniac derailments and paranoid reactions with an almost schizophrenia-like character.

On the basis of an already abnormal personality, the tendency to excitability and irascibility, which had already been shown earlier, increased to severe mood disorders and explosive irritability with destructive rage.

Dr. Ochernal, the chief psychiatrist for the prison hospital, designated "Nagell for the entire period after his craniocerebral injury from 1954 to the present day as mentally incompetent." His final diagnosis was "Severe changes in character following craniocerebral injury on the basis of an already abnormal personality structure in conflict situations and predominantly paranoid syndrome."

As a result of this conclusion, the charges against Nagell were dropped.

Verfügung vom 23. 1o. 68

Das gegen

         N A G E L L , Richard Case,
         geb. am 5. 8. 193o in Greenwich/USA,
         zuletzt ohne festen Wohnsitz

eingeleitete Ermittlungsverfahren wird gemäß § 148
Abs. I Ziffer 2 StPO eingestellt.

Die Ermittlungen ergaben, daß der Beschuldigte im Sinne des
§ 15 Abs. I StGB für die ihm zur Last gelegten Handlungen
strafrechtlich nicht verantwortlich ist.

Die gesamte Verhaltensweise des Beschuldigten war in zu-
nehmendem Maße durch paranoide Reaktionen gekennzeich-
net.

Die Handlungen sowie Einlassungen des Beschuldigten stehen
weiterhin mit einem festgestellten Wahnsystem im Zusammen-
hang.
Diese Geisteskrankheit ist auf eine durch einen im
Jahre 1954 überlebten Flugzeugabsturz erlittene schwere
Kopfverletzung sowie auf eine mehrjährige Haftzeit in
den USA zurückzuführen.

Die erfolgte psychiatrische Untersuchung ergab eine Unzu-
rechnungsfähigkeit im Sinne des § 15 Abs. I StGB.

Aus diesem Grunde wurde das Verfahren mangels gesetz-
licher Voraussetzungen zur Strafverfolgung eingestellt.

                                 (Wagner)
                               Staatsanwalt

This is the order that discontinued the investigation of Nagell. It says that he is not criminally responsible for his actions because "the psychiatric examination revealed insanity."

Here is Nagell's discharge paper signed by Erich Mielke, head of the Stasi.

Regierung der
Deutschen Demokratischen Republik
Ministerium für Staatssicherheit

GVS
BSTU
0010

Verw. / Bez.-Verw.
Abt. / Krsdst. HA IX/1

Berlin , den 17. 10. 1968 195

Entlassungsanweisung

für die Haftanstalt in

Der / Die am 14. 6. 1968 eingelieferte:

Name N A G E L L

Vorname Richard Case

Geburtstag u. Ort 5.8.1930 in Greenwich

Beruf ohne

Familienstand geschieden

Wohnungsanschrift keinen festen Wohnsitz

ist zu entlassen.

Hinweise zur Durchführung der Entlassung:
Die Entlassung ist am 23. 10. 1968
durchzuführen.

Der Leiter der Abteilung / Kreisdst.:

(Siegel)

Bestätigt: i.V.

Entlassen am 23. 10 1968

D 20 653 20.0 Form C 25-53

Two law partners, Wolfgang Vogel and Juergen Stange, who had offices in East and West Berlin negotiated Nagell's return to the west in October 1968. Bruce Flatin, the chief of the public safety section of the U.S. mission in Berlin, arranged for a psychiatrist to be present when Nagell was handed over. However, when Nagell was told he was now in West Berlin, he accused Flatin of wanting to kill him, and he ran back to East Berlin. Several conferences were held with East German authorities, and they forcibly expelled Nagell from East Berlin. The police were ordered to restrain Nagell, and he was confined to a mental hospital where he was examined by a U.S. Army psychiatrist, Dr. George Babineau.

E. Germany Frees
U.S. Ex-Officer

Washington Post, October 25, 1968

Nagell told Babineau he believed it was his head injury that led to his "unstable personality and immature or impulsive behavior." His bank holdup was "bred out of his feeling of hopelessness and desperation." Nagell said he was fearful of being subpoenaed to testify in the Clay Shaw trail in New Orleans and, in any case, had no useful information. It was Garrison who planted in his mind that the CIA was going to try to "eliminate" him. The only way he could convince the East Germans to release him was to "feign mental illness." He wanted to return to the United States to begin his appeal to get a full disability pension.

Babineau concluded that we are "dealing with a person who has had a personality disorder for a number of years, manifested by emotional instability, impulsive behavior, a tendency to be litigious, and a general suspicious or paranoid orientation." But while Nagell might have been "delusional," Babineau felt he was not psychotic and was competent enough to negotiate his own affairs.

Nagell's last words in the interview: "Well, I'll tell you one thing, that's the last time I ever take a train through East Germany."

Nagell flew back to the United States to continue his quest for full disability. He was examined by VA Dr. Benjamin Kagwa on December 12, 1968, who concluded that Nagell suffered from "chronic brain syndrome, associated with brain trauma, with behavior reaction characterized by passive-aggressive and paranoid features." The VA found that Nagell's issues were service-connected and rated him 100 percent disabled, effective April 21, 1967, but not retroactive to his injury or date of separation.

In January 1969 Nagell complained of severe headaches and was admitted to the VA hospital in Brooklyn, New York. He was examined by Dr. Iris Norstrand, a staff neurologist, who said his headaches were "due to emotional causes." She wondered about "the possibility of underlying paranoid schizophrenia," but Nagell did not remain long enough for any psychological studies.

Just before the start of the Clay Shaw trial in February, according to Jim Garrison, Nagell turned up in New Orleans ready to testify:

> I met him at the New Orleans Athletic Club and had a long session with him. He was as intense as he had been when I last talked to him. He was as accurate and precise in his recollection of details. He felt as strongly as ever about J. Edgar Hoover's silence after his early letter of warning about the operation to assassinate President Kennedy.
>
> However, he was also as inflexible as ever about identifying the intelligence agency with which he had been associated—and might still be associated. I understood his concern about the non-disclosure agreement which he apparently had signed with his parent agency. But it was all too clear to me what a field day the defense lawyers would have when they discovered on cross-examination that he would not disclose his affiliation. In short order they would be coming at him just as the sharks had come at Santiago's fish. By the time they finished with Nagell, the jury would have been left with the impression of a crackpot. One such incident, one such discrediting, is all it takes to undo an entire case. I decided that with Nagell we could not take that risk.

Of course, this would later be contradicted by Nagell. Garrison's theory of the case was that Oswald had been at an assassination planning session in the fall of 1963. But Nagell wrote Senator Richard Russell in April 1967 and said, "I can only point out that my knowledge of Mr. Oswald's contacts and associations during the summer of 1963 indicate that he had no relationship with the persons identified as Messrs. Clay L. Shaw, David W. Ferrie and Perry R. Russo." That would not have helped Garrison's case.

In addition, Nagell told author Dick Russell in the mid-1970s that the real Lee Harvey Oswald was in his company during the night in question. Since this would clash with Garrison's theory, it was felt he could not testify.

As if all of this was not ridiculous enough, there is a third reason why he did not testify. He also told Russell that an inert "practice Mark IV grenade" had been thrown at him in New York City from a speeding car. He thought it would thus be "inadvisable" to testify and claimed that he turned over what remained of the grenade to Garrison. If this were true, you'd think that Garrison would have mentioned it his book.

It was time to go back to Europe.

On February 27 and 28, Nagell visited the Zurich consulate and made his "usual complaints against the U. S. government." His last appearance was on March 7, and he said that if he "received no satisfaction by five o'clock that afternoon he would carry out his threats and expose the U. S. government on radio, television and in the press."

He then went to the Barcelona consulate on March 10. He asked to see the consul or anybody who could help locate his wife and children. The receptionist sent him to see the protection and welfare officer, Lela Luther. Nagell told her that he wanted to see a higher-ranking official because he had something "big" to say. She then introduced Nagell to Richard Brown, the American consul.

Nagell told Brown that he had just come from the American consulate in Zurich, where he had received the "run-around" and that he was "damn sick and tired of being given the brush-off by the Department of State." Nagell explained that the reason he had been arrested in 1963 was because he had worked with Oswald on an assignment with a "U.S. intelligence agency." He was held in prison for a long time because he had refused to tell the FBI about his intelligence activities and that the CIA had visited him in prison and told him to shut up about his ties with Oswald.

During his time in prison, Nagell said, he had not been allowed to see his wife or children, and he speculated that he might be divorced. He went to Zurich and asked for help but got nowhere. During his last visit, he said he issued a threat to consular officials that if he did not find his wife and children, he would "reveal the whole story about the assassination to the press." He gave them two weeks. He came to Barcelona because someone was "leaning" on him in Zurich.

The consul calmed Nagell down but promised nothing. Nagell left by repeating his threats and then said that he had been offered money to "go over to the other side" and would think about it if he believed he would never see his children again.

On March 12, Nagell returned to the consulate, and they explained that they had contacted Zurich, which had asked the State Department about the whereabouts of his family. That calmed Nagell down, and he left.

He returned two days later and asked if they had received an answer. They told him to be patient, and he returned on March 17 and March 18. The consul wrote that Nagell expressed "signs of depression and desperation" and threatened that he would do something dramatic like "blowing someone's head off" if he did not get an answer from the States.

Nagell then went to the embassy in Madrid on March 20 and accused US government agencies of "leaning on him" and demanded that they pass the word around to "lay off" or he would blow up. He also said that his children meant everything to him and that if he could not find them, he "would take leave of this world and would take somebody with him."

A Department of State telegram dated March 26, 1969, provided guidance on dealing with him:

```
2. ON ZURICH REQUEST FOR GUIDANCE HANDLING NAGELL, POSTS MUST
REMEMBER HE IS MENTALLY UNBALANCED AND MAY BE DANGEROUS. ABOVE
INFORMATION SHOULD BE CONVEYED NAGELL IN SUCH MANNER AS TO
CONVINCE HIM DEPARTMENT AND POST MAKING EVERY EFFORT ASSIST HIM
AND EXTREMELY SORRY UNABLE PROVIDE HIM WITH DESIRED INFO.
SINCERELY BELIEVE HIS BEST SOURCE INFO LOCAL POLICE AT WIFE'S
LAST RESIDENCE OR IF HE DESIRES IT WOULD BE ADVISABLE HE EMPLOY
PRIVATE INVESTIGATOR (NEW YORK PHONE BOOK LISTS MANY).
ANY FUTURE CONTACTS WITH NAGELL SHOULD BE CONDUCTED SO AS TO
CONVEY SYMPATHETIC UNDERSTANDING HIS PROBLEM AND WILLINGNESS
CONSIDER ANY ACTION HE PROPOSES. DO NOT REPLY HIS REQUESTS WITH
ABRUPT QUOTE NO UNQUOTE NO MATER HOW WILD SUCH REQUESTS MAY BE.
TELL HIM CONSIDERATION AND CONSULTATION NECESSARY AND REPLY

CAN BE GIVEN AT LATER TIME OR DATE. KEEP DEPARTMENT INFORMED
OF DEVELOPMENTS. UNQUOTE
```

He visited the embassy again on April 3 and requested admission to the Torrejon Air Force Base hospital for his "nervous condition." He again accused the embassy of breaking their promise to find his wife and children. A cable from the embassy indicated that they had contacted the chief of police in Los Angeles to get some information.

Nagell's last meeting with the consul was on April 7, and he was upset that there were two Marine guards present in the interview and by the consul's refusal to allow him to tape record the session. Nagell harangued the consul for two hours and accused him of deliberately provoking him to harmful actions. The consul told Nagell that they had tried, without success, to find his wife and children. Nagell also threatened to reveal that in 1957 he had been the courier of treasury plates from the United States to Japan for counterfeiting North Korean currency. He showed the consul two North Korean bills, one marked real and the other counterfeit, and said that his could be a story of interest to the media.

On his way out, Nagell said he was leaving Spain and requested the consul forward the State Department's reply to Paris. The embassy alerted Paris about Nagell and sent them all the relevant documents. They also suggested the State Department alert all western European posts about Nagell. A State Department memo indicated that they could not give Nagell information about the location of his wife without her permission.

On April 10, Nagell appeared at the Berlin station. He told them that from August 1962 to October 1963, he was an informant or investigator for the CIA. In April of 1963, he investigated the marital status of Marina Oswald and her supposed desire to return to the Soviet Union. Nagell also claimed that he investigated Lee Harvey Oswald's activities during July, August, and September of 1963.

Nagell also claimed that his conviction and subsequent incarceration was a result of his knowledge of Oswald and the JFK assassination. While he was in prison, Nagell said he was "beaten, intimidated, threatened, tortured, and kept incommunicado" and that this treatment was because he refused to "talk." Nagell also said he was "roughly treated and subjected to various forms of torture and intimidation" while detained in East Germany.

After his release, Nagell said the Berlin mission promised a complete physical examination, dental care, and help in finding his wife and children. However, after he returned to the United States, these promises were not kept, and Nagell returned to Europe. He got some help in Madrid but decided to go to West Berlin. He wanted them to pressure the State Department and the CIA to keep their promises. If they did not, he would take his story to *Der Spiegel* and embarrass the American government.

After hearing his story, the mission asked Nagell to write out an account of his story and come back on April 14. He did come back but had failed to write anything because of his emotional state. He was then told to go to the consular office for help, which then urged Nagell to visit an Army psychiatrist, which he did the next day. The psychiatrist said he was mentally ill and should be hospitalized.

The mission concluded that "it was obvious throughout both interviews with SUBJECT that HE was mentally disturbed. SUBJECT broke down and cried on numerous occasions, usually when the conversation concerned HIS attempts to locate HIS family."

Nagell then went to the West Berlin Police Office, and he told them he had information about East Bloc countries. He regaled them with various stories about his stay in an East German prison. They asked him why he had not contacted American agencies, and he replied that he had done so today but was mad at them because they do not trust him. He then got up and left but said he would come back. He called them on the phone later that day to say he was too far away to keep his appointment.

The police officer noted that "according to the conversation between KHK Werner and Mr. Winter [Norman Winter, U.S. liaison officer to the West Berlin police], Richard Nagell is mentally disturbed."

Here is a memo written by the Secret Service:

UNITED STATES GOVERNMENT

Memorandum

U. S. Secret Service

CO-2-34,412

TO : SAIC Towns - ID

DATE: April 17, 1969

FROM : SAIC Hanly - Paris

SUBJECT: Richard Case NAGELL

Enclosed is Berlin cable 0668 of April 16th reporting that subject has returned to Berlin. He was last reported in Barcelona.

This man is apparently psychotic. He has a fixation revolving about his alleged connection with Lee Harvey OSWALD. He has a grievance against the United States and according to the consulate at Barcelona he has stated that he would do something dramatic like "blowing someone's head off" if he did not get satisfaction. Copy of file memos of conversations had by consular officers at Barcelona are also attached.

Should he return to the USA NAGELL definitely should receive attention from us since he clearly comes within our criteria for a security risk. I am therefore asking Berlin and other posts in Europe to inform us at once and furnish details of itinerary if NAGELL returns to the USA.

It is suggested the appropriate agencies in Washington be informed of our interest and requested to furnish any background information they may have on this subject.

Enc.

John H. Hanly
Special Agent in Charge

The mission in Berlin considered Nagell's presence in Berlin to be "undesirable," and they hoped they could persuade him to leave.

On April 22, 1969, while still in Berlin, Nagell was taken to the Hospital Wilmersdorf for treatment. He had a wound in his head, and he told doctors that someone had hit him. But a witness at a restaurant said that he fell from a bar stool. He told the hospital he was an agent of the U. S. Information Service. The German police report noted that "Mr. N. was member of CIA. He had the appropriate card with him." I wonder what kind of card Nagell had manufactured. Interestingly, he had told the East Germans that he had bought several fake passports and other fake IDs. He departed Berlin on a train to Frankfurt on April 26 to return to the United States.

Four days later, Nagell went to the New York regional office of the VA and said he wanted to go to a VA hospital to be examined for injuries sustained while he was in East Germany. He was told he would have to wait for an appointment, and he then threatened to go the press. He also said that the White House was afraid of him and had stopped the DC press from writing stories about him. He further claimed he had been on an espionage mission in East Berlin for the CIA. The Secret Service report about this visit noted:

> The undersigned was further informed by the above mentioned representatives of the Veterans Administration that the subject is constantly appearing at their office and complaining of physical ills and requesting hospitalization. He is also constantly telling stories of his espionage activity and his importance to the United States Government. They further advised the undersigned that the subject has at times been boisterous and that GSA Guards have assisted him in escorting him from the offices of the Veterans Administration.

At the end of June, an article about Nagell appeared in *The Family*, a weekly tabloid catering to U.S. servicemen in Europe. The article, entitled "I want to find my children," was by Thomas C. Lucey, who also worked as a freelancer for Radio Free Europe.

'I want to find my children'

Ex-Army spook who fingered Oswald claims Uncle Sam hides his family / by Thomas C. Lucey

Lucey wrote that Nagell had not seen his children since 1963 and that "officials inside the Federal government—most likely FBI and CIA agents—know where they are and deliberately isolated him from his family." The article claimed that Nagell staged the bank robbery "because he had refused to kill Kennedy-assassin Lee Harvey Oswald and was afraid he would be killed himself." In addition, "the CIA used the promise of reuniting Nagell with his family as part of the incentive for him to undertake a one-man CIA assignment inside East Germany."

The article also claimed:

- Nagell first went to work for the CIA as an informant in August 1962.

- Nagell's last assignment was to penetrate the Fair Play for Cuba Committee, where he met Lee Harvey Oswald. In September 1963, Oswald told Nagell, "We will kill him [Kennedy] before the month is out." The "we" were Oswald and two Latins—possibly Cubans—who belonged to anti-Castro organizations.
- Nagell reported this to his CIA contact, and their instructions were to "take care" of Oswald. He replied that he was not a killer.
- He then tipped off J. Edgar Hoover, and the FBI then questioned Oswald but released him.
- Two months later, Nagell heard the assassination news and realized the FBI had screwed up.
- Six days before what Nagell thought was the assassination date, he shot up the bank in El Paso and waited to be arrested. He expected to be held briefly for discharging a firearm and that police custody would keep him safe from the CIA.
- Once he was in prison, Nagell was not allowed any mail to or from his wife and children. His sister wrote and told him that his wife wanted to know where he was and why she had not heard from him.
- After his release, a man met Nagell at JFK airport and gave him $500 and said more will come. He told Nagell, "We appreciate your cooperation in prison." But Nagell never received any additional money.
- In New York, Nagell met a CIA official he knew only as Buehel, who was going to brief him on a new assignment. He was to have himself arrested by East German authorities and find out if a certain U.S. naval officer who had allegedly defected was there and get information on their techniques of interrogation and methods of treatment.
- After being held in East Germany for over four and a half months, Nagell believed that the CIA had deserted him, so he decided to "play crazy."
- When Nagell was released, he was driven to the U.S. mission and drank some coffee that had been drugged. He had to

stand to keep awake. The people at the mission told him to go back to the United States. At the airport, Nagell was promised they would help get his disability retirement.

- After Nagell arrived in Zurich, he went to the U.S. consulate to get a doctor because he was sick. A civilian doctor told him he had been given an overdose of Seconal—a sleeping drug. He went back to the consulate, but because they would not help him, he flew back to New York.
- Nagell then got an appointment in Washington for a physical, which he said only took two and a half minutes. They awarded him a 100 percent disability allowance for a nervous condition. They told him they wanted to "tag him with a nervous condition to destroy his credibility."
- He flew back to Zurich, where there was an attempt on his life. He then went to Barcelona. With no luck getting information on his wife and children, he went back to Berlin. They told him they had been unable to locate his children, but they were still trying. He then realized he was under surveillance, and in a bar two men came toward him, and he was hit on the back of the head. The consulate told him that he must get out of Berlin and that the German police believe it was either a mistaken identity or that MfS (the Stasi) were after him.
- A consulate official told Lucey that "ninety-nine and a half percent of his [Nagell's] story is fantasy."

Nagell then wrote a three-page addendum to the story and had it all bound into a booklet.

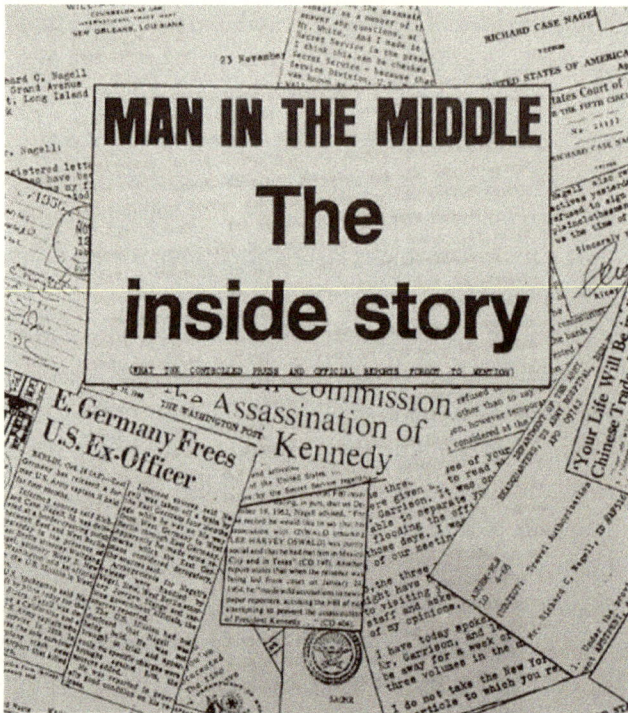

Cover of Nagell's booklet. The subtitle says, "What the controlled press and official reports forgot to mention."

Nagell wrote that while he was in the military, he was an informant for the CIA. After he left the military, he continued to serve with the CIA and was also paid. From August 1962 until his arrest in September 1963, he was a CIA agent. Here is just a sample of what he wrote:

Texas on 20 September 1963, I was employed by the Agency in a capacity which can be accurately described as that of an agent, in every sense of the word. My assignments varied and necessitated travel to three Latin American nations and many states, including the Commonwealth of Puerto Rico. They also necessitated my taking on cover employment for one week in New York and for about ten weeks in Los Angeles, though usually I posed as a tourist, an investigator for the Immigration & Naturalization Service or as a researcher for a private firm, the appropriate credentials being furnished to me by the CIA. To sum it up briefly, I operated in Mexico City at the onset of the Cuban Missile Crisis in an effort aimed chiefly at the Soviet government; I conducted inquiries relative to "dissident" members of several Cuban refugee groups based in the United States; I checked out an alleged connection between a Miami resident named Eladio Del Valle and New Orleans CIA informant Sergio Arcacha-Smith; I investigated an associate of the now deceased right-wing extremist David W. Ferrie of New Orleans, as I did the activities of left-wingers Vaughn L. Snipes and his wife, Priscilla, near Venice, California, and others; I conducted a surveillance on a man, said to have been an ex-CIA employee, observed talking to MRP leader Manuel Artime and former Cuban senator/racketeer Rolando Masferrer; I inquired into an allegation that Marina Oswald intended to divorce her husband and return to the U.S.S.R. (although I never stated that I met her personally, as was reported by the FBI and Secret Service); and I performed courier duties and acted as a cut-out. At the time of my arrest I was operating in an undercover role, having become involved in a domestic-inspired plot to assassinate President Kennedy and, leastwise ostensibly, other highly-placed government officials.

Nagell concluded his commentary by noting that he had never "been certified psychotic by any U.S. medical authority or adjudicated mentally-incompetent in a court of law."

Bruce Flatin noticed that Nagell's article claimed he was a "longtime CIA member" and that he claimed that Flatin was not his real name.

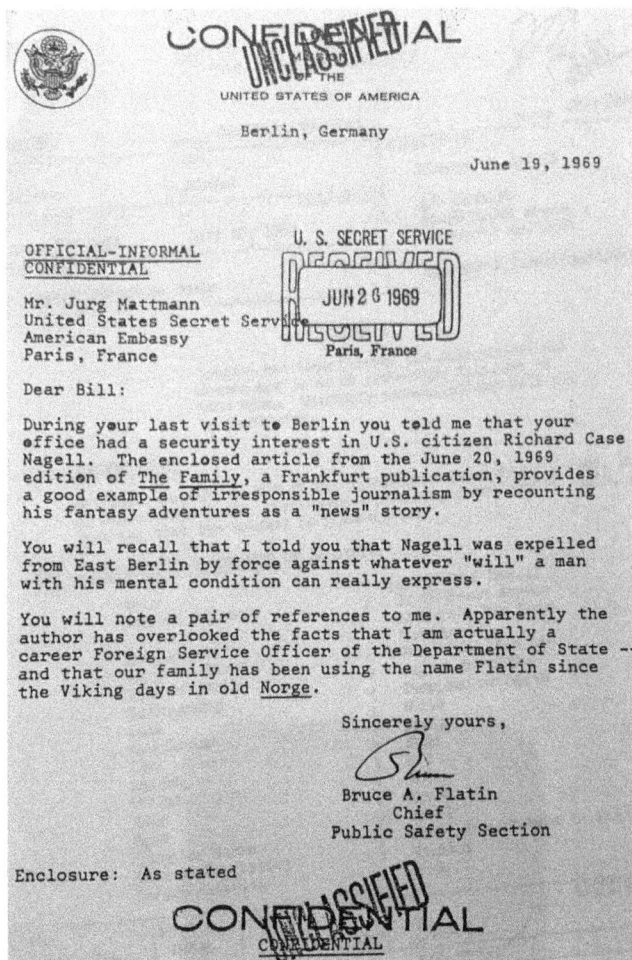

CONFIDENTIAL

UNCLASSIFIED

THE
UNITED STATES OF AMERICA

Berlin, Germany

June 19, 1969

OFFICIAL-INFORMAL
CONFIDENTIAL

U. S. SECRET SERVICE
RECEIVED
JUN 2 6 1969
Paris, France

Mr. Jurg Mattmann
United States Secret Service
American Embassy
Paris, France

Dear Bill:

During your last visit to Berlin you told me that your office had a security interest in U.S. citizen Richard Case Nagell. The enclosed article from the June 20, 1969 edition of The Family, a Frankfurt publication, provides a good example of irresponsible journalism by recounting his fantasy adventures as a "news" story.

You will recall that I told you that Nagell was expelled from East Berlin by force against whatever "will" a man with his mental condition can really express.

You will note a pair of references to me. Apparently the author has overlooked the facts that I am actually a career Foreign Service Officer of the Department of State -- and that our family has been using the name Flatin since the Viking days in old Norge.

Sincerely yours,

Bruce A. Flatin
Chief
Public Safety Section

Enclosure: As stated

CONFIDENTIAL

In August 1969, Nagell placed a personal ad in the *East Village Other*, an alternative newspaper published in New York.

> "Caught In The Act. Notice to the CIA and all SY
> shitheads who participated in Project Purple Shaft:
> After that fiasco in the GIR you worms did your best
> to screw, blue and tattoo me. You even tried to have
> my ass dusted in Berlin . . . you fuckups. Now its
> my turn to do a little shafting.
>
>   Cordially, R. C. NAGELL."

This ad was noticed by the office of security in the State Department, who wrote that "while Nagell may be something of a crackpot, the item does appear to contain somewhat of an implied threat. For this reason, the information is forwarded for your consideration and for any action which may be necessary."

In mid-April 1970, Nagell was back in Zurich, and he reported to police that his raincoat had disappeared. He claimed that an especially important document, intended for American military authorities in Berlin, was in one of the pockets. The raincoat was found in another hotel but without the document.

> 5. BONN FRANKFURT BERLIN: SUBJ IS FABRICATOR AND MENTAL
> CASE WHO PERIODICALLY CAUSES TROUBLE FOR SWISS AND LNPURE
> CONSULATES IN SUISSE.

CIA Cable from Bern regarding Nagell's raincoat.

Here is a routing sheet from a 1970 dispatch from the Berlin mission:

☐ UNCLASSIFIED	☐ INTERNAL USE ONLY		☐ CONFIDENTIAL	☒ SECRET
ROUTING AND RECORD SHEET				

SUBJECT: (Optional)

FROM:		EXTENSION	NO.
CI/R&A/Hartman	2C-29	6748	DATE 17 April 1970

TO: (Officer designation, room number, and building)	DATE RECEIVED	DATE FORWARDED	OFFICER'S INITIALS	COMMENTS (Number each comment to show from whom to whom. Draw a line across column after each comment.)
1. Chief, SRS Office of Security	4-20-70		Paul,	
2. Mr. Paul Gaynor				This material arrived attached to a dispatch from Berlin. I thought you might want to index Richard Case NAGELL as a crank because he is mentally deranged. He was the sole survivor of an air crash of a military craft in ca. 1956 and suffered brain damage. He has claimed CIA employment but was never connected with the Agency.
3. Milligan	4/24/70			
4. Mr Hall	4/20/70			
5.				
6.				
7.				

On August 17, 1971, Nagell was granted legal custody of his two children. I found this somewhat curious, and I asked his son Robert about this:

> My father reappeared in our lives when I was ten years old. I had been told he was dead. He had just returned from Russia. He was unhappy with my mother's care of us and wanted custody. My mother was disinclined to fight with him over the issue. My sister wanted to go with my dad, but I did not. However, my mother told me to just go so he would not cause problems for her. We remained in his custody until my sister ran away in 1975, and about a year later he decided fatherhood was not for him and took me back to my mother in Hollywood and left me there. Shortly after I left my mom's home and lived with two gay dudes that helped me out.

On January 2, 1973, Nagell filed an action to get full disability. In March, the government informed him that the Corrections Board would reconsider his case, but they needed a letter from him with an opinion by Dr. Weinstein. Weinstein wrote the Department of Justice on July 23, 1973:

> As I have testified in several court appearances, personality and behavioral changes are common sequelae of brain injuries such as were sustained by Mr. Nagell. These include lapses in memory, denial of illness, outbursts of temper and violence and anti-social behavior. Any medical evaluation of Mr. Nagell made in 1959 should have considered his severe brain injury as a causal factor in his behavior. After his injury he was in my opinion unfit to be any Army officer.

On November 23, 1973, the board informed Nagell that a formal hearing would be held in January. Nagell told them he did not intend to appear as a witness because the board lacked the ability to subpoena witnesses. The board convened to consider Nagell's case on April 3, 1974, and disallowed his claim because they believed that the medical treatment he received after the crash made him fit to serve.

In June 1975, conspiracy author Richard Popkin started sending out mailgrams to various government officials.

```
THIS MAILGRAM IS A CONFIRMATION COPY OF THE FOLLOWING MESSAGE:

7144535956 MGM TDRN LA JOLLA CA 100 06-13 0120A EST
ZIP
SENATOR FRANK CHURCH
US SENATE
WASHINGTON DC 20510




IF GRANTED IMMUNITY RICHARD CASE NAGELL WILL TESTIFY TO A MEETING IN
SEPTEMBER 1963 THAT LEE HARVEY OSWALD ATTENDED WITH TWO FAKE CUBAN G-2
AGENTS IN JACKSON SQUARE NEW ORLEANS WHO WERE IN FACT MEMBERS OF A
VIOLENCE PRONE FACTION OF A CIA FINANCED GROUP OPERATING IN MEXICO
CITY. AT THE MEETING THE ASSASINATION OF JOHN F KENNEDY WAS DISCUSSED.
NAGELL WILL ALSO TESTIFY TO THE REASONS FOR OSWALD'S TRIP TO MEXICO AND
WHO FINANCED IT ALONG WITH MANY OTHER MATTERS CONNECTED WITH THE
CONSPIRACY TO ASSASSINATE JOHN F KENNEDY.

RICHARD H POPKIN
```

Mailgram sent to Senator Frank Church by Richard Popkin. Nagell told Church and others that he did not tell Popkin he would testify before Congress.

Popkin was the author of the 1966 book *The Second Oswald*, which argued that there was an Oswald impostor trying to incriminate the real Oswald. Nagell had written Popkin a letter saying there was something to his theory. Popkin had met once with Nagell and had also talked with him on the phone several times.

Dick Russell, a former writer for *TV Guide*, was researching a possible book on the JFK assassination and flew to San Diego to see what Popkin had discovered. Popkin had two stories about the assassination—one was about a U.S. lab that produced "robot murderers (Manchurian Candidates)," one of which was a young Puerto Rican who took part in the assassination. The other story was about Richard Case Nagell.

Popkin gave Russell a copy of Nagell's notebook, in which he had scribbled notes about Mexico City, Cuba, and the CIA. Russell flew to El Paso to review the local newspaper coverage of Nagell's 1963 bank incident. He also interviewed one of the arresting officers, Jim Bundren, and asked him if Nagell had ever mentioned Oswald. Bundren said yes but could not say if he was mentioned before or after the assassination.

Russell believed there was a concerted effort to "discredit Nagell as either a would-be bank robber or a madman," and he knew he had to track Nagell down.

He noticed an address in the notebook, drove out there, and found Richard Case Nagell. He told Russell that his life had been periodically threatened "but that he had 'life insurance'—certain documents and photographs being kept in a foreign country" that would be "released in the event of my death."

In September 1975, Nagell's attorney filed a document that listed the facts they expected to establish at trial to get full disability:

- Since 1953, Nagell has suffered from a mental disorder known at Anton's disease, the major manifestation of which is a complete denial by the sufferer that he is unfit either mentally or physically.
- As a result of his several injuries in 1954 in the plane crash, Nagell suffered permanent brain damage, including organic brain disease and disturbed brain function.
- Nagell's brain damage and symptoms were exacerbated by psychological stress and physical exertion.
- Nagell underwent a complete personality change after the 1954 plane crash.
- Nagell's brain damage rendered him physically, mentally, and psychologically unfit for military duty after the plane crash.

The brief further argued that by performing his counterintelligence duties after the crash, Nagell's "mental condition gradually became so aggravated and worsened that it caused a permanent functional impairment of his ability to perform thereafter in any capacity commensurate with his training, experience and status as a commissioned officer of the Army." It concluded that Nagell "is permanently and totally disabled at the present time."

Nagell did not say much else, but over the next couple of years, Russell met him several times, and they exchanged many letters. Russell stopped talking to Nagell in 1978 and then published an article about him in the March 1981 issue of *Gallery* magazine:

Here, for the first time, is the story of

THE MAN WHO HAD A CONTRACT TO KILL LEE HARVEY OSWALD BEFORE THE ASSASSINATION OF PRESIDENT JOHN F. KENNEDY

Investigative report by **Richard Russell** with **Dave Navard**

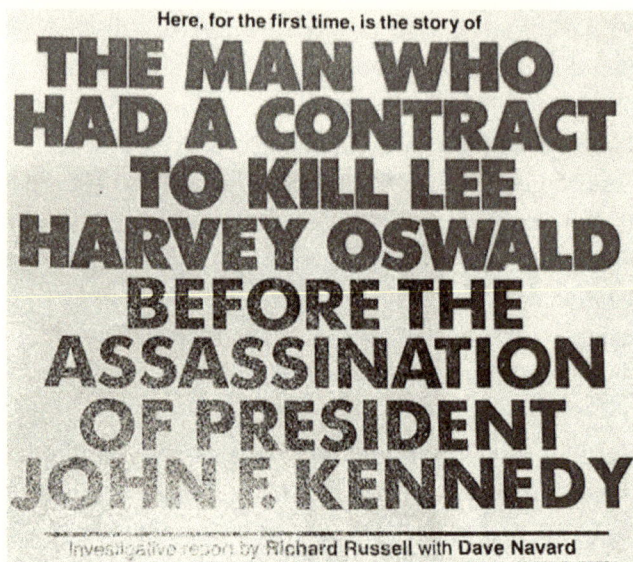

Headline from *Gallery* magazine, March 1981

Here is my summary of Russell's article about Nagell:

In 1962, Nagell signed a contract with the CIA to act as a 'double agent,' and would appear to work for the KGB. The CIA had him contact a KGB officer in Mexico City to feed 'disinformation' to the Russians. The Soviets gave Nagell an assignment to return to the U. S. and monitor Cuban exiles. They gave him a photograph of Lee Harvey Oswald and Nagell was to keep tabs on him in Dallas. Nagell followed two plots to kill JFK—one when JFK was addressing Bay of Pigs veterans in Miami and the other at the premiere of the film *PT-109* in L. A. in June 1963. The next plot was scheduled for late September in Washington, D.C. Nagell said that Cuban exiles, masquerading as G2 intelligence officers had solicited Oswald's help to kill JFK. This was retaliation for plots against Castro. Nagell recorded a planning meeting of this group in August in New Orleans. The KGB then told Nagell to persuade Oswald that the "deal was phony" and if this didn't work then to get rid of Oswald. They didn't want Castro to be blamed for the assassination and thus bring the world close to nuclear war. Nagell met with Oswald in New Orleans in September but he denied that a plot was underway. Nagell then wrote

Hoover warning him of the conspiracy to kill JFK. Nagell started to have doubts about killing Oswald and did not know if he was working for the CIA or the KGB. So, he decided to shoot up the bank so that he would be in federal custody.

How much of this was actually told to Russell by Nagell is hard to tell.

On July 2, 1982, the court ruled that Nagell was entitled to a full military pension from the time of his resignation in 1959. The court noted Nagell's mental disability:

Plaintiff's brain syndrome has been manifested by severe personality and behavioral disturbances. They took the form, over the years since the airplane crash, of suicidal preoccupation, deliriousness, restlessness, and violence, paranoid trends and passive-aggressive behavior, hysteria, psychotic states, severe headaches, dizziness, confusion, impaired judgment, confabulations, and delusional formulations, anosognosia or Anton's disease. Plaintiff attempted suicide in 1962 by shooting himself, and according to Dr. Weinstein in 1963, when he tried to slash his wrists after this arrest, and in 1964, when he took a drug overdose. Dr. Weinstein described plaintiff's suicidal behavior too, immediately after the 1954 plane crash. Plaintiff has been in various mental institutions and psychiatric wards almost a dozen times between 1955 and 1969.

The evidence is unhappily abundant of likely confabulations, or fictitious stories told by plaintiff with no awareness of their falsity. One example surrounds plaintiff's attempted suicide in 1962. He has variously suggested that he shot himself (the most likely), that his wife shot him, and that it was an unknown assailant. Stories told by plaintiff throughout the years after his discharge involve work for the CIA and, alternatively, persecution by the CIA. He has suggested that the bank shooting incident in 1963 involved undercover CIA activities, that he had dealings with Lee Harvey Oswald prior to the Kennedy assassination as part of an undercover CIA assignment, and also that he sought by the shooting to be taken into protective custody because he felt his life threatened by the CIA. These stories are unsubstantiated and are likely confabulations, continuing symptoms of plaintiff's brain injury.

The court concluded that Nagell "was entitled to better treatment than he got. The least that can be done for him now is monetary justice." The government appealed, but on March 2, 1983, the Court of Appeals affirmed the judgment. Bob Nagell informed me that, in the end, Nagell only received $12,000 and added, "After that he traveled around staying in cheap motels and spent all the money he received."

In 1992, Dick Russell published his magnus opus, *The Man Who Knew Too Much*. It came in at a whopping 824 pages, including a fifteen-page cast of characters. I remember visiting a friend in Brooklyn Heights for dinner, and before arriving I walked into a bookstore on Montague Street. I had never heard of Nagell, and I instantly bought this book to read on my way back to Europe, where I was working. But I couldn't get through it. There were just too many names, and I couldn't keep the whole story straight. And Nagell just kept continually promising some piece of substantiating evidence that never seemed to arrive.

One of Russell's last conversations with Nagell was in March of 1990, in which he "implored" him to "once again, to sit down and lay out his full story the sake of history." Nagell once again said that "the truth will come out if I die," but he was not going to budge: "I'm not going to take a chance on losing my money from the government." Russell interpreted all this to mean that Nagell was "using the threat of full disclosure to me as a stick en route to that carrot. Once he won his case, in 1983, quote the raven, 'Nevermore.'"

In March 1995, Russell testified before the ARRB and implored them to get Nagell's files and to offer him immunity to testify. The board was unfortunately too late.

On October 31, 1995, Jeremy Gunn, the associate director of the ARRB, sent Nagell a letter asking him to contact the board. Unfortunately, Nagell was found dead in his apartment on November 1. One analyst, Douglas Horne, who was prone to conspiracy theories, found it very suspicious:

FYI

Assassination Records Review Board
600 E Street NW · 2nd Floor · Washington, DC 20530
(202) 724-0088 · Fax: (202) 724-0457

[handwritten: ANNE — VERY DISTURBING. — Doug 6:15 PM 11/2/95]

October 31, 1995

Mr. Richard Case Nagell
P.O. Box 3673
Los Angeles, California 90078

Dear Mr. Nagell:

As you are probably aware, the "President John F. Kennedy Assassination Records Collection Act of 1992," 44 U.S.C. § 2107, was established to collect, in the National Archives, records related to the assassination of President Kennedy. The law also created the Assassination Records Review Board to oversee the process and to provide a mechanism for collecting the records.

It has been suggested to us that you may have in your possession records or information that might be appropriate to include in the National Archives. I would very much like to discuss this and other matters with you at a time and in a manner that is agreeable to you. I would very much appreciate it if you would contact me either by mail, telephone (call collect at 202-724-0088), or by fax (202) 724-0457.

I look forward to hearing from you.

Sincerely yours,

T. Jeremy Gunn
Associate Director for Research and Analysis

[handwritten: FOUND DEAD IN APARTMENT LATE ON NOV 1ST, 1995. THIS LETTER MAILED OCT 31. KEY WORD →]

However, Richard Case Nagell had a full forensic autopsy, which noted "the decedent is a 65-year-old man with a history of heart disease, ulcerative colitis and alcohol abuse." The autopsy noted "significant coronary artery disease," which was "consistent with the scene suggesting sudden unexpected death."

Nagell was a heavy smoker, as you can see from this excerpt from the 1969 article in *The Family*:

> Officials inside the Federal Govern-
> ment — most likely FBI and CIA agents
> — know where they are and deliberately
> isolated him from his family, the tall, lean
> chain-smoker claims.

When Nagell was hospitalized in 1962 in Bay Pines, Florida, the hospital's final summary noted that he "smoked continuously during the interview."

Nagell's death was noted in newspapers across the United States with an unfortunate sub-headline:

RICHARD CASE NAGELL
CIA double agent, 65

ASSOCIATED PRESS

LOS ANGELES — Double agent Richard Case Nagell, the subject of the 1992 book "The Man Who Knew Too Much," has died of heart disease. He was 65.

Mr. Nagell was found dead Nov. 1 in his Silver Lake area apartment, said Scott Carrier, a spokesman for the coroner's office.

Author Dick Russell's book "The Man Who Knew Too Much" described Mr. Nagell's work for the CIA and Soviet spy networks. It also delved into Mr. Nagell's mys-terious link to Lee Harvey Oswald.

Mr. Nagell knew Oswald prior to the assassination of President John F. Kennedy, Russell said Monday from his Boston home.

"Nagell was a very strange guy," Russell said. "He certainly wasn't crazy. I spent a lot of time with him and talked to a lot of people who knew him. He never lied to me.

"I believe he is the key to unlocking the mystery of who was behind the assassination."

Mr. Nagell didn't want a funeral, Russell said.

San Diego Union-Tribune, November 7, 1995

On November 7, 1995, Tom Samoluk, associate director of the ARRB, flew to Los Angeles to help search Nagell's apartment. The ARRB listed the records they were hoping to find:

Possible JFK Records Formerly in Custody of Richard Case Nagell

Item	Location
Polaroid picture of himself and Oswald in Jackson Square, N.O. taken in SEP 63	In a bank vault in Switzerland (exact location of city and name of bank unknown)
Audiotape recording of Oswald, two Cuban exile co-conspirators, and Nagell himself, taped surreptitiously in late AUG 63	Unknown; however, Nagell has stated that he has made arrangements for this evidence, and more, to surface after his death
Copies of letters sent to numerous Government officials and members of Congress, including FBI Director J. Edgar Hoover circa SEP 63, a CIA official in SEP 63, Senator Richard Russell, Congressman Don Edwards, the Warren Commission, and the House Select Committee on Assassinations; and copies of letters to relatives and personal acquaintances	Nagell himself frequently bragged of his careful record-keeping of both copies of personal letters and mail receipts; it is reasonable to assume that some, or many of these items may have been in his lodgings, or that perhaps clues as to where they are located may be in his lodgings or amongst his possessions
A footlocker was known to exist circa 1965 at the house of his half-sister, Eleanore Gambert (now deceased), which reportedly contained photographs, audio tape recordings, and documents which would clearly be classified today as "assassination records"	As of 1992, her second husband, Louis Gambert of Tarpon Springs, FLA was 88 years old, and had two sons who were also aware of the footlocker: Robert (then 62) and Roger (then 54). Present whereabouts of this footlocker and/or the material in it is unknown. Following an FBI visit to view the contents of this locker in the summer of 1965, a break-in occurred and some of the contents of the footlocker were stolen.

Dick Russell claimed that "In the event of his demise, Nagell made arrangements for this [the Polaroid photograph] and more to surface." But none of these materials were found. However, Samoluk did find a notation on a credit card slip about a storage locker in Tucson, Arizona. On November 26, 1995, Samoluk flew to Los Angeles to meet Nagell's niece and son to review five footlockers they found in Tucson. Once again, nothing of interest was found.

In fact, nothing has ever showed up.

Richard Case Nagell was a decorated war veteran who suffered brain damage in a plane crash in 1954. He was never the same, and his family and friends realized that he needed help. Unfortunately, despite his pleas for help—and the shoot-up in the bank in El Paso was a plea for help— he never got the help he needed and the help he deserved.

That is the Richard Case Nagell story. He was not the man who knew too much; he was the man who needed help. And he turned into the man who loved to entice.

For instance, shortly after Nagell's second trial in 1966, he told his sister to contact Mark Lane. Fortunately for us, Lane was promoting his book *Rush to Judgment*. Otherwise, he might have fallen for the Nagell story, and he would have turned it into a very public circus.

What did Nagell want his sister to tell Lane? Well, if Lane would represent Nagell, he could tell his sister about "a location where I have photographic *evidence* relating to the Main Topic." A standard Nagell ploy. He then wrote to Richard Popkin, and then he contacted Jim Garrison. He was on his way.

Nagell needed someone to help him with his writ of habeas corpus, and what better hook than to tell a JFK conspiracy theorist that he had some incredible evidence—be it a tape recording of the conspirators or perhaps photographs of him with Lee Harvey Oswald. It was always too good to be true.

He always knew what buttons to push. Paul Hoch, publisher of the *Echoes of Conspiracy* newsletter, wrote that "Nagell seemed to have served as a Ouija board, helping Russell fit the usual wide range of stories together. Go to him with the right question, and you'll get an answer."

Nagell was an excellent student of the assassination. When he first met William Martin, the assistant district attorney from Jim Garrison's office, Nagell said he was following Garrison as best he could. He then wanted to hear *Garrison's* theory of the assassination. Only then would he talk about some of what he knew.

And it was the same with Dick Russell:

I also sent Nagell a detailed outline of what I believed to be the "high-lights" of his relationship to Oswald and the assassination, which he returned to me with typewritten corrections.

Nagell knew how to play these people and strung them along, first for some legal help and second for God knows what. Perhaps he just wanted some attention, or perhaps he wanted some meaning to his life. Since he was a very disturbed man, we will never fully understand his motivations. He had been on his way to a successful military career, but the plane crash damaged him permanently.

I asked his son Bob his thoughts on his father's possible CIA/KGB connections, and he replied:

I know very little about that aspect of my father's life as he was very tight-lipped. My dad spoke several languages, among them excellent Russian and Japanese. He used to receive letters and packages frequently from Russia including Lenin's complete works in Russian, and he had travelled there a few times that I knew of, so he did have friends in Moscow when it was unpopular, but I don't know directly about any CIA/KGB connections; Anything like that was never evident in the time that I lived with him. I have my doubts as we always struggled financially, and dad never had anything that would cause me to believe he was profiting from any clandestine activities. He intensely disliked the US Government more and more as his lawsuit for 100% disability rating progressed and always commented that "the masses are asses". He held disdain for many people, including Dick Russell and his book, which I never read in its entirety, terming it garbage. However, as an adult looking back on everything I see two parallel threads, one involving what I view as a coincidental timing of political events interwoven with the domestic turmoil in his marriage to my mother, which had resulting in his departure from the only career he had, the army, and his subsequent inability to secure suitable work because of his appearance and his later arrest for domestic violence vis-a-vis my mom, due to which he lost his job at the ABC in Los Angeles which caused him to become destitute. It was after this that he went into the bank in El Paso. His confinement at Springfield weighed heavily on him. He felt he was punished by being confined despite recommendations that he be released. I never saw anything to suggest that he was actually mentally ill. He was very smart but had personal demons that followed him from childhood when he and his sister were put in an orphanage by his mother who kept the other children in the family. He always said the truth would come out after he died, but there was no revelation. Despite the governments taking of some of his belongings, this one fact alone causes me to have my doubts about the whole JFK involvement because he wouldn't have been so careless as to have left things to end with his passing, that was how much he despised his adversaries.

At the end of the second edition of *The Man Who Knew Too Much*, Dick Russell recounts a conversation he had with Nagell in 1978:

So, I'm still hanging in there, with no guarantee, only this faith that there've got to be some people in this world who won't just let me fade away.

Nagell's faith was justified. Conspiracy theorists will never let him fade away. Virtually every major conspiracy book has the Nagell story. If Nagell were still alive, I think he would be thrilled that he is the still the talk of the town in conspiracy land.

8

DID FRENCH INTELLIGENCE SOLVE THE JFK ASSASSINATION?

In February 1968, Jim Garrison called Bill Turner, author of an article in *Ramparts* on the Minutemen (a right-wing paramilitary organization), for some advice on how to move his JFK investigation forward. Turner told him that the KGB "probably had a thick file on Lee Harvey Oswald" but that the press would go crazy if Garrison approached the Soviets. Garrison agreed., "The wolves out there would never stop howling if they caught us asking the time of day of the K.G.B."

According to Warren Hinckle, editor of *Ramparts*, Turner then told Garrison, "Never mind that, *Ramparts* would make the Russians an offer they couldn't refuse."

And Turner knew just the right man to contact the Russians.

His name was Jim Rose. The ultimate adventure man. A former contract pilot for the CIA who had flown bombing raids over Cuba.

Later that month Rose went to Mexico City and visited the Russian embassy. He was there for two hours and told them Garrison's theory of the assassination. Rose asked them for the KGB file on Oswald and anyone else involved. "Our assumption is that you must have information about these matters that we do not."

The Russian sent Rose back to his hotel and told him that "it may be necessary for you to stay in Mexico City for a few days." Rose was followed as he left the embassy. At dinner that night, a man "in a rumpled suit" watched him intently. He then got a message to come back the next day. He was told that "What you request is not impossible. But it is not necessary that it will happen. The only way it could possibly occur is in a way that would be most unexpected, and untraceable to its source. Something might be left in your hands, for instance, by a visitor to your country. That is all for now."

Warren Hinckle wrote about this in a 1973 article for *Esquire* magazine, and so did Bill Turner in his 2001 memoir. But had Jim Rose really visited the Soviet embassy in Mexico City? There are two reasons to be skeptical: Turner and Hinckle could not even get the dates right for the supposed visit.

And Jim Rose had a knack for making up stories.

In November 1967, Garrison part-time investigator Steve Jaffe, then only twenty-three years old, met radio broadcaster Ed Foley at the offices of Stanley Sheinbaum, who was involved with the Center for the Study of Democratic Institutions, a progressive think tank, and who was one of the investors in *Ramparts*. Foley gave Jaffe the names of some conservatives who could help with the Garrison investigation and also mentioned that he knew someone who was extremely knowledgeable about anti-Cuban groups.

Jaffe wrote that:

FOLEY stated that this person was known to him as "VINCE" although that was not his real name. He told us that VINCE had been a pilot during the Invasion [Bay of Pigs] and was connected with the CIA. Since then, he'd broken all relations with the CIA and was being pursued by that agency for arrest.

On the third of January 1968, Jaffe and Foley met with "Vince," whom Jaffe now dubbed Jim Rose.

Explaining his background to me Mr. Rose told of his anti-Castro flights before, during, and after the Bay of Pigs invasion of April 17, 1961, and said that because of his "having morals" he was no longer useful to the CIA and was being sought by them for arrest on no apparent grounds.

Rose was particularly interested in Rolando and Kiki Masferrer, two brothers who were purported leaders of the anti-Castro movement. He told Jaffe that if any anti-Castro Cubans were involved in the assassination that one of the brothers would be his first choice. He proposed to visit Tom Duncan, a journalist for the *Atlanta Journal*, to find out more.

At the end of his memo, Jaffe noted that:

> He [Rose] stated that a friend of his who is a former CIA employee specializes in Spanish languages and "crypto." This friend has a vast knowledge of Cuban movements, and with his knowledge of code-breaking would be able to aid us in de-coding any materials which we might want to have analyzed. I have directed ROSE to do nothing in this regard and will await any instructions.

Sheinbaum then sent Rose to be vetted by Bill Turner, who noted the "the possibility" that "this man is a plant" but who now felt this was remote. He recommended to Garrison that he be hired "in the some three months he has in this country before going overseas on a flying contract." Turner noted that "of course, we have to make sure that he does not learn more than we do from him, but I am inclined to trust him and to believe that he would be extremely valuable to us."

To help prove his bona fides, Rose showed Turner a clipping from the *Fresno Bee* of March 7, 1965:

'ExFresnan's' Death In Cuba Poses Puzzle

Rose had excised his name from the article with a razor blade. The article said that Rose (called Carl M. Davis in the story) had been lost, and was thought to be dead, while flying a B-26 back from a raid on Cuba that had been staged by Dr. Orlando Bosch's anti-Castro group. Bosch said that Davis had done volunteer work for his organization and was a reserve pilot for the Bay of Pigs invasion.

Turner wrote that "with not much more than a gut feeling, I cleared him for action." Warren Hinckle wrote that Rose "loved adventure, and second only to that he loved talking about adventure."

But Turner did not know about the article in the next day's edition of the *Fresno Bee*.

'Cuba Raider' Report Is Held Hoax, Forgery

A report that a Carl M. Davis, described as a former Fresnan, was lost on a fire bombing mission for anti Castro forces today was branded as a hoax and a forgery.

Dr. Orlando Bosch of Miami, Fla., coordinator of the Insurrectional Revolutionary Movement (MIRR), denied making the report and said the rebel group has never heard of Davis.

"It was a forgery, a false letter, you can be sure of that," Bosch said.

"We haven't lost any airplanes, and we haven't heard anything about an airplane going down in Cuba."

Fresno Bee, March 8, 1965, found by researcher Larry Haapanen.

Bosch told the newspaper that the report about Davis was a "hoax and a forgery." In fact, the anti-Castro group had never heard of Davis.

The *Lindsay Gazette* and the *Visalia Times Delta* also received the same article about Carl Davis being a pilot for Bosch's anti-Castro group. The Times Delta checked and took back the story, saying that "Davis, who is well known locally as a young man with an eye for adventure, is wanted for questioning about some rented cars that have not been returned." The *Lindsay Gazette* commented:

> If the letter to the newspaper was an attempt to throw the police off the trail of a suspected auto thief, it was a clever device. Dr. Bosch denies authorship of the letter, and it does not stand to reason that he would commit his signature to it and then deny it on the telephone two days later.

You would think that a former FBI man like Turner might have been a tad more skeptical.

While in Mexico City, Rose met two girls who were on holiday and joined them for dinner. He introduced himself as Vince and regaled them with tales of buying aircraft and said that he was about to be deported because of his activities. The girls decided that he "was a big talker trying to impress two young midwestern girls." They asked him why they should believe his stories, and he explained that he had worked for the CIA at one time. They felt he was "some kind of a nut" and could not understand why he would tell such stories, if they were true, to complete strangers.

So, who knows if he really visited the Soviet embassy?

On March 9, 1968, Garrison gave Turner $300 to give to Rose so he could come to New Orleans and start as a new investigator. Tom Bethell, a Garrison staffer, wrote in his diary that Turner "told us some story about Rose simply burgling some guy's house when he wanted to get some information" from a person of interest to Garrison. Supposedly the guy came back when Rose was still there, but Rose "had some kind of gun which squirts a disabling gas or fluid, fired it at the guy and escaped."

Rose's first job was to go to Miami and check out the Masferrer brothers. Bethell thought it "seems like a waste of time" But, on March 28, Rose contacted Don Bohring, Latin American editor of the *Miami Herald*, who was actually the source he had previously mentioned to Jaffe. By this time, the Garrison team had given Rose the codename Winston Smith.

Bohring reported to a contact at the CIA that he "gained impression Smith was a disorganized soldier of fortune type who had been on fringes of many different ventures in recent years." Rose told Bohring that "he had planned" to offer his services as a B-26 pilot in 1966 to support an invasion of Haiti. Bohring told him that he was not willing to help with the Garrison investigation since "he did not take it seriously." The conversation concluded with Rose saying that he was leaving for Biafra to fight as a mercenary but hoped to finish the job for Garrison before he left.

Bohring checked around and found that Smith had contacted other people using the name Carl McNabb. Later that day, Smith returned and Bohring asked him about that. He said, "I use many names for different purposes and I used to have still a different war name with 'the company.'" He would not tell Bohring which name was correct.

Researcher Larry Haapanen did some checking and found that Rose was born in Jacksonville, Florida, in 1936 to Emery C. and Helen K. McNabb. They divorced during World War II, and she married Private Francis Davis of the U. S. Marine Corps in 1943. Rose probably used his stepfather's last name from time to time.

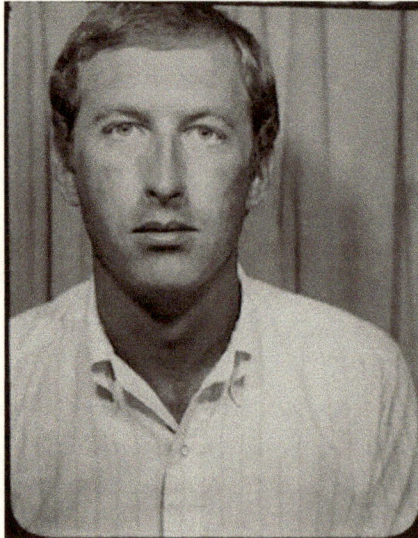

Photo of E. Carl McNabb from the files of Jim Garrison.

Some Garrison staffers thought Rose's activities were suspicious. Harold Weisberg wrote that he rummaged around the garbage of certain people in Los Angeles trying to uncover some sort of S&M ring. And here is one of his crazier theories:

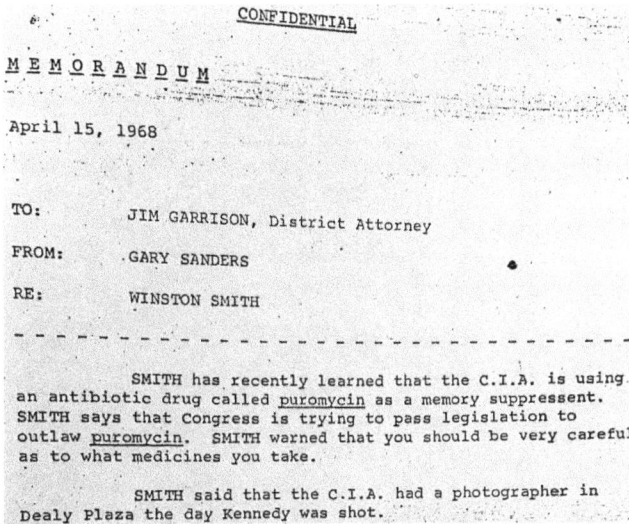

```
                    CONFIDENTIAL

M E M O R A N D U M


April 15, 1968



TO:        JIM GARRISON, District Attorney

FROM:     .GARY SANDERS

RE:        WINSTON SMITH


- - - - - - - - - - - - - - - - - - - - - - - - - - - - -

        SMITH has recently learned that the C.I.A. is using
an antibiotic drug called puromycin as a memory suppressent.
SMITH says that Congress is trying to pass legislation to
outlaw puromycin.  SMITH warned that you should be very careful
as to what medicines you take.

        SMITH said that the C.I.A. had a photographer in
Dealy Plaza the day Kennedy was shot.
```

In March 1968, a deliveryman dropped off a package at Garrison's office. It contained three manuscripts, bound in black binders. It was entitled *The Plot*, purportedly written by James Hepburn. But Garrison's office received lots of parcels, and it lay in a pile for a few weeks. Garrison read the manuscript in early April on a flight to Los Angeles and was very enthusiastic about its style and content. He felt it was a "collective effort because expertise was demonstrated in diverse areas (e.g., economics, weapons systems, ballistics, marksmanship, intelligence, etc.)"

Garrison then met with Steve Burton, Steve Jaffe, and researcher Maggie Field at her house. Xerox copies of the manuscript were handed out, and they were told to keep the existence of the book highly secret. Jaffe said that manuscript "was filled with details that only people involved with the plot could know." He also overheard a telephone conversation in which Garrison told Bill Turner that it was "beautifully written."

They all felt that the manuscript was written by the KGB and had arrived because of Rose's trip to Mexico City. Inside the package was a note saying, "call this number" and a card titled "Fiduciaire Wanner" with a Geneva and Paris address. Garrison immediately sent a telegram to Geneva asking for fifty copies of the book and further communications.

Jaffe called them up and they said we will be in touch. He then received this telegram:

They wanted Jaffe to go to Europe so they could show him the evidence that supported the manuscript. They also wanted to discuss publication in the United States. Jaffe called Garrison and asked for permission to travel to Europe.

It was time to find out the truth about *The Plot*.

So, what was in the manuscript?

Most of *The Plot* was a commentary on social conditions in the United States. Chapters discussed the oil industry, race relations, the power of corporations, and poverty. It also discussed Kennedy's foreign policy and quoted heavily from his speeches.

The group of men who organized the assassination was "the

Committee." They came from Texas or Louisiana with technical advisers from New York, California, and Washington. The plot to kill JFK "required the participation of several dozen people, and the number of people who knew what was going to happen on November 22nd was probably much higher than that."

> The collaboration on which the Committee was dependent, and the coop-
> eration of those who did nothing to stop it, turned the assassination into a
> national conspiracy in which not only the local police and certain judicial
> officers, but also the FBI through its negligence and the CIA through its
> double agents and its operational units, the Army with its dissident
> generals, Congress and its corruption, and the entire economic systems
> through its ideals and certain members of the Committee were impli-
> cated. A plot on this level is equivalent to a revolt, Kennedy's assassins
> were the arms of a counter-revolution.

Once the Committee decided to kill JFK, they then "turned their attention to political camouflage and technical arrangements." The manuscript estimated that the "cost of preparation, the assassination itself, and the post-assassination clean-up at between $5 and $10 million." About one hundred people contributed the money, with donations varying between $10,000 and $500,000.

One person on the Committee followed Kennedy's trips in 1963. One plan was to shoot Kennedy in his car on a highway in Virginia; another was to kill him in Chicago, and there was also a suggestion to blow up Air Force One. These were all rejected, "for they required accomplices among the President's staff. It was too risky." They wanted to also kill him in Florida, but they had doubts about the Florida State Police and the Tampa and Miami police departments, and the "operation was postponed until Dallas on November 22nd."

The plot extended to the top ranks of Dallas Police. and all of them were "on the special payroll."

> [Dallas Police Chief Jesse] Curry and his deputies were accustomed to
> covering minor offenses, but the assassination of a President was in a

class by itself. The plan didn't shock them. The rewards were especially attractive, and so many of their superiors were involved that they had little to fear. But their subordinates presented a problem. Many Dallas policemen were admirers of Kennedy. Many others were cowards. The plot did not extend beyond the official hierarchy. The rank of a Dallas policemen was in direct proportion as his degree of corruption.

Policemen that Curry felt were unreliable were removed that day.

The attack was carried out by a team of ten men, including four gunmen, "each seconded by an assistant who would be responsible for their protection, evacuation, and radio liaison, and who would retrieve the shells." The ninth man was a radio operator, and the tenth was to create a "last-minute diversion to enable the gunmen to get into position." The gunmen were chosen for their marksmanship, and "they were provided with excellent weapons." The organizers of the plot "delimited an exact firing zone sixty feet long which took into account the distance of each gunman from his target and the trajectory of the bullet, and which offered the maximum for success." The gunmen were evacuated by the police in "official cars." The bullets used were frangible bullets, which disintegrated on contact.

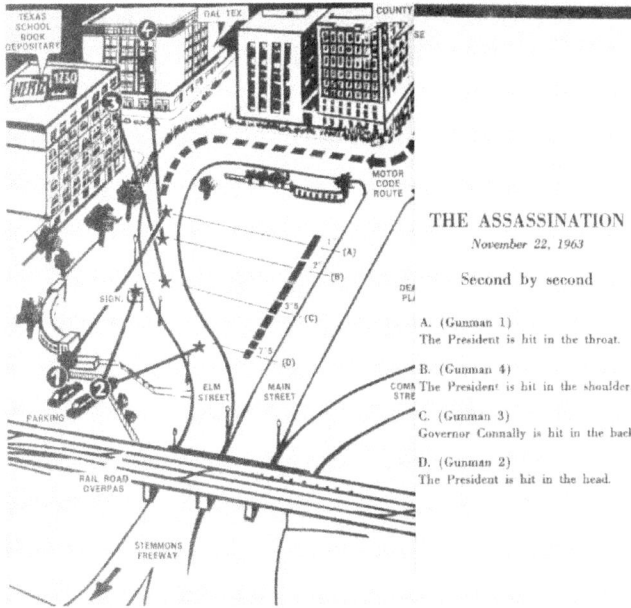

THE ASSASSINATION
November 22, 1963

Second by second

A. (Gunman 1)
The President is hit in the throat.

B. (Gunman 4)
The President is hit in the shoulder.

C. (Gunman 3)
Governor Connally is hit in the back.

D. (Gunman 2)
The President is hit in the head.

Pages 356–357 of *Farewell America*.

They also needed a scapegoat. Enter Lee Harvey Oswald, and here it starts to get confusing. "The plan consisted of influencing public opinion by simulating an attack against President Kennedy ..." In addition, the attack on General Edwin Walker in April "also designed to arouse public feeling, had been simulated."

Oswald had no special reason to suspect this new mission. In four years he had seen and done worse, and he was so psychologically involved in intelligence work that at times he would confuse his assignments for the CIA and the FBI, and his "Marxist" and "anti-Marxist" activities. Furthermore, he was in the habit of asking questions. There is no doubt that he considered himself well-covered on November 22.

The Plot was designed to appeal to Garrison by including various characters from his investigation. It claimed that Clay Shaw was an intermediary for the Committee, and Guy Banister (consistently spelled wrong throughout the manuscript) and David Ferrie were described as

CIA agents. The Rose Cherami story was also included, but with errors, including the claim that she was killed in a hit-and-run in a Dallas suburb.

And that error came from Jim Garrison's October 1967 interview with *Playboy Magazine*:

> *The Plot*: She [Cherami] repeated her story on November 20, but the doctors concluded that she was hysterical and put her under sedation. She recovered and returned to Texas, where she was killed in a hit-and-run accident in a Dallas suburb.
>
> *Playboy Interview*: After the assassination, she was killed by a hit-and-run driver on a highway outside Dallas.

Of course, Cherami (see Chapter Six) died in 1965 on a highway in Louisiana.

The Plot was also potentially libelous. For instance:

- "[Dallas Police Chief] Curry and his deputies were accustomed to covering [up] minor offenses, but the assassination of a President was in a class by itself."
- Ruth Paine was described as a lesbian.
- George de Mohrenschildt, a friend of Oswald's, was alleged to be a CIA man who kept Oswald under surveillance. He noted that "the publishers are in Luxembourg where they cannot be sued."
- Clay Shaw was named as an "intermediary for the Committee."

And have a look at these two paragraphs:

> At 12:23 on November 22, from his office on the 7th floor of the Mercantile Building, Haroldson Lafayette Hunt watched John Kennedy ride towards Dealey Plaza, where fate awaited him at 12:30. A few minutes later, escorted by six men in two cars, Hunt left the center of Dallas without even stopping by his house.

At that very moment, General Walker was in plane between New Orleans and Shreveport. He joined Mr. Hunt in one of his secret hideaways across the Mexican border. There they remained for a month, protected by personal guards, under the impassive eyes of the FBI. It was not until Christmas that Hunt, Walker and their party returned to Dallas.

Besides libeling H. L. Hunt and General Walker, it was also untrue. Walker was out of town during the assassination but returned on December 2, 1963, and you can see his picture in a variety of Texas newspapers.

It was also clear that the author or authors of the manuscript were unfamiliar with the United States. For instance, Hugh Hefner is referred to as a "gifted psychologist." Roy Cohn, hardly an important commentator, is mentioned fourteen times, and they quote him about the prospect of a second Kennedy term from remarks he made at the Stork Club in 1963. The book says that "A secret service agent whose code name was 'Dentist' was in charge of the President's pleasures." This was lifted from a satirical article about William Manchester's book *The Death of a President* in the May 1967 issue of *The Realist*.

The Plot could not even get the correct date for the assassination. The manuscript said that "On October 15, Oswald visited the warehouse, and on October 16 he began taking inventory and moving boxes of books … One week later, President Kennedy drove beneath the windows of the Depository." The *Wall Street Journal* of December 9, 1963, is quoted talking about the assassination of "last Friday morning."

And there were some plain ridiculous notions. The book says that after the assassination some Dallas police "muttered their disapproval" of the assassination, that three Dallas policemen were then murdered, and that others flew the coop. The sources: Mark Lane and Jim Garrison. In fact, the manuscript refers to Mark Lane's book *Rush to Judgment* as a "scholarly work." The book also claims there was a man carrying a two-way radio set standing on the corner of Houston and Elm Streets. The last-minute diversion, mentioned earlier, was actually just a man by the name of Jerry Belknap who had a seizure in Dealey Plaza. *The Plot* says the police took him away, but an ambulance took him Parkland Hospital.

Researcher John Locke wrote that "the authors' antipathy does not derive from an actual acquaintance with America" and that "the real authors weren't much acquainted with the assassination, but instead hastily pulled the book together from a collection of research materials."

How anybody could have taken this manuscript seriously is beyond me.

Garrison did not hear back from Geneva and then sent a second letter:

DISTRICT ATTORNEY

PARISH OF ORLEANS
STATE OF LOUISIANA
2700 TULANE AVENUE
NEW ORLEANS 70119

JIM GARRISON
DISTRICT ATTORNEY

May 10, 1968

Frontiers Establishment
c/o Fiduciaire Wanner
18 Cours des Bastions
Geneva, Switzerland

Gentlemen:

Reference is made to the recent request I made concerning the book by James Hepburn which you are publishing. This is to confirm our interest in obtaining information concerning the amount of cost of fifty copies, although the actual number purchased by us might be less.

As I advised, I am very interested in any background material available as the result of Mr. Hepburn's study. It is apparent that he knows his subject well and has done effective research.

I sent my earlier request by cable some weeks ago and possibly you did not receive it.

Please let me know also the shipping costs for any purchase of the books which this office might make.

Sincerely,

JIM GARRISON
District Attorney

Jaffe traveled to Europe in the second week of May, and he returned on July 1. Because of the riots in Paris, he landed in Brussels and took a bus to Paris. He was picked up by Herve Lamarre, the "director of the production" of *The Plot* in a "beat-up Citroen" and was taken to the office of a lawyer who represented Frontiers. At that meeting, Jaffe was offered a percentage of the profits if he helped find an American publisher. They told him that the documentation for the book was in a bank vault in Lichtenstein.

The next day they both drove to Geneva, where they went through the manuscript point by point.

Jaffe wrote that Lamarre was thirty-four years old and had attended Harvard University in "some mysterious way." He was a former combat officer in the infantry during the French-Indochina war, had diplomatic training, and was the publisher of *Mademoiselle* magazine between 1962–1965. Jaffe claimed that he was "considered to be one of the top men in the French Intelligence" and that he "was assigned to infiltrate the Oil Industry Social Circles in Texas and New York."

Lamarre told Jaffe that *The Plot* was "gathered through a combination of intelligence offices" in France and the UK and "personal contacts" in the United States. Lamarre claimed that Robert Kennedy interrogated all the Secret Service agents right after the assassination and then sent Senator Daniel Patrick Moynihan to investigate the Dallas police. He also said RFK told him to contact his campaign manager, Stephen Smith, who then either referred him to Moynihan or gave him the information directly.

The information in *The Plot* about the "ambush team, their activities and performances; intelligence information concerning ballistics and weapons and crime" came from:

- A French intelligence agent known as "Philippe," who had met with one of the Cubans involved.
- A conference with Andre Ducret, who was responsible for the protection of President Charles de Gaulle, and his brother in the French police.
- Interpol files on international crimes.

- A French intelligence weapons expert.
- The French intelligence agency and the British intelligence agency, MI5.

The information about the members of "the plot" came from French intelligence agents who had infiltrated the oil industry and certain businesses in New York. One particular target was Lloyd Hilton Smith, who was the head of an independent oil company—one agent worked as a gigolo in Paris and slept with his wife, and Lamarre knew both of his daughters. Another agent in Tokyo knew Oswald when he was stationed in Japan, and one agent was in contact with the employer (and possible CIA contact) of David Ferrie.

Jaffe reported that the manuscript was written by one man who was an established American writer. James Hepburn was just a pseudonym created by Herve Lamarre, largely because of his appreciation of Audrey Hepburn, with whom he had an affair, and the French word *j'aime*, which means "I love." In addition, Jaffe wrote that "all information for the book which is included in the final text is supported by at least two independent sources." Any information that could not be sourced was not used.

On June 21, 1968, Jaffe met with Philippe, a representative of the French Deuxieme Bureau. His speciality had been the oil business but was now moving to nuclear. Lamarre said that Phillipe had been responsible for "gathering information about the oil industry people involved in the plot." Jaffe wrote that "at one time Phillipe had met with a man in Mexico who had been part of the ambush group which murdered the President in Dealey Plaza."

Phillipe was a careful study:

> I found that Phillipe did not want to tell things directly but that if an analogy or humorous metaphor were suggested as a vehicle for discussion purposes he would follow along carefully allowing certain new information to be known.

So let me get this straight. Jaffe claimed to have met with a man who had met part of the supposed "ambush group," and we end up learning almost nothing about what happened on November 22.

The highlight of Jaffe's trip was his visit to Elysee Palace, where he was taken into the office of Andre Ducret, who was in charge of President Charles de Gaulle' security. Ducret confirmed that French intelligence had provided the information in the manuscript, and that Garrison was on the right track. Jaffe claims he asked him if he could get a letter to de Gaulle. Ducret took the letter, left the room, and returned about fifteen minutes later with de Gaulle's card, with the words "I am very grateful for the trust you have placed in me."

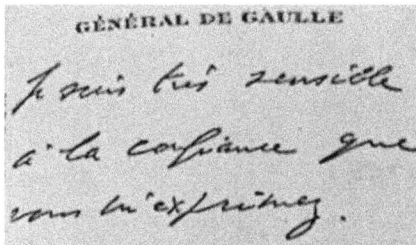

De Gaulle calling card that Jaffe brought back from Europe. It reads
"Je suis tres sensible a la confiance que vous m'exprimez."

Jaffe also claimed that Ducret called him into the hallway, where he saw de Gaulle, who nodded and "kind of gave me a salute." In response to a 2020 survey by researcher David Mantik, Jaffe wrote that he "briefly met with President de Gaulle."

Jaffe asked Ducret about getting some help in checking out some suspects with French intelligence. Ducret said he would help put Jaffe in touch with Interpol. He then asked Ducret for a copy of the Zapruder film, and Ducret replied that he could not give it to him because it might be intercepted. And then Ducret pulled out "kind of a frame," which contained a German Mauser. Ducret told Jaffe that this was the weapon that killed JFK —not that very rifle, but that model had been used in the assassination.

Lamarre and Jaffe then drove out to Interpol and met with a man named Nepote. Lamarre told Jaffe not to tell him that his inquiry was about the JFK assassination, just that he had certain business and could they check their files. Jaffe submitted a list of people to be checked out.

Note the inclusion of Richard Case Nagell, David Ferrie, and
Edgar Eugene Bradley on the list. In December 1967, Garrison
had charged Bradley, a promoter of Christian radio, with
conspiring to kill JFK. There was no evidence to back up the
charge, and years later Garrison apologized to Bradley.

They gave Jaffe a note saying that "the individuals do not appear in
our files. All are unknown."

Burton wrote that while in Geneva, Jaffe was in Lamarre's hotel room
when two Americans knocked on the door. They wanted to buy the
rights to *The Plot* and were prepared to make an incredibly good offer.
Jaffe thought that they could not have known where they were unless
they were tailing one or both. Fred Newcomb had another theory: it was
all done to "impress Steve [Jaffe]."

There was one other element to Jaffe's trip. He sent two telegrams to
Warren Report critic Raymond Marcus asking for negatives of the
Moorman photograph, which was taken of JFK just after he had been
shot in the head.

Second telegram sent to Jaffe. The first was sent on June 1.

Jaffe wanted the photograph to use in an article he was writing for a newspaper in France. Jaffe might not have known it then, but Lamarre was planning to turn *The Plot* into a film, and that photograph would come in handy. Lamarre also asked about getting a copy of the Zapruder film, and Jaffe told him to ask Jim Garrison or Mark Lane.

Jaffe retuned to the United States convinced that *The Plot* was written by the Service de Documentation Exterieure et de Contre-espionage (SDECE), France's external intelligence agency. Jaffe told Burton that he "returned with substantial evidence" and said that "Garrison had been impressed."

Once Jaffe had informed Garrison that the manuscript was put together by French intelligence, Garrison reached out to the press.

The *New Orleans Times-Picayune* reported on July 12, 1968, that Garrison had told them that "his office has exchanged information with the intelligence agency of a foreign country 'that successfully penetrated the assassination operation' against President John F. Kennedy." Garrison said that "the great amount of detailed information" he received corroborated his previous claims that JFK was killed "by elements of the Central Intelligence Agency." Garrison would not identify the country and only said that it was one on "friendly terms with the United States."

FOREIGN GROUP HAS FACTS--DA

CIA Role in JFK Death
Confirmed, He Says

He also said the foreign intelligence service had the names of Dallas policemen who had participated in the plot, had established contact with one of the assassins and thus knew the shooting points in Dealey Plaza, and had information about a pre-assassination trip David Ferrie had taken to Dallas. He added that the intelligence agency "has been extremely cooperative and they have made a great deal of detailed information available." The assassination was done by an element of the CIA "and a handful of extremely powerful individuals in the industrial complex of the Southwest."

Garrison also phoned the *New York Times:*

GARRISON CLAIMS FOREIGN SPY LINK

Says He Exchanged Data About President Kennedy

By PETER KIHSS
District Attorney Jim Garrison asserted yesterday that his office had been exchanging information with a foreign intelligence agency that he said had "penetrated the forces involved in the assassination" of President Kennedy.

July 12, 1968

Garrison told them that the "foreign intelligence agency" had arrived "by a completely different route" to the same information as his investigation. They had a "penetration" of the pre-assassination planning group "for other reasons unconnected with the assassination." The men who shot JFK were trained by the CIA—Oswald "didn't shoot anybody."

Author Edward Jay Epstein wasn't impressed by Garrison's foreign agents:

As to Garrison's foreign agents, they are of course just bunk.
Some time ago, the N.Y. Review of Books received a manuscript
from a writer using the psuedonymn "Mr.Hepburn", which outlire
a plot involving Texas oil millionaires,etc. It was a transparantly
ridiculous book,written by some 3rd-rate Mark Lane(which is saying
a lot), and they rejected it. Last March, Garrison fowarded copies
of the same manuscript to Ramparts, suggesting it must have been
written by the KGB--seeing it had so many details. An editor
from Ramparts talked to me about it, and gave me a list of details
"no one could possibly know". I gave him back a list of citations
int the Manchester book showing that the book was lifted fromth there
and the Garrison interview in Playboy,etc. Even Ramparts turned
it down as transparent nonsense. Garrison's "foreign intelligence
agency" is that manuscript--which he assumes now must have been
written by French intelligence.

Letter to Elmer Gertz from Edward Jay Epstein dated August 3, 1968.

L'Amerique Brule [America Burns] was published in France in mid-July 1968.

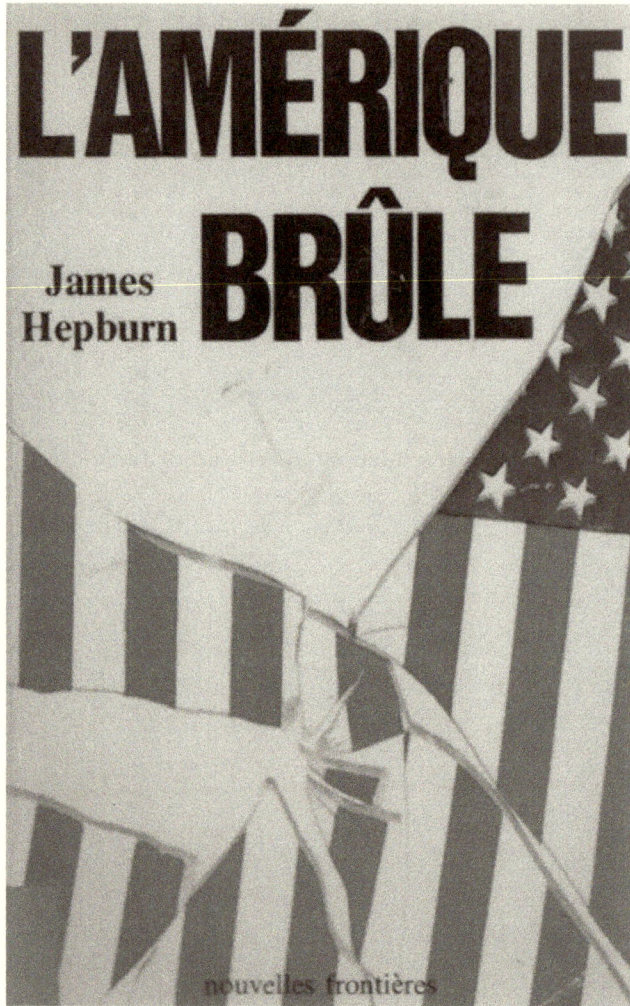

The book's jacket said James Hepburn was thirty-four years old and had studied in London and Paris and ended up with a PhD in economics. It claimed he met Jacqueline Bouvier in 1951 and that he twice met Senator John Kennedy during the 1960 presidential campaign. It also claimed that Hepburn had chatted with Robert Kennedy in 1964 in Japan and once again in 1967 after the publication of William Manchester's book *The Death of a President*. Last, work on the book started in the spring of 1967 "with the assistance of various European and American specialists."

On August 4, Jaffe received a telegram from Herve Lamarre, using the name Marie Herve, requesting that he phone him:

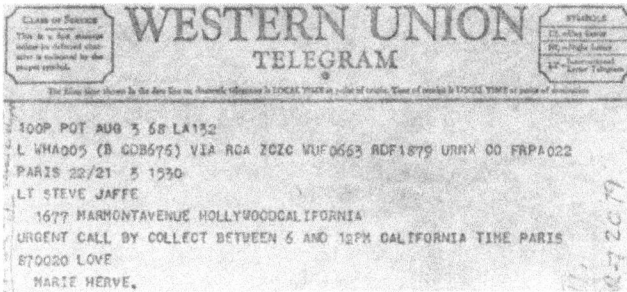

Jaffe had sent Lamarre a letter three days earlier asking for additional information about *The Plot*. He wanted details about any participants who were inside the limits of New Orleans, obviously for prosecution purposes. He also wanted Lamarre to tell him "any details at all regarding the conspiratorial acts committed by the men we discussed particularly in the case of Clay Shaw." Jaffe also asked if Lamarre wanted him to help find a publisher in the United States.

Lamarre told Jaffe that a representative of Frontiers would be in the United States on August 8 and could meet afterward. That person would not be Lamarre but somebody that Jaffe had already met. Perhaps this might be the mysterious Philippe. Jaffe said he would try to arrange a meeting with this representative and Garrison on the weekend of August 10 and 11. Lamarre also said that the book was scheduled to be released in the UK in September.

In fact, Lamarre was the person who visited the United States in August. He gave copies of *L'Amerique Brule* to Jaffe, Garrison, and Mark Lane. Garrison said, "let's hope the book does some good." He suggested that the name of the book in English be changed to *Farewell America*. It was at this point that Lamarre told Jaffe that they were also producing a film to accompany the book. Jaffe wanted to help, and over the next couple of months sent Lamarre a copy of the film he was working on as well as the photographic work of several Warren Report critics.

The book was serialized in June in four installments in the *Bild-*

Zeitung, then Germany's largest circulation newspaper, and then a German-language edition was published in late September.

In the beginning of November, Jaffe phoned Burton and told him that Lamarre had made a film and that it contained the Zapruder film. He asked Burton to contact the UCLA Film Commission to set up a showing.

On November 14, 1968, Burton called Fred Newcomb and asked if he would prepare an ad for the showing of *Farewell America* at UCLA on November 22. The film was to arrive by special courier from France, but Jaffe was worried "something could happen." The film did not show up, and the date was moved to the twenty-fifth. A huge crowd of about seven hundred people showed up, but the film never arrived. Jaffe actually thought that the courier might have been killed by the CIA.

A.S.U.C.L.A.
FILM
COMMISSION

presents

THE AMERICAN
PREMIERE
OF:

"FAREWELL
AMERICA"

A EUROPEAN
MEMORIAL FILM
COMMEMORATING THE
FIFTH ANNIVERSARY
OF THE DEATH OF

President John Fitzgerald

KENNEDY

MONDAY
NOVEMBER 25,
1968   4P.M.

UCLA Dixon Art Center
Rm. 2160
North Campus End
(Near Sunset)

ADMISSION: FREE

(FILM IN ENGLISH)

showings:

"FAREWELL
AMERICA"·

NOVEMBER 20 - PARIS
NOVEMBER 21 - LONDON
NOVEMBER 25 - LOS ANGELES

LA Free Press, November 22, 1968

Lamarre later called Jaffe and said that he had been terribly ill in Paris and that was why the film did not show up.

By this time, Garrison had told Jaffe to disassociate from the film because it could bring about a legal trap for his prosecution of Clay

Shaw. At some point, there was a blowup in the Garrison office. As best I can tell, Vincent Salandria accused Jaffe of being a CIA agent. At one point, Jaffe had a scuffle with Lou Ivon, Garrison's chief investigator, and his DA credentials were taken away.

Jaffe then wrote an article for the December 5, 1968, issue of the *LA Free Press*, under the name of Jay Singer, about the kerfuffle with the film:

> For if the allegations of the expert critics of the Government's official position on the case (Warren Report: Oswald was alone; definitely not a plot; the CIA was nowhere in sight) are correct, it is not inconceivable that the film's courier received some interference when he attempted to enter the country.

On December 13, 1968, the film *Farewell America* was shown at a screening room in Los Angeles. Present were Steve Burton, Maggie Field, Jim Rose, Steve Jaffe, Herve Lamarre, Fred Newcomb, and a few other researchers. Unfortunately, Steve Burton felt that most of it was "either so irrelevant or so incorrect as to discredit totally the value and damning evidence in the Zapruder film."

Farewell America named [Dallas Police Captain] Will Fritz, Jesse Curry, Guy Banister, Clay Shaw, and David Ferrie as "actively participated in the planning" of the assassination. Burton noted that "no evidence whatsoever was presented to substantiate these accusations."

Burton wrote that "the accusation against Clay Shaw is clearly prejudicial to the current legal proceedings in New Orleans. Such actions are intolerable. Second, any group or person who presents this film is very much subject to libel actions by the living accused."

One massive error in the film was the inclusion of the "walkie-talkie man." Researcher Fred Newcomb initially believed that a line on the top of the man's hand in the background of a photograph was a radio antenna. He then changed his mind when he finally noticed that the "antenna was a just a line from Lyndon Johnson's limousine." The walkie-talkie man was presented as fact in *Farewell America*.

The film also included the claim that Edgar Eugene Bradley, a man Garrison had erroneously indicted for conspiring to kill Kennedy, was in a photograph of men being escorted from the Texas School Book Depository. By the time of the film, most researchers realized that Bradley had nothing to do with the assassination.

All the people at the screening, except Lamarre, "were of the opinion that the film was poor; most felt that no responsible person could have anything to with its promotion."

But there was one question in the minds of everyone concerned. Where did Lamarre get his copy of the Zapruder film?

Jim Garrison had issued a subpoena to *Life* magazine for a copy of the Zapruder film on March 15, 1968. A *Life* photo lab technician was sent to New Orleans on March 28 with a copy of the film that was to be shown to the grand jury. *Life* agreed that the film could stay with Garrison for use at the Shaw trial but that it could not be used for any other purposes. Mark Lane wrote in an article for the *Midlothian Mirror* that "an excellent first generation color reprint was delivered."

On December 16, 1968, a meeting was held at Maggie Field's house with Fred and Marilyn Newcomb, Ray Marcus, and Steve Jaffe. They wanted to know how Lamarre had gotten the Zapruder film, and Jaffe told them a story about getting it from the Kennedy family. But then he said he had another explanation and asked for the tape to be stopped.

Here is an excerpt from a transcript of the tape:

Raymond Marcus: What is the very first time, to your recollection, that the subject of doing a promotional film came up? How did it come up? Did it ever come up in Europe?

Stephen Jaffe: Yes, he asked me in Europe. He said, "you know, you have, or there exists a Zapruder film," I think he said, "you have," because by that time, we did, although I'm not so sure if we didn't acquire it during the time I was in Europe.

Maggie Field: That film came, I think, after you were there. Didn't it? [No, the film arrived in Garrison's office before Jaffe went to Europe.]

Stephen Jaffe: Well, anyway he talked about the Zapruder film. And he said, why don't you show that to me? That's the most important piece of evidence. All you have to do is just show it, you know. You can worry about the consequences later. So, I gave him the logical explanation that

Garrison is a district attorney. He is an official. He uses legal means. He does not depart from those legal means, although he is criticized for it, but that his sole integrity is that he had not departed from those functions. He only has, he only has a small amount of power as a district attorney, anyway. He's no national investigator, because it's quite a different thing to be the FBI and be a local DA. And he's not going to break the law. And I said, other than that, the Archives has a copy of the film, and Life has a copy of the film, neither of them showing it, except the archives showing it to people who make appointments. But he said, "well, you should really show it,' and he asked me if he could get a copy of it. And I said, "well, you can go to the Archives, you know, ask them or ask Life." And he said, "no." And then at different times, he asked me if Garrison would give him a copy. And I said, "you ask him, I don't know." And then I know that he did ask Garrison, and he asked Mark Lane to ask Garrison, or he asked me to ask Mark to answer. And anyway …

Maggie Field: What did Garrison say, no?

Stephen Jaffe: Garrison said no.

Maggie Field: Where did he get the copy then?

Stephen Jaffe: Well, he told me that he got it through sources within Kennedy's office, Robert Kennedy's office. Now I have personal knowledge of the possibility of another place where he got it, and I refuse to say that on tape or here.

Marilyn Newcomb wrote that Jaffe then said that Lamarre had gotten a copy from Garrison's office. Lamarre had taken the film to Canada but was not able to make a decent copy, so he flew it to Paris and copies were made. The original was then returned to Garrison along with two copies. Harold Weisberg also wrote that "Ray Marcus had earlier told me of three occasions on which Jaffe told others he had given a copy of the Z film to Lamarre."

This is why the showing of the film *Farewell America* had to be stopped. The inclusion of the Zapruder film and the citation of Stephen Jaffe as a photographic consultant to the film would have allowed *Life* magazine to point a finger at Jim Garrison as the source of the film. This would have put Garrison in violation of the subpoena, and his ability to show it at the upcoming Shaw trial would have been in jeopardy. In addition, Lamarre told Jaffe that he had put Clay Shaw into the film "as a courtesy to Jim Garrison." Naming him as a conspirator was libelous and would have caused huge problems.

Lamarre then realized his attempts to show this film were going nowhere, and he returned to Paris. At the end of December, Maggie Field went to Paris and met with Lamarre. He disparaged the Garrison investigation, particularly the use of "kids" like Jaffe and Burton. He felt that not much would come from New Orleans. He wined and dined Maggie and her husband but did not reveal any evidence about the case. She felt that he was a "nervous wreck, impolite," and with "no humor."

The *New York Times* wrote about *Farewell America* on January 1, 1969.

BOOK ON KENNEDY SEES A WIDE PLOT

Origin of French Bestseller Remains a Mystery

By JOHN L. HESS
Special to The New York Times

PARIS, Dec. 31—A book of mysterious origin accusing the entire American power structure of complicity in the assassination of John F. Kennedy has spread through Western Europe and is now crossing the Atlantic.

Lamarre was quoted as saying the manuscript had been rejected by "practically all" publishers in the United States. He said the book had sold sixty thousand copies in France and that they had printed thirty thousand copies of the English edition. The "fear of libel action" was one reason for its American rejection. Interestingly, the *New York Times* noted that "no new evidence is offered to support the allegations, which are generally conclusions or suppositions drawn from previously published material." The president of Farrer, Straus & Giroux said they had rejected the book because it contained "nothing new on the assassination of President Kennedy."

No one was going to touch the book in the United States. Frontiers then printed an English-language edition of the book in Belgium and sold it through Canada. A stack of six hundred books ended up in Bill Turner's garage.

LA Free Press, September 5, 1969

There were very few reviews of *Farewell America*. An article in the South Carolina *Anderson Independent* newspaper said:

For evidence, the book offers only assertions; for facts, only hallucinations.

We think that anyone who would believe this malicious garbage would believe anything, or—and it is saying much the same thing— would believe nothing. We regret to say that some people will and do.

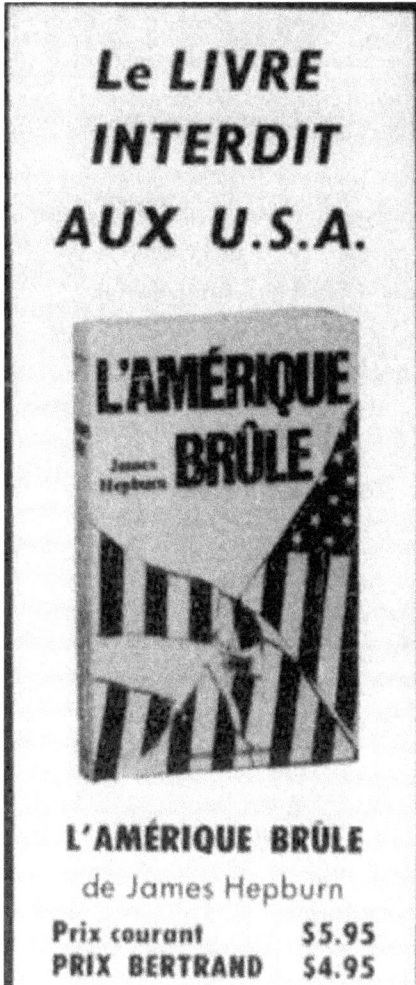

Le Devoir, March 1, 1969, "The Book Banned in the U.S.A."

The French language edition was sold in Quebec and was serialized in *La Presse*, the largest Montreal daily newspaper.

In 1973, *San Francisco Chronicle* columnist Herb Caen noted that "the book strikes this reader as what you'd get if you crossed a crocodile with an abalone. Right. A crocobalone."

So just who was responsible for *Farewell America*? Hinckle wrote that

> Back home, we at last developed a good hunch about who was dealing in the bridge game in which *Ramparts* was playing a dummy hand. The droopy fleur-de-lys of French intelligence overshadowed the cardboard publishing house of Frontiers, but that in itself was of little specific help in tracing the river of data in *Farewell America* to its source, because the French S.D.E.C.E. was so notoriously, and almost hilariously, ridden with K.G.B. double agents that, as a matter of course, Frenchmen were offered vodka before wine at international spy gatherings.

The truth is that we do not really know.

It might have been a Gaullist disinformation attempt. Certain passages indicated a French origin—for instance, quoting the Chevalier de Beaujour and the Baron de Montlezun. Charles de Gaulle is routinely praised in the book:

> He [JFK] did not belong to that great family of emperors who, from Peter the Great to Frederick of Prussia to Charles de Gaulle, have always placed the interest of the state above sentiment—even when it caused their heart to suffer.

There also might have been a Soviet hand in the affair.

The French Communist Party played a role in the resistance during World War II, and de Gaulle put communist ministers in his provisional government in 1944. Historian Christoper Andrew noted that because of this fact, "Soviet intelligence had much greater freedom of action in France than in either the United States or Britain."

In 1945 alone, KGB agents resident in Paris sent 1,123 reports to Moscow from seventy different sources. In 1946 an agent was placed into the new French intelligence agency DGER which then became the SDECE. Two more agents joined SDECE in 1947. Ivan Ivanovich Agayants, a KGB agent in France, said in 1952 that French intelligence was "that prostitute I put in my pocket."

Mitrokhin and Andrew claim that there were at least fifty KGB agents resident in Paris from 1946–1958, including four officials in the SDECE. They note that "in 1954 30 per cent of all reports to the Centre from the Paris residency were based on information from its agents in the French intelligence community." This made British and American intelligence agencies cautious about sharing information with the SDECE.

Besides sending classified information back to Moscow, another important aspect was influencing Western opinion. Between 1947 and 1955, a "series of bogus memoirs and other propaganda works" were published. Andrews and Mitrokhin note that "KGB penetration of the French intelligence community continued during the 1960s."

In 1961, the French blamed the CIA for a coup attempt against de Gaulle despite the fact there was absolutely no evidence to sustain the charge. These allegations were then amplified by the KGB. Mitrokhin noted that "In April 1961 the KGB succeeded in planting on the pro-Soviet Italian daily *Paese Sera* a story suggesting that the CIA was involved in the failed putsch mounted by four French generals to disrupt de Gaulle's attempts to negotiate a peace with the FLN which would lead to Algerian independence."

In 1962, Anotoliy Golitsyn (code-named Martel), a KGB defector, stated that there were Soviet agents within French military intelligence and even within de Gaulle's cabinet. JFK sent a letter to de Gaulle discussing the situation. Golitsyn was interrogated by French counterintelligence officers, and they came away convinced they had a problem. This led to a three-year breakdown in intelligence sharing between France and the United States.

Philippe Thyraud de Vosjoli was posted in Washington in 1960 as a liaison officer between the SDECE and the CIA. In 1963, he alerted the SDECE that a Soviet spy ring was operating within the organization. When Vosjoli received an order to return to France, he believed it was a death warrant and defected to the United States. He then worked with author Leon Uris, who published a book, *Topaz*, about a Soviet spy ring within the French Security Services.

The April 26, 1968, issue of *Life* magazine featured an article by Vosjoli detailing Soviet penetration into the SDECE.

LIFE THE FRENCH SPY SCANDAL

The former chief of French Intelligence in the U.S. reveals the fantastic story of Soviet espionage that penetrated De Gaulle's official family

We still do not know the true extent of Soviet penetration into French intelligence.

But we do know that the KGB was extremely interested in manipulating American public opinion regarding the assassination. A KGB official who worked in the Soviet delegation at the United Nations, codenamed Shamrock, contacted the CIA on January 16, 1967, and began to share information. He told the CIA he had had two meetings with Mark Lane, a prominent critic of the Warren Report. The KGB would go on to funnel $1,500 to Lane through a "trusted contact" and $500 for a trip to Europe, which was eventually canceled.

A CIA memo notes that "other investigators and Kennedy assassination buffs were supplied by the KGB not only with money, but also with circumstantial evidence that made the affair appear to be a well-concealed political conspiracy."

Shamrock also said there had been a KGB commission to investigate the JFK assassination:

> Essentially, the report contains two basic elements: the information about the KGB commission established to investigate the circumstances of President Kennedy's death and information on Lee Harvey Oswald's relationship with the KGB. As far as we know, there has been no previous reporting on the existence of such a commission. It is important to note, however, that the alleged conclusions of this commission—that President Kennedy was killed by a conspiracy of right wing monopolists—have long comprised the standard Soviet line on this subject. To cite but two examples, KHRUSHCHEV took this tack in an interview he granted to columnist Drew Pearson in early 1964; a complete statement of the Soviet line on Kennedy's death is to be found in a book called "Where do the

Tracks Lead?" by A. TORYSH and B. SERGEYEV, which was submitted for publication on 2 September 1964. This book spells out the theory of a right wing conspiracy in great detail.

In 1978, Vosjoli was contacted by the HSCA, and he had a rather interesting story:

> At another time, which coincided with the period when he was replaced by Paris as Chief of Intelligence in Washington, subject states that he was in New York City ... about three days before Kennedy was shot in Dallas.
>
> He had a mail drop at 555 Fifth Avenue as a precaution. While picking up his mail one day he spotted the French Chief of Station for New York, a Monsieur Herve, walking along Fifth Avenue with a Colonel George de Lannurian, whom he recognized as a member of SDECE and whom subject also knew was a Soviet agent planted in the French Services. He was intrigued what the Colonel was doing in the United States and why he was obviously having a clandestine meeting in New York, so he followed them. The Colonel went to the Harvard Club on West 44th Street, and subject states he had lunch there with a group of right wing extremists from Texas.

Was the "Herve" Herve Lamarre, or was it Herve Alphand, the French ambassador to the United States? I do not know, but it all sounds familiar—remember that Lamarre told Jaffe that French intelligence had "infiltrated the Oil industry in Texas, and certain businesses in New York." He also told Jaffe he had spent time in New York and Washington.

Steve Jaffe eventually turned that "crocobalone" into the 1973 feature film *Executive Action*. In the film, a shadowy group of right-wing members of the military-industrial complex decide to kill JFK. Jaffe was the technical consultant and supervising producer.

The book of the film, written by Mark Lane and Donald Freed, even included a remarkably similar chart to that in *Farewell America*, with two gunmen in front of and two gunmen behind the presidential limousine:

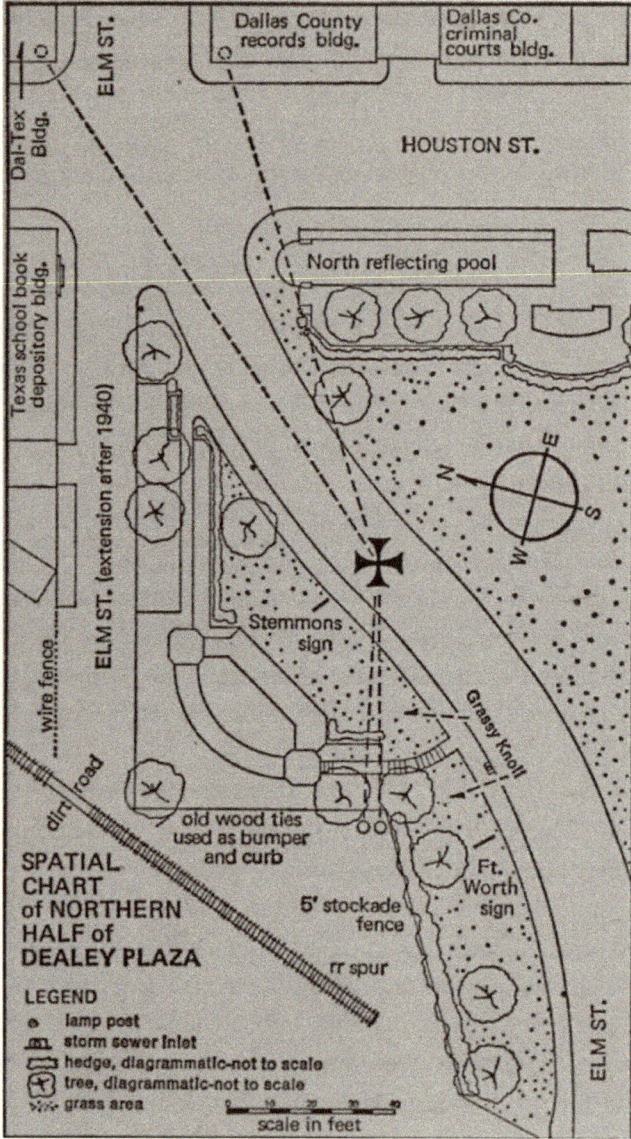

SPATIAL CHART of NORTHERN HALF of DEALEY PLAZA

LEGEND
- lamp post
- storm sewer inlet
- hedge, diagrammatic-not to scale
- tree, diagrammatic-not to scale
- grass area

scale in feet

We will never know for sure just who was behind *Farewell America*. Was it an SDECE production with KGB help? Or was it the work of some crafty entrepreneurs who tried to take advantage of Jim Garrison's investigation? In any case, Garrison was very receptive to hearing that he was on the right track and that his suspects were indeed responsible for the JFK assassination. Had the perpetrators been a little less clumsy, Garrison might have shouted *Farewell America* from the rafters.

9

THE BOLTON FORD INCIDENT

I n January of 1961, two men visited the Bolton Ford dealership in New Orleans to buy some trucks. They represented Friends of Democratic Cuba, an anti-Castro organization created by several New Orleans business and political figures. The contact for the group was Joseph Moore.

Right above Moore's name on the quote is the name Oswald. But it could not have been Lee Harvey Oswald since he was living in the Soviet Union at the time.

Here is the quote for the trucks:

Three days after the assassination, Oscar Deslatte, a salesman at Bolton Ford, called the FBI to tell them what had happened. He could not remember any identifying data about Joseph Moore or his friend.

The FBI showed him a photograph of Lee Harvey Oswald, and Deslatte said he could not recall having seen him before. In fact, he could not really describe any of the two men since it had been almost three years since the event and they were only at Bolton Ford for a brief time.

BOLTON FORD
announces the opening of
The TRUCK CENTER
1483 North Claiborne

Specialized Service-by Specialists
TRUCKS ONLY
SALES AND SERVICE
Free Pick-Up! Free Delivery! Servicing All Makes
WE SELL AND SERVICE FORD DIESELS

This staff of experts combine 220 years of experience!

1483 NORTH CLAIBORNE • WHItehall 7-1490

New Orleans Times-Picayune, November 11, 1960

Moore told Deslatte that they should get the trucks for no profit and that the name on the quote should be changed to Oswald, who was the person with the money and who would pay for the trucks.

There the matter rested until the Garrison investigation. He called in Oscar Deslatte for questioning, but Deslatte refused to say anything and denied the incident ever happened. Garrison then spoke to Fred Sewell, who was Deslatte's boss at Bolton Ford. And now, Sewell remembered that the man said his name was "Lee Oswald." But his memory was fraying—it was now six years after the incident—and he said he "can't remember that long." Garrison repeated the question:

Garrison: Did it have "Oswald" on it or "Lee Oswald"? Do you remember looking at it?

Sewell: I can't remember that. It's been six years but I know that the man who identified himself as Oswald was in the office and made that remark [about paying for the trucks]. Now, I do know that.

I certainly discount Fred Sewell's story. There is no contemporaneous record of the person identifying himself as Lee Oswald. And Mr. Sewell did not come forward in 1963 or 1964. And in a February 1968 interview, Sewell could not even remember Deslatte's name.

Two things piqued Garrison's interest. First, there was the possibility that somebody was impersonating Lee Harvey Oswald. Second, Guy Banister was one of the officers of Friends of Democratic Cuba, and he was a suspect in the assassination.

Here is how Jim Garrison described the discovery that Banister was behind Friends of Democratic Cuba:

I pondered the implications of this staggering information. In the very month that John Kennedy was inaugurated, an intelligence project being run by Guy Banister was using the name "Oswald" in bidding for pickup trucks for apparent use in the Bay of Pigs invasion.

Of course, we do not know what purpose the trucks were intended for.

Friends of Democratic Cuba did not last long and closed its doors on February 2, 1961.

To determine the meaning of all this, Garrison brainstormed with his assistant Frank Klein. Here is an excerpt from his book *On the Trail of the Assassins*:

Garrison: You don't think Sewall [*sic*] and Deslatte were lying, do you?

Klein: No. But the story doesn't make sense. Oswald was in Russia in January 1961. He couldn't possibly have been at Bolton Ford.

Garrison: Someone was playing Oswald's part.

Klein: Playing Oswald's part? But why?

Garrison: I don't know yet. But the important point is we now know that whoever was behind the assassination was inclined to have someone impersonate Lee Oswald.

Klein: You're headed somewhere but I don't know your direction yet.

Garrison shows Klein some job applications from the Warren Commission documents.

Garrison: Notice anything odd?

Klein: That's the wrong height. In every one of these applications, he's [Oswald] got the wrong height down.

Garrison: Exactly. If they'll impersonate you in 1961, they'll impersonate you in 1963.

Klein: But why would someone fill out these applications at all these places and continually put down the wrong height?

Garrison: Because the impersonator was only five feet nine. Since he was interviewed in person, he had to put down his real height or close to it. Just because someone could imitate Oswald's handwriting perfectly doesn't mean he could stretch himself to Oswald's real height.

Klein: You know, you haven't mentioned the most significant thing of all.

Garrison: What's that?

Klein: The time of the visit to Bolton Ford. Using Lee Oswald's name as early as January 1961. That was the month of Kennedy's inauguration.

Garrison: You're asking me if I think the plan to eliminate John Kennedy had begun as early as January 1961. I would find that hard to believe. My answer would have to be no.

Garrison understood that it was ridiculous to believe conspirators were already plotting when Kennedy was just being inaugurated.

But Garrison goes on to say that he learned in 1977 that the CIA had prepared, after Kennedy's election win in 1960, a psychological profile of how Kennedy would react in certain circumstances.

Nowadays I often think back to Frank's question about the implications of the 1961 impersonation of Oswald. And when I do, I wonder—if I had known then about the C.I.A.'s remarkably early psychological profile of Kennedy—whether my answer would have been the same.

So now Garrison is now saying that indeed people may have been plotting back in January 1961.

Garrison made the CIA report sound creepy. But the CIA just wanted to understand the right way to brief Kennedy. Their assessment, according to former intelligence officer and author, William Corson, was "made in order not to offend him by the method of presentation, or to trigger subjective, antagonistic response to well established operation and practices in the intelligence community." This was hardly nefarious.

The Bolton Ford story made the film *JFK*:

BACK AT GARRISON'S HOME—(1967)

SUSIE: ... now it gets positively spooky. In January 1961—in New Orleans, at the Bolton Ford Dealership—when the Oswald we know is in Russia—there is a man using the name "Oswald" to buy trucks for the Friends of Democratic Cuba. The salesman never saw him again, but guess who's on the articles of incorporation of the Friends of Democratic Cuba? Guy Banister. (reactions from the others) Banister has someone using the name "Oswald" to buy the trucks.

The film makes the illogical leap that Guy Banister was behind this impersonation of Oswald.

The whole thing makes no sense. Why would they impersonate Oswald? Were the conspirators plotting to kill Kennedy before he had even taken office? Why would they frame a man who was in the Soviet Union? They had no idea when or if he would return.

Garrison also had an interest in the man that accompanied Oswald. He noted in *On the Trail of the Assassins* that "one of the men was a powerfully built Latin with a thick neck and a distinct scar over his left eyebrow." He then adds:

After Lee Harvey Oswald returned to New Orleans and began handing out pro-Castro leaflets, this man with the scar was always present on the edge of the crowd. It is standing operating procedure for an intelligence agent engaged in a provocative activity to have a nearby bodyguard to protect him against a violent reaction from the crowd. It seems probably that this man with the scar was Oswald's bodyguard because of the regularity of his presence—invariably on the outer edge of the scene and invariably wearing sunglasses. The sunglasses were large, but they could not conceal the vertical scar that ran up through this man's left eyebrow. We learned of his consistent attendance from our questioning of persons present at the leaflet handout, many of whom we had identified from our copies of the news photos.

Garrison told Edward Jay Epstein that the man with a scar was Oswald's CIA babysitter. But why on earth would an Oswald impostor need a babysitter?

To be honest, I was never that interested in the Bolton Ford incident. The allegations never made any sense, and I figured that since there were at least twenty-six Oswalds in the New Orleans phone book back then, someone else accompanied Joseph Moore.

But in January 2022, I got lucky. I did a search on Google for "Bolton Ford" and Oswald. And up popped this court case:

Schulingkamp v. Bolton Ford, Inc.

This case presents a suit by Oswald A. Schulingkamp, the owner of Schulingkamp Motor Company, for damage to his property on North Claiborne Avenue in the City of New Orleans, which resulted from a fire on November 13, 1960. The fire originated in the adjacent building, leased and occupied by Bolton Ford, Inc., and spread from there to plaintiff's property. Named as defendants are Bolton Ford, Inc., and its insurer.

Bolton Ford and Schulingkamp Motor Company were adjacent to each other. The owner of Schulingkamp Motors was Oswald Schulingkamp, and his brother Oliver was a judge in New Orleans.

Oliver Schulingkamp's picture appeared in the July 5, 1961, edition of the *New Orleans Time-Picayune* standing next to Guy Banister, who was one of the founders of Friends of Democratic Cuba. They were both at a Fourth of July rally organized by the National Confederation for Conservative Government, whose president was Delphine Roberts, Banister's secretary.

Perhaps Oliver Schulingkamp sent the Friends of Democratic Cuba to see his brother Oswald for help in buying trucks. He then took them next door to Bolton Ford, which specialized in trucks. The salesman, Oscar Deslatte, wrote "Oswald" because it might have been a lot easier than spelling his difficult last name.

In January 1961, Lee Harvey Oswald was just twenty-one years old living in the Soviet Union. Why would anybody associated with Friends of Democratic Cuba even know his name? And why would they impersonate Oswald just as JFK was being inaugurated?

The impersonation of Lee Harvey Oswald at Bolton Ford never made any sense.

AFTERWORD

The stories presented in this book illustrate some of the nonsense swirling around Jim Garrison's investigation into the JFK assassination. Unfortunately, some of the more popular conspiracy books leave their skepticism at home when considering some of this material.

Why would anybody still believe that Raymond Broshears is a credible witness? How on earth could people still think that Richard Case Nagell held the key to understanding the assassination? Does it make any sense that someone like Rose Cherami would have foreknowledge of JFK's murder? And was there ever any good reason to think that Bootsie Gay really saw a map of Dealey Plaza on David Ferrie's desk?

Let's examine these stories through the eyes of three JFK conspiracy books:

- *JFK and the Unspeakable: Why He Died and Why it Matters* (James W. Douglass, 2008, Orbis Books)
- *Destiny Betrayed: JFK, Cuba and the Garrison* Case (James DiEugenio, 2012, Skyhorse Publishing)
- *Honest Answers About the Murder of President John F. Kennedy* (Vince Palamara, 2021, Trine Day)

Douglass completely buys the Richard Case Nagell story. In his opening chronology of the assassination, he provides the following note for September 20, 1963:

> In El Paso, Texas, U.S. counterintelligence agent Richard Case Nagell, who has met with Kennedy assassination planners, walks into a bank and fires two pistol shots into a plaster wall just below the ceiling. He waits outside to be arrested and tells the FBI, "I would rather be arrested than commit murder and treason."

Well, Nagell did fire two shots into the ceiling of the bank, but nothing else in that statement is correct. He didn't wait outside to be arrested; he tried to drive away and was stopped by a policeman. Nagell said nothing about murder and treason *before* the JFK assassination.

Douglass devotes five pages to the Nagell story, and all of his material is taken from Dick Russell's book *The Man Who Knew Too Much*. He even repeats Russell's claim that there was something suspicious about Nagell's death:

> Russell asked an investigator for the Los Angeles coroner, Gary Keller-man, if a heart attack could be induced. Kellerman said it was indeed possible to kill in such a way, while leaving no clues:
> "I'm not sure what chemical you have to use, but I've heard of it," he said. "From what I understand, it's a chemical that gets into the system and then it's gone. You can't find it."

Douglass does not mention that Nagell was a lifelong smoker, nor does he mention Nagell's forensic autopsy. Not surprisingly, he also does not discuss Nagell's plane crash or any of his mental health issues.

James DiEugenio, the author of *Destiny Betrayed*, also believes Nagell's story and spends five pages in his book discussing him:

> Jim Garrison referred to Nagell in these terms: "Richard Case Nagell is the most important witness there is." No serious and objective writer in the field can disagree with that to any great extent. If Nagell was not the

most important of the cooperating witnesses, he was certainly in the top five.

Nagell is the most important witness? Witness to what?

And here is what DiEugenio says about Nagell's mental health:

In the wake of Russell's book and the revelation of a plane accident Nagell had previous to the assassination, commentators like Mark Zaid and Paul Hoch have questioned Nagell's utility on the basis of his possible mental instability. *Probe* [DiEugenio's newsletter] has decided not to engage in telepathic psychiatry.

Is there any need for telepathic psychiatry? Nagell himself petitioned the courts to recognize his brain damage from the plane crash.

DiEugenio also took the Nagell story from Dick Russell, who will seemingly believe almost anything.

For instance, he wrote in the first edition of his book that he had been looking for a "smoking gun, some official document that might lend credence to Nagell's revelations." And lo and behold in 1986, Nagell mailed Russell one page from a military intelligence document (see below).

FOR OFFICIAL USE ONLY

AGENT REPORT
(SR 380-320-10)

1. NAME OF SUBJECT OR TITLE OF INCIDENT	2. DATE SUBMITTED
NAGELL, Richard Case	2 May 1969
DOB: 5 August 1930	3. CONTROL SYMBOL OR FILE NUM
POB: Greenwich, New York, USA	

4. REPORT OF FINDINGS

October 1959, promoted SUBJECT, retroactively, to the rank of permanent Captain, as of 1 August 1959. On 29 October 1959, SUBJECT received an Honorable Discharge.

From 14 December 1959 through 22 June 1962, SUBJECT was employed as a special investigator for the State of California, Fraud Section, Department of Employment, and the Department of Alcoholic Control. On 8 June 1962, SUBJECT was suspended for unauthorized release of information to the newspapers and the Los Angeles Police Department. During the period from August 1962 to October 1963, SUBJECT was intermittently employed as an informant and/or investigator for the Central Intelligence Agency (CIA). In April 1963, SUBJECT conducted an inquiry concerning the marital status of Marina Oswald and her reported desire to return to the USSR. During July, August, September, and on one occasion prior to this, SUBJECT conducted an inquiry into the activities of Lee Harvey Oswald, and the allegation that he had established a Fair Play For Cuba Committee in New Orleans, Louisiana. SUBJECT stated that while working for the CIA, HE had operated in Mexico, Florida, Louisiana, Texas, California, Puerto Rico, and New York. HE was primarily concerned with investigating activities of Anti-Castro organizations and their personnel in the United States and Mexico. On 20 September 1963, SUBJECT was arrested in El Paso, Texas on the charge of entering a Federal bank with the intent to commit a felony. In May 1964 and September 1966, SUBJECT was twice tried and twice convicted on this charge. The conviction of the May 1964 trial had been subsequently reversed, thus the reason for the second trial. SUBJECT was sentenced to a maximum of ten years imprisonment, but was released after four and one-half years. SUBJECT claimed that HIS conviction and subsequent incarceration was a result, not of HIS supposed intent to commit a felony, but rather as a result of HIS knowledge of Lee Harvey Oswald and the assassination of President Kennedy. SUBJECT claimed that while HE was in prison HE was beaten, intimidated, threatened, tortured, and kept incommunicado. SUBJECT stated that this treatment resulted from HIS refusal to "talk," although SUBJECT did not make clear exactly what it was that HE was being asked to talk about. SUBJECT also claimed that HE was denied due process of law during HIS respective trials. On 29 April 1968, the US Court of Appeals for the Fifth Circuit at New Orleans acquitted SUBJECT, due to insufficient evidence. On 30 May 1968, SUBJECT was given $500 by two people who refused to identify themselves, and told to leave the US. SUBJECT went to Geneva, Switzerland, though HIS reasons for picking Geneva were never made clear. SUBJECT was apparently trying to determine the location of HIS family. SUBJECT next

THIS PROTECTIVE MARKING IS EX-CLUDED FROM AUTOMATIC TERMINATION

PAGE 2 OF 4 PAGES

Russell was certainly taken in:

What was so striking about this report was that, unlike any other government file I had seen about him, it stated directly that Nagell had been monitoring the activities of Oswald, his wife, and "Anti-Castro organiza-tions" on behalf of the CIA. The beginning sentences of the report were not phrased in a manner attributable to Nagell. In other words, they did not say "SUBJECT alleged" or "claimed" or "stated"; the facts about Nagell were simply stated as facts.

It seemed obvious that this information came directly from Nagell. It did not take me long to track down the entire document. Have a look at the opening sentence from page one:

```
                  ' UN UFFIUIAL UST 'UNi
                    AGENT REPORT
                     TSR 380-370-107

1. NAME OF SUBJECT OR TITLE OF INCIDENT          2. DATE SUBMITTED
NAGELL, Richard Case                              2 May 1969
DOB:  5 August 1930                              3. CONTACT SYMBOL, OR F.
POB:  Greenwich, New York, USA

4. REPORT OF FINDINGS

        On 11 April 1969, SUBJECT appeared as a walk-in at Berlin Station
and stated in substance as follows:
```

The entire document is a summation of what Nagell told them. No wonder Nagell only sent one page to Russell. Of course, he never would have sent Russell page four, which has the agent's notes:

AGENT'S NOTES: It was obvious throughout both interviews with SUBJECT that HE was mentally disturbed. SUBJECT broke down and cried on numerous occasions, usually when the conversation concerned HIS attempts to locate HIS family. SUBJECT'S allegation that HE received no cooperation from VA Hospitals or the State Department could quite possibly stem from SUBJECT's extreme emotional state and HIS propen-sity to interpret anything but immediate response to HIS demands as an indication of non-cooperation. Subsequent investigation revealed, in fact, that measures have been taken to fulfill the promises made to SUBJECT.

This "smoking gun" clearly was using smokeless powder. At some point Russell realized that the document didn't substantiate any of Nagell's allegations, and it was removed from the second edition of his book.

Russell also believed Nagell when he said he had met Fidel Castro:

Nagell indicated to me that he met personally with Fidel Castro, apparently to inform the Cuban premier of what was transpiring—a "domestic-
inspired, domestic-formulated, and domestic-sponsored" plot to assassinate Kennedy, where the intent was to make it look like Castro had engi-
neered it. "Cuban authorities had been informed of his [Oswald's]
association with anti-Castro elements (posing as pro-Castro agents) in the
USA before September 1963," Nagell has written. During one interview,
when I asked him whether Castro ever knew what was going on, Nagell
replied: "That's a loaded question."

Russell added this in a footnote:

RCN [Richard Case Nagell] on Castro: At our May 19, 1978, interview,
RCN mentioned that should I ever go to Cuba, Castro was an excellent
Ping-Pong player—"and he'll play you, too." He added that I ought to
brush up on my game.

I don't know whether Dick Russell took Nagell's advice to "brush
up" his game.
    Russell did have an inkling of what the Nagell story was really about.
In a November 1993 *Boston Magazine* article "From Dallas to Eternity," he
wrote:

Nagell had been largely dismissed as a nut by numerous assassination
researchers. Only Bernard Fensterwald, Jr., and Jim Garrison—both now
deceased—believed as strongly as I did that he held the key to solving the
mystery of the century. If only he would tell all …
    That was why I waited so long, hoping that eventually Nagell would
decide to produce his photographs and tapes, meet me in some secluded
rendezvous, and come totally clean about his days as a double agent. I
realize in retrospect that, since he was suing to get a big pension from the
Pentagon, Nagell was just using the threat of full disclosure to me as a
stick en route to the carrot. Once he won his case, in 1983, quoth the
raven, "Nevermore."

Actually, Nagell's major interest was to get JFK conspiracy theorists to help him with his legal cases. Once he won his disability suit, he had little use for these people.

In 2018, Russell spoke at Judyth Vary Baker's JFK assassination conference in Dallas. She claims that she was Oswald's lover in New Orleans in 1963. Few researchers take her seriously, but some conspiracy theorists will speak anywhere. In his presentation, Russell discussed the East German Stasi files on Nagell.

He claimed there are several thousand pages, but I only received 280 from the Germans. Russell believed that Nagell was on some sort of a CIA mission when he went to East Germany. And, of course, Nagell was indeed charged with espionage. But Russell doesn't say one word about the Stasi's twenty-six-page psychiatric report, which found that Nagell had serious mental health issues and that the charges were dropped because of insanity.

Had the East Germans believed that Nagell was really on a CIA mission, or was an actual CIA agent, they would have tried to trade him for a person of interest. They didn't. They just handed Nagell back to the West. I think they were happy to get rid of him.

Russell said that Nagell told him the East Germans sent him to Russia for questioning. Here is an excerpt from a transcript of his presentation:

Russell: There's a lot of questions and a lot of things that still haven't surfaced in these East German documents. I know that there were 39 missing days. Nagell was held there for four months, and he was released in the fall of '68 in a prisoner exchange where Wolfgang Vogel, who was a major spy master at the time for the for the communists, was very involved in negotiating this. And shortly … then there's a story in the *Washington Post*, no reference to the bank robbery or anything—attempted bank robbery, so called—but to this guy being released at the border. And so, Nagell's last 39 days behind the Iron Curtain, and he told me that he wasn't only in East Berlin, East Germany, that he was taken to Moscow, and that he wrote out a confession, or if you call it that, but he wrote out all the reasons why he did what he did in walking into the bank.

There is absolutely nothing in the Stasi files to indicate that Nagell was taken to Moscow. This is just another one of his false stories, and Russell was only too willing to buy it. Of course, he also believed Nagell's story about sending a letter to Hoover with all the details of the "plot."

Russell also believes the stories of Raymond Broshears. He wrote that "Broshears had once been called in to talk to the Garrison investigation but revealed little." Broshears was actually interviewed twice in New Orleans, and they couldn't shut him up.

Toward the end of his interview with Russell, Broshears said that if he were subpoenaed to testify before Congress, he would refuse. "They never tried." However, Broshears did testify before the HSCA, and I have even posted his session on YouTube. You would think Russell wouldn't just take Broshears's word.

James DiEugenio, author *Destiny Betrayed*, also believes Raymond Broshears.

> A friend [of Ferrie's] said in a Los Angeles TV interview with Stan Bohrman that Ferrie actually confessed the plot to him in one of the erratic moods that then began to consume him, and which he tried to combat with pills and alcohol. He stated that his function was to fly the assassins from Houston to South America. From there, they would fly to South Africa, which has no extradition treaty with the U.S.

That was the same TV interview in which Broshears said he had channeled Lee Harvey Oswald at a séance. Somehow, that did not make it into DiEugenio's book.

That story was removed from the second edition of DiEugenio's book. But he still used Broshears as a witness, accepting a story taken from Jim Garrison's book, that Broshears had drinks and dinner with Clay Shaw and David Ferrie. DiEugenio also claims that Broshears corroborates his theory that a Leon Oswald was an Oswald impersonator —he wrote that Broshears "spoke about a Leon Oswald."

Both Douglass and DiEugenio believe that Rose Cherami talked about the assassination before it happened. Douglass is definitive: "At the East State Louisiana State Hospital on November 21, Rose Cheramie

[sic] said again, this time to hospital staff members, that President Kennedy was about to be killed in Dallas."

Douglass footnotes that paragraph to an HSCA staff report on Rose Cherami which says, "Dr. Bowers allegedly told Weiss that the patient, Rose Cherami, had stated before the assassination that President Kennedy was going to be killed." As I showed in Chapter Six, Bowers denied that he said that. His other source is a memo that Garrison investigator Frank Meloche wrote on May 22, 1967, to his boss, Louis Ivon:

M E M O R A N D U M   U

May 22, 1967

TO: LOUIS IVON, CHIEF INVESTIGATOR

FROM: FRANK MELOCHE, INVESTIGATOR

- -

         I received information from LT. FRANCES FRUGE, State
Police, on May 22, 1967, that we should talk with one MARY YOUNG
who is manager of the business office at Charity Hospital. MARY
YOUNG was recruited by LEE OSWALD to join some type of women's
club while OSWALD was in New Orleans.

         Also, there is an operator of a computer, name unknown,
now employed by Charity Hospital who has been with them about a
week who also was an operator of a computer at Standard Coffee
Company while OSWALD was employed there.

         Information was also received that several nurses
employed at Jackson Mental Hospital who were watching television
along with ROSE CHERAMI the day Kennedy was assassinated stated
that during the telecast moments before Kennedy was shot ROSE
CHERAMI stated to them, "This is when it is going to happen,"
and at that moment Kennedy was assassinated. Information states
that these nurses had told several people of this incident.

         FRUGE said that he will drive to Jackson, Louisiana,
to investigate this matter further and will contact us on Tuesday,
May 23, 1967.

Of course, JFK's motorcade in Dallas was not televised, so it would have been impossible for Cherami to tell the nurses that "this is when it is going to happen." And by the way, no nurse ever came forward with such a story about Cherami.

Joan Mellen, in her book *A Farewell to Justice*, recreated this very scene:

> On Friday, November 22nd, at twenty minutes before noon, Rose was watching television in the hospital recreation area. Scenes in Dallas flashed on the screen. President Kennedy was on his way.
>
> "Somebody's got to do something!" Rose shouted. "They're going to kill the president!" No one paid any attention. The motorcade pulled into view. "Watch!" Rose cried out. "This is when it's going to happen! They're going to get him! They're going to get him at the underpass!" "POW!" Rose yelled as the shots rang out.

Douglass accepts Cherami's supposed assertion that Oswald and Ruby were lovers:

> Rose Cheramie was a witness not only to participants in the Kennedy assassination traveling to Dallas but also to Ruby and Oswald knowing each other. She said she knew that the two of them had an intimate relationship "for years." Her testimony, if heard, would have contradicted the Warren Report's assertion that Ruby and Oswald were lone killers and had never met.

Her testimony, if heard? But is there any evidence at all that Oswald and Ruby even knew each other, let alone that they were gay lovers?

Vince Palamara's 2021 book *Honest Answers About the Murder of President John F. Kennedy* also repeats some of these stories. His lists fifteen pieces of evidence that "vindicates" Jim Garrison's "case for conspiracy." His number ten is Bootsie Gay:

> A declassified HSCA document, a 1977 memo from Garrison to L. J. Delsa and Bob Buras, recounts the story of Clara Gay, a client of G. Wray Gill whose office David Ferrie shared. She happened to call Gill right after Ferrie was interviewed by Garrison and the FBI and overheard the secretary deny Gill's knowledge of Ferrie's activities. Clara then went to the office, and noticed on Ferrie's desk a diagram of Dealey Plaza with "Elm

Street" on it, which she unsuccessfully tried to snatch it in order to turn over to the FBI.

He believes the Bootsie Gay story, hook, line, and sinker.

As for Richard Case Nagell, Palamara thinks that his "assassination prediction" is one of the smoking guns that proves conspiracy. Palamara agrees with DiEugenio that Nagell "was one of the most important witnesses there was in the JFK case."

One witness that Palamara believes rivals Nagell's importance was Rose Cherami. He cites her "assassination prediction" as yet another smoking gun of conspiracy. And he adds that it's hard to ignore the circumstances of her death.

The "Crafard impersonated Oswald" story is still around. In 2024, DiEugenio published an article on his website that claimed the Warren Commission had the same suspicion:

> Unpublished WC papers in a dossier now in the Kennedy files show that Warren Commission staff had a suspicion that Laverne "Larry Crafard" was 1 of 4 persons who they suspected might be impersonating Oswald. (Memo from Burt Griffin to staff, March 13, 1964)

Here is the document in question:

There is nothing in that memo about impersonation. The Warren Commission was simply interested in mistaken identities.

Then the article veers into silliness:

> The purpose of an impersonation in the form of Crafard would be a decoy operation to establish the narrative that the person to be blamed for the assassination of Kennedy, namely Oswald, was a lone gunman who'd escaped without assistance. A duped Oswald would need to be shot, and blamed. Case closed.

A decoy operation?

DiEugenio presents the Bolton Ford episode as proof that Guy Banister knew Lee Harvey Oswald.

In fact, there is evidence that Banister had heard of Oswald before he even arrived in New Orleans in the summer of 1963. This is the famous

Bolton Ford incident, which occurred on January 20, 1961, the day President Kennedy took the oath of office.

Palamara uses Bolton Ford as further evidence that there was a second Oswald. He claims that "Oswald's name was curiously placed on 1/20/61 on the original bid form for Bolton Ford, Inc." It wasn't Lee Harvey Oswald's name but just the name Oswald.

In fact, James DiEugenio accepts most of these stories in this book. Crafard was impersonating Oswald; Richard Case Nagell and Rose Cherami both had foreknowledge of the JFK assassination plot; *Farewell America* was a CIA operation to divert Garrison's attention away from the true culprits; David Ferrie's ice-skating trip to Houston was suspicious; Bootsie Gay did retrieve a map of Dealey Plaza from Ferrie's desk; Broshears was a reliable witness; and the Bolton Ford incident proves Banister knew Oswald.

You would think that we had heard the last about Richard Case Nagell. But no, Rob Reiner spent half of an episode on Nagell in his 2023 ten-part podcast series, *Who Killed JFK?* Nagell is presented as a CIA operative, and Reiner repeats the entire narrative as fact. Nagell's mental health issues are mentioned only in the context of an attempt by the authorities to marginalize him.

And guess who his main researcher was? Yup, Dick Russell.

Reiner claimed that CIA operative Bill Harvey, who worked on ousting Castro through JFK's Operation Mongoose, was the strategist of the JFK assassination plot. It is all nonsense. Harvey was in Rome for almost a year prior to the assassination—rather hard to pull off such an operation and cover-up from overseas. In fact, he was drunk at the time of the assassination and had to be wakened by a deputy. Reiner presented no evidence that Harvey was involved in the JFK assassination.

I asked Gus Russo, author *Brothers in Arms: The Kennedys, the Castros, and the Politics of Murder* [with Stephen Molton], what he thought of the idea of Bill Harvey being behind the assassination:

Bill Harvey was an exceptional CIA officer with an exceptional drinking problem. He was key to the building of the CIA's Berlin Tunnel, the unmasking of KGB spy Kim Philby, and was honored with the CIA's Distinguished Service Medal. But you won't hear any of that from the conspiracy nuts who think he killed JFK.

Harvey's five-a-day martini problem had escalated after the Kennedys kicked him off of the Cuba Project assassination operation, and the CIA exiled him to Rome. It was the martinis that had likely loosened his lips when he told AG Robert Kennedy that he, Kennedy, was an amateur at covert operations (he was). The exchanges grew so ugly that it almost came to fisticuffs.

Over the years, I have interviewed over two dozen people who were close to Harvey, both as family and fellow CIA officers (e.g., CIA's Anita Potocki, Mark Wyatt, Sam Halpern, David Murphy, Dick Helms, Ted Shackley, Dino Brugioni, etc., as well as spending two days in Indianapolis with his widow, CG Harvey, and other family members. CG kindly sent me a box of Bill's papers.) I also interviewed friends and family of Harvey's "son," Johnny Rosselli, the patriotic mobster.

Here's the skinny: Harvey despised RFK for his ego-maniacal and sloppy running of the sensitive Cuba ops. His colleagues at the Agency were in unanimous agreement on that (details in my books). But he was not a killer of anyone, let alone the President. He was in fact another patriot, one who believed that the Kennedys had bit off far more than they could chew (they had), and he worried that RFK's ineptitude at espionage could start the nukes flying.

The sad irony is that Robert Kennedy ultimately came to agree with Harvey. About a month before his own assassination, he told Peace Corps executive/journalist Bill Moyers, "I have myself wondered at times if we did not pay a very great price for being more energetic than wise about a lot of things, especially Cuba." The great price was his brother Jack's life.

He knew that his Cuba Project had not only infuriated the hard-drinking CIA man, but also propelled a violent pro-Cuba terrorist also named Harvey—Lee Harvey Oswald—into a murderous rampage that gained him the recognition he had long craved.

And now Steve Jaffe is claiming that the French intelligence people he met in Paris in 1968 named Bill Harvey as one of the plotters. In an interview with journalist Jefferson Morley, Jaffe said the following:

Jaffe: I had not planned to talk about this until later, when I published my book. But in light of what … David Talbot and Jim Douglass had put together—the only name that they gave me out of that meeting with the head of French intelligence, the head of Secret Service, was William K. Harvey, and they said that he, as far as they were concerned, was a very, very high level key member of the team that masterminded the assassination.

I asked Steve Jaffe why Harvey's name did not make it into a contemporaneous memo. He replied:

There were some things that I had to simply commit to memory based on procedures I agreed to follow. This was something that Garrison instructed as well as my French intelligence contacts. It had to do with highly sensitive evidence or information.

But didn't Jaffe tell Garrison? Garrison's book *On the Trail of the Assassins* says nothing about Harvey being the mastermind.

And the nonsense continues. Here is an excerpt from a Jefferson Morley article on JFK assassination records:

In his campaign, Robert F. Kennedy Jr. repeatedly expressed his belief that rogue CIA officers were complicit in his uncle's death, the scenario amply documented in Rob Reiner and Soledad O'Brien's popular podcast "Who Killed JFK?" Fact-checking organizations, Politifact and Factcheck.org, have not disputed the accuracy of Reiner and O'Brien's reporting.

Well, I can't speak for *Politifact* or *Factcheck*. But they should give me a call. I can tell them a few things about the Reiner podcast series.

Conspiracy theorists are skeptical about every detail of the Warren Commission investigation. Vincent Bugliosi, author of the magisterial *Reclaiming History: The Assassination of President John F. Kennedy*, offered some important advice:

A substantial majority of the conspiracy community is also extremely gullible believing every story they hear without bothering to check it to see if it is accurate or makes any sense. As long as the story helps their theory, they buy it. They would improve the quality of their research appreciably by simply embracing rule number one of the journalistic profession: "If your mama says she loves you, check it out."

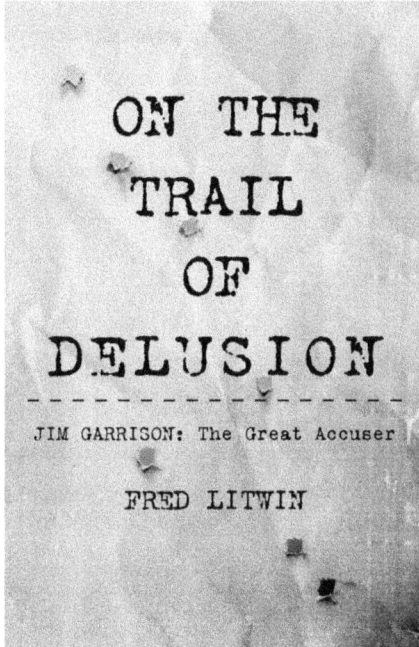

ON THE TRAIL OF DELUSION

JIM GARRISON: The Great Accuser

FRED LITWIN

Fred Litwin exposes the truth about Jim Garrison, the New Orleans district attorney, who "solved" the JFK assassination in 1967.

On the Trail of Delusion shows how Garrison persecuted an innocent gay man in order to spout his crazy conspiracy theories. There is also a touch of bribery and intimidation, the story of his attempt to charge a dead man with being a grassy knoll assassin, the former Marine he believed was a "second Oswald," several con men who turned the tables and fooled Garrison, the use of truth serum and hypnosis to recover memories, the ugly story of Oliver Stone's homophobic film *JFK*, and a lawyer from Montreal who was unjustly accused of operating an international assassination bureau. There's even a chapter with flying saucers. And a whole lot more.

ACKNOWLEDGMENTS

I want to thank my dear partner Andrew Yip, who has endured yet more stories about the JFK assassination. I'm sure his eyes glaze over whenever I tell him about my latest research.

This is the fifth book of mine that Michael Totten has prepared for publication, and I greatly appreciate his editing, his comments, and his efforts to produce a readable and well laid-out book. Thanks, Michael.

I would like to thank Dr. Norbert Eschborn for his help obtaining Richard Case Nagell's Stasi files. He kindly directed me to the proper German government portal that allowed me to submit an application.

Larry Haapanen worked with me on the *Farewell America* chapter. He supplied some important background material on Jim Rose, in particular the Orlando Bosch story, which substantially improved my chapter.

Steve Jaffe kindly answered my questions about the Garrison investigation and *Farewell America*.

I owe a great debt of gratitude to David Reitzes, an amazing researcher who did yeoman's work on the Nagell and Cherami files. His website provides important commentary on the Garrison investigation and Oliver Stone's film *JFK*.

Bob Nagell, the son of Richard Case Nagell, was kind enough to send me a file of Nagell's letters to his sister and graciously answered all my questions.

Steve Roe supplied research for my chapter on Rose Cherami. I am truly fortunate to know Steve since he regularly comes up with important pieces of evidence. He is a tremendous researcher, and I strongly recommend that people watch my interview of Steve on YouTube. His blog (*SR's Historical Research*) also offers many important articles.

Matthew Kordelski is a great editor and creator of videos. He edits all my video podcasts, and his work is second to none. And he is a helluva nice guy who is always there to help. Thank you, Matt.

Paul Hoch read this manuscript and offered many helpful suggestions and has been a continual source of help for my blog. Paul's wisdom comes from his sixty years of perspective on the JFK assassination controversies. I greatly appreciate his help.

I also want to thank Ken Owens, who supplied photographs of Breck Wall.

The Mary Ferrell Foundation is an indispensable resource for JFK assassination research. I couldn't have written this book without taking advantage of its document collection. I strongly recommend that everybody become members.

Any error or mistake is mine and mine alone.

NOTES AND SOURCES

A document with all the notes and sources will be available at www.onthetrailofdelusion. com/documents. This will allow purchasers of a printed copy of this book easy access to all the links contained below.

Author Patricia Lambert: She is the author of *False Witness: The Real Story of Jim Garrison's Investigation and Oliver Stone's Film JFK* (M. Evans and Company, 1999). I strongly recommend her book.

Sixth Floor Museum: https://www.jfk.org/; You can see my oral history interview here, https://emuseum.jfk.org/objects/69366/fred-litwin-oral-history

1. Was Larry Crafard the Grassy Knoll Assassin?

A lot of documents related to this chapter are on my blog:
onthetrailofdelusion.com/post/jim-garrison-names-the-grassy-knoll-gunman

Judge Herbert Christenberry's permanent injunction:
https://www.onthetrailofdelusion.com/post/the-christenberry-decision

Garrison appealed: Here is a link to the Wisdom decision which affirmed the Christenberry ruling.
https://www.onthetrailofdelusion.com/post/the-wisdom-decision

Garrison's nine-page press release:
https://www.onthetrailofdelusion.com/post/1972-jim-garrison-releases-crazy-statement-after-the-u-s-supreme-court-rules-against-him

JFK's death certificate: https://www.maryferrell.org/showDoc.html?docId=587

Ron Rosenbaum called Garrison: http://jfk.hood.edu/Collection/Weisberg%20Subject%20Index%20Files/S%20Disk/Shaw%20Clay%20Perjury%20Trial%203-4-69/Item%2043.pdf, also Rosenbaum wrote this article, "Taking a Darker View" for *Time Magazine*, https://time.com/archive/6719384/taking-a-darker-view/

Larry Crafard biography: https://www.maryferrell.org/showDoc.html?docId=232910#relPageId=291

Larry Crafard testimony before the Warren Commission: Crafard spends a lot of time talking about his various jobs, https://www.maryferrell.org/showDoc.html?docId=47#rel PageId=412; https://www.maryferrell.org/showDoc.html?docId=50%23relPageId=9#relPageId=9

Impeach Earl Warren sign: https://www.maryferrell.org/showDoc.html?docId=10755#relPageId=45; https://www.maryferrell.org/showDoc.html?docId=1141#relPageId=747

Ad in the Dallas Morning News *signed by Bernard Weissman*: https://www.onthetrailofdelusion.com/post/jfk-destiny-betrayed-misleads-on-jack-ruby; https://www.maryferrell.org/showDoc.html?docId=1138#relPageId=746

Mark Lane quote on Crafard: *Rush to Judgment*, page 20, Holt, Rinehart, Winston, 1966.

Ruby tells Crafard that the assassination would ruin Dallas: https://www.maryferrell.org/showDoc.html?docId=47#relPageId=462

Crafard telling Ruby he wanted to leave: https://www.maryferrell.org/showDoc.html?docId=1136#relPageId=373

Crafard testifying at Jack Ruby trial: https://www.maryferrell.org/showDoc.html?docId=217789#relPageId=94

Mark Lane on the meeting at Ruby's club: https://www.maryferrell.org/showDoc.html?docId=38#relPageId=66

Crafard admission that his recollection of Weissman was wrong: https://www.maryferrell.org/showDoc.html?docId=62374#relPageId=113

Garrison's annotation of Crafard's testimony: I am not certain exactly when Garrison scribbled his annotations. Some of his annotations in his files are from the 1970s, https://archive.org/details/GarrisonPapers/Mancuso%2C%20Marlene/page/n77/mode/2up

Tom Bethell's diary entry on callsigns: entry for September 22, 1967, https://www.jfk-assassination.net/bethell2.htm

Boxley's memo on Crafard's testimony: https://archive.org/details/GarrisonPapers/Mancuso%2C%20Marlene/page/n93, Garrison thought that Boxley was a CIA plant which was just ridiculous. You can read more about Boxley here, https://www.onthetrailofdelusion.com/post/fact-checking-james-dieugenio-part-two

Joesten quote on "planting false clues to incriminate Oswald: p. 41, *How Kennedy was Killed*, Joachim Joesten, Peter Dawnay Ltd, 1968. https://archive.org/details/HOWKENNEDYWASKILLEDByJoachimJoesten1968VeryReadablePDF/page/n39/mode/2up

Joesten quote on Crafard shooting at Connally: p. 364, *Oswald: The Truth*, Joachim Joesten, Peter Dawnay, 1967, https://archive.org/details/OswaldTheTruthByJoachimJoesten1967/page/n185/mode/2up

Penn Jones on Crafard: p. 64, (*Forgive My Grief*, Volume IV, Penn Jones, 1974; https://archive.org/details/ForgiveMyGriefPennJonesJr/Forgive_My_Grief_04/page/n81/mode/2up

Garrison memo to Jonathan Blackmer: https://www.onthetrailofdelusion.com/post/why-do-conspiracy-theorists-still-believe-julia-ann-mercer

David Scheim's quote on Crafard behaving strangely: p. 133, *Contract on America: The Mafia Murder of President John F. Kennedy*, Shapolsky Publishers, Inc., 1988.

David Scheim quote on the fleeing Larry Crafard: p. 148, Ibid.

Peter Whitmey's article on Larry Crafard: "Creating a Patsy," *JFK/Deep Politics Quarterly*, April 1988, https://www.jfk-assassination.net/creatingapatsy.htm

Joan Mellen on Crafard: p. 260, Joan Mellen, *A Farewell to Justice: Jim Garrison, JFK's Assassination, and the Case That Should Have Changed History*, Potomac Books, Inc., 2005.

Gale Cascaddan on Crafard: FBI report from June 5, 1964, by S. A. Douglas Cannell https://www.maryferrell.org/showDoc.html?docId=11589#relPageId=110

Gaeton Fonzi speech: Kennedy Assassination Chronicles, Volume 4, Issue 4; https://www.maryferrell.org/showDoc.html?docId=4265#relPageId=29

Hasan Yusuf article on Crafard: https://jfkthelonegunmanmyth.blogspot.com/2014/12/did-larry-crafard-kill-jd-tippit.html

The Ballad of Larry Crafard: https://www.everand.com/podcast/594779333/Ep-67-The-Ballad-Of-Larry-Crafard-This-week-we-take-a-closer-look-at-the-man-himself-Larry-Crafard-Classified-by-the-Warren-Commision-as-Jack-Ru

Burt Griffin on Larry Crafard: p. 118 of the Kindle edition, *JFK, Oswald, Ruby: Politics, Prejudice and Truth*, Burt W. Griffin, McFarland & Company, 2023.

2. Galveston, oh Galveston

Breck Wall's decision to leave Dallas: page 604; https://www.maryferrell.org/showDoc.html?docId=50#relPageId=607

Ruby's phone call to Breck Wall lasting two minutes: https://www.maryferrell.org/showDoc.html?docId=1141#relPageId=281

David Ferrie's trip to Houston and Galveston: A lot of this information comes from Stephen Roy's unpublished biography of David Ferrie: *Likely Villain: David Ferrie and the JFK Mystery.*

Also, please check these three blog posts on Ferrie's trip:

https://www.onthetrailofdelusion.com/post/david-ferrie-s-strange-ice-skating-trip-part-one; This blog posts contains FBI reports, Garrison documents, and testimony on Ferrie's trip

https://www.onthetrailofdelusion.com/post/david-ferrie-s-strange-ice-skating-trip-part-two; Lots of documents here on Breck Wall and the trip.

https://www.onthetrailofdelusion.com/post/dave-ferrie-s-strange-ice-skating-trip-part-three; A blog post about the weather during Ferrie's trip; Stephen Roy on the weather: https://www.jfk-online.com/dbdfhouston.html

Here is what Ferrie told the FBI: https://www.maryferrell.org/showDoc.html?docId=139368#relPageId=170

Chuck Rolland was interviewed by the FBI: https://www.maryferrell.org/showDoc.html?docId=10702#relPageId=92

Tom Bethell on Garrison's theory of propinquity: p. 62, *The Electric Windmill: An Inadvertent Autobiography*, Regnery Gateway, 1988.

Garrison's memos on Propinquity: https://www.onthetrailofdelusion.com/post/garrison-s-weird-investigative-technique-the-theory-of-propinquity; https://www.onthetrailofdelusion.com/post/garrison-s-weird-investigative-technique-propinquity-part-two

Garrison and Phelan in Las Vegas: Dialogue is taken from Phelan's chapter "Jim Garrison v. Clay Shaw" in his book, *Scandals, Scamps and Scoundrels: The Casebook of an Investigative Reporter*, Random House, 1982.

Garrison told Schiller that Wall ordered Jack Ruby to kill Oswald: The Peter Vea index, page 9; this is from an interview of Garrison by Lawrence Schiller in a memo dated March 3, 1967.

Andrew Sciambra's interview of Chuck Rolland: https://archive.org/details/GarrisonPapers/Miscellaneous%20Investigative%20Reports%20and%20Memorandum%202/page/n19/mode/2up

Gurvich at Bottoms Up in Las Vegas: Phelan, op. cit., page 164.

Breck Wall oral history at the Sixth Floor Museum: https://www.jfk.org/collections-archive/breck-wall-oral-history/

Hank Greenspun and Breck Wall: Ibid.

Breck Wall and the Playbill Club: https://www.maryferrell.org/showDoc.html?docId=50#rel

PageId=610; https://www.maryferrell.org/showDoc.html?docId=217816#relPageId=445

Garrison memo on military industrial complex: https://www.onthetrailofdelusion.com/post/jim-garrison-s-memo-on-the-military-industrial-complex

Earle Cabell and the CIA: "Bombshell or Dud? Earle Cabell's CIA Connections" by Steve Roe; https://www.washingtondecoded.com/site/2018/04/roe.html

Garrison on Breck Wall: https://www.onthetrailofdelusion.com/post/david-ferrie-s-strange-ice-skating-trip-part-two; this blog post also includes an excerpt from a Garrison memo on open Dallas leads; https://archive.org/details/NewOrleansConference921196812Of17/page/n99/mode/2up

McWillie at the Thunderbird: https://www.maryferrell.org/showDoc.html?docId=11085#relPageId=17

McWillie leaves Thunderbird Hotel: https://www.maryferrell.org/showDoc.html?docId=79001#relPageId=3

Questioning of Perry Russo by the Garrison team:

Perry Russo Talks - in Baton Rouge, Part One
Russo went to the press before he was interviewed by Sciambra.

Perry Russo Talks - in Baton Rouge, Part Two
James Phelan wrote a memo about the contradictions in Perry Russo's story.

Perry Russo Talks - in Baton Rouge, Part Three
An interview with Perry Russo from 1971.

Perry Russo Talks - in Baton Rouge, Part Four
Tom Bethell sends a memo to Sylvia Meagher about Dick Billings and Andrew Sciambra.

Perry Russo Talks - in Baton Rouge, Part Five
Jim Garrison's hypocrisy is on display in this post.

Perry Russo's first hypnosis session: https://www.jfk-assassination.net/session1.htm

Garrison annotation on FBI report: https://www.onthetrailofdelusion.com/post/did-breck-wall-order-jack-ruby-to-kill-oswald

Garrison quotation on Ferrie trip to Galveston: p. 19 of *On the Trail of the Assassins*, Kindle edition.

Death of Breck Wall: https://www.classiclasvegas.com/clv-history-blog/2010/11/16/show-producer-breck-wall-has-died.html

3. The Lost Map of Dealey Plaza

A lot of documents related to this chapter are in this blog post: https://www.onthetrailofdelusion.com/post/did-david-ferrie-have-a-map-of-dealey-plaza-in-his-desk-drawer

Garrison's handwritten memo to the HSCA: https://www.onthetrailofdelusion.com/post/jim-garrison-s-memo-to-the-hsca-regarding-fred-crisman-and-thomas-beckham-part-one

Thomas Beckham and Ricky Nelson: https://www.onthetrailofdelusion.com/post/why-did-jim-garrison-want-to-speak-to-thomas-beckham

Anonymous letter to Jim Garrison: https://www.onthetrailofdelusion.com/post/jim-garrison-s-exhibits-to-his-hsca-memo-on-fred-crsiman-and-thomas-beckham

Beckham's testimony to the Garrison grand jury: https://www.maryferrell.org/showDoc.html?docId=1175#relPageId=29

Beckham telling jury he was a former member of the CIA: https://www.maryferrell.org/showDoc.html?docId=136904#relPageId=2

Acquittal of Thomas Beckham in promoting concert: New Orleans Times-Picayune, July 29, 1977.

Beckham in Pine Bluff, Oklahoma: Arkansas Gazette, February 24, 1977.

Beckham interview with the HSCA: Memo dated October 9, 1977 at the Holiday Inn in Jackson, Mississippi, https://www.onthetrailofdelusion.com/_files/ugd/325b1c_432f6e0027e04e02bb100a3afb9cf760.pdf

Garrison memo to Buras and Delsa: https://www.onthetrailofdelusion.com/post/did-david-ferrie-have-a-map-of-dealey-plaza-in-his-desk-drawer

Delsa and Buras report on G. Wray Gill: https://www.onthetrailofdelusion.com/post/did-david-ferrie-have-a-map-of-dealey-plaza-in-his-desk-drawer

Bootsie Gay in Who's Who in Poetry: https://archive.org/details/internationalwho00erne/page/160/mode/2up

Harold Weisberg interviews at Dixieland Hall: Memo from Harold Weisberg to Jim Garrison, dated November 8, 1967, regarding interview with Al Clark and Clint Bolton, https://archive.org/details/GarrisonPapers/Lead%20Files%203/page/n7/mode/2up

Memo to Garrison on new leads: Memo from Andrew Sciambra to Jim Garrison, dated March 27, 1969, regarding the New Shaw Lead File, https://www.onthetrailofdelusion.com/post/did-david-ferrie-have-a-map-of-dealey-plaza-in-his-desk-drawer

Soule interview of Al Clark: Memo from Captain Fred Soule to James Alcock, dated April 22, 1969, regarding interview with Al Clark, https://archive.org/details/GarrisonPapers/Andrews%2C%20Dean%20re/page/n1/mode/2up

Soule interview of Bootsie Gay: Memo from Fred Soule to James Alcock, dated April 24, 1969, regarding interview with Clara Flournoy "Bootsie Gay," https://archive.org/details/GarrisonPapers/Additional%20Thornley%20material/page/n99/mode/2up

Soule interview of two receptionists: Memo from Capt. Frederick Soule to James Alcock, dated June 6, 1969, regarding Shaw Leads – Report on interview with Alice Guidroz and Regina Franchevich, https://archive.org/details/GarrisonPapers/Additional%20Thornley%20material/page/n99/mode/2up

Joan Mellen on Bootsie Gay: Mellen, op. cit., page 82 in the Kindle edition.

James DiEugenio on Bootsie Gay: page 216, *Destiny Betrayed*, Second Edition, James DiEugenio, Skyhorse Publishing, 2012. Unless specified, I always quote from DiEugenio's second edition.

Joan Mellen adds dialogue: Mellen, op. cit., page 84 in the Kindle edition.

Bootsie Gay's letter to F. Edward Hébert: https://www.onthetrailofdelusion.com/post/did-david-ferrie-have-a-map-of-dealey-plaza-in-his-desk-drawer

Papers of F. Edward Hébert: https://library.search.tulane.edu/permalink/01TUL_INST/1vh4m5n/alma9945304741706326

Bootsie Gay's letter about David Ferrie: https://www.onthetrailofdelusion.com/post/did-david-ferrie-have-a-map-of-dealey-plaza-in-his-desk-drawer

Thomas Beckham's testimony before the HSCA: https://www.onthetrailofdelusion.com/_files/ugd/325b1c_1e8c669ce0ba41038686c998ad43bb3a.pdf

Bootsie Gay poem in the Congressional Record: page 1266; https://www.congress.gov/91/crecb/1969/01/17/GPO-CRECB-1969-pt1-11.pdf

4. The Man Who Channeled Lee Harvey Oswald

My blog contains many articles on Raymond Broshears: https://www.onthetrailofdelusion.com/blog/tags/raymond-broshears; You'll be able to find many of the documents referenced in this chapter.

Broshears Secret Service File: RIF #154-10003-10058. The ARRB said that they released 32 pages from his Secret Service file, but they actually released 52 pages. I will be uploading this document to my website.

Raymond Broshears on the Stan Bohrman's show: https://www.onthetrailofdelusion.com/post/exclusive-raymond-broshears-on-the-stan-bohrman-show-july-1968; https://youtu.be/uuiqDbeeZyY?si=ud5uJd6nFHx-VjpC

Light of Understanding from May 1968: https://link.gale.com/apps/doc/AMWPUY044597288/AHSI?u=glbths&sid=bookmark-AHSI&xid=21f78d9b&pg=123

David Ferrie autopsy: https://www.onthetrailofdelusion.com/post/the-death-of-david-ferrie; https://web.archive.org/web/20060411130552/https://mcadams.posc.mu.edu/ferrie_autopsy.htm

Broshears at Los Altos Public Library: "Outer Space Chef Tosses Bewildering Saucer Salad," *Long Beach Independent Press-Telegram*, July, 9, 1968; http://historiadiscordia.com/the-raymond-broshears-files-part-00003-flying-saucer-attack/

Eric Markowitz on Raymond Broshears: "The Most Dangerous Gay Man in America Fought Violence with Violence," https://www.newsweek.com/2018/02/02/most-dangerous-gay-man-america-789402.html

Broshears' serious injury to the head: Ibid.

Broshears beaten up in the Navy: Ibid; *Gay Crusader*, No. 15. 1975; https://digitalassets.lib.berkeley.edu/sfbagals/Gay_Pride_Crusader/1975_Gay_Crusader_No15_Feb.pdf

Broshears dropped by Hargis: *Bay Area Reporter*, January 14, 1982; https://archive.org/details/BAR_19820114/mode/2up

Broshears arrest in East St. Louis: *Belleville News Democrat*, November 12th, and November 13th, 1964.

Broshears admitted to VA Hospital in New Orleans: Report of SAIC Anthony Gerrets on September 28, 1965, contained in RIF #154-10003-10058.

Broshears attempted to send a postcard to President Johnson: Letter from Special Agent Anthony Gerrets to U. S. Attorney Louis LaCour dated October 25, 1965, contained in RIF #154-10003-10058.

Broshears visited by Mr. Victor LeBeau: Report of SAIC Anthony Gerrets on September 28, 1965, contained in RIF #154-10003-10058.

Broshears on Mac Bell: Report by Special Agents Richard Taylor and Gary Stigall dated September 17, 1965, contained in RIF #154-10003-10058.

Broshears' longstanding interest in the JFK assassination: Report of SAIC Anthony Gerrets on September 28, 1965, contained in RIF #154-10003-10058.

Quote from Dr. Richard Stone: Ibid.

Broshears diagnosed as schizophrenic paranoid potentially dangerous: Ibid.

Broshears' combat disability: Ibid.

Broshears lookout worksheet: Contained in RIF #154-10003-10058.

Broshears relocating to Long Beach: Report from Special Agent Larry Newman, dated January 17, 1968, contained in RIF #154-10003-10058.

Universal Life Church Credentials: https://link.gale.com/apps/doc/BHJLYB311480558/ AHSI?u=glbths&sid=bookmark-AHSI&xid=9dead916&pg=5

Broshears showing up at Secret Service office in Los Angeles: Report by Special Agent Anthony Sherman dated February 15, 1968, contained in RIF #154-10003-10058.

Broshears' quote that he admits he is mentally ill: Ibid.

David Snelling letter to Jim Garrison: Contained in the files of Maggie Field.

Turner memo to Steve Burton: https://www.onthetrailofdelusion.com/post/david-ferrie-s-roommate-reveals-the-assassination-plot

Burton met with Snelling and Dixon Gates: Memo from Burton to Jim Garrison dated March 21, 1968, contained in the papers of Maggie Field.

Burton called Broshears on the phone: Memo from Burton to himself, dated April 12, 1968, contained in the papers of Maggie Field.

Burton interview of Broshears on April 12, 1968: Memo of Burton to Jim Garrison, dated April 15, 1968, contained in the papers of Maggie Field; https://www.onthetrailofdelusion.com/post/first-garrison-interview-with-reverend-raymond-broshears

Burton called Broshears in late April: Memo from Burton to Jim Garrison, dated April 29, 1968, contained in the papers of Maggie Field.

Burton interviews Broshears at his home: Memo from Burton to Jim Garrison, dated April 30, 1968, contained in the papers of Maggie Field.

Caller to the Stan Bohrman show was Steve Jaffe: Memo from Burton to Jim Garrison, dated July 8, 1968, contained in the papers of Maggie Field.

Séance as a cover story: Peter Vea Index, memo from Jaffe to Jim Garrison, dated July 15, 1968.

Mark Lane and Steve Jafee visit Broshears: Broshears #1 memo, From Stephen Jaffe to Jim Garrison, dated August 8, 1968; https://archive.org/details/GarrisonPapers/Thornley%2C%20Kerry%2002/page/n39/mode/2up; https://www.onthetrailofdelusion.com/post/reverend-raymond-broshears-tells-all-to-stephen-jaffe-and-mark-lane

Broshears letter to Mark Lane: https://archive.org/details/GarrisonPapers/Thornley%2C%20Kerry%2002/page/n51

Steve Jaffe re-interviews Broshears: Broshears memo #1, From Stephen Jaffe to Jim Garrison, dated August 8, 1968; https://archive.org/details/Broshears1234/page/n29/mode/2up; https://www.onthetrailofdelusion.com/post/reverend-raymond-broshears-reveals-the-shaw-ferrie-link

Jaffe article for the LA Free Press *on Broshears*: https://archive.org/details/Broshears1234/page/n25/mode/2up; https://www.onthetrailofdelusion.com/post/david-ferrie-s-roommate-reveals-the-assassination-plot

Raymond Broshears in New Orleans: His first interview - https://archive.org/details/Broshears1234/page/n1/mode/2up; https://www.onthetrailofdelusion.com/post/reverend-raymond-broshears-tells-even-more-in-new-orleans;

Raymond Broshears in New Orleans: His second interview - https://archive.org/details/ GarrisonPapers/Bank%20of%20New%20Orleans%206%20of%2017/page/n13/ mode/2up;   https://www.onthetrailofdelusion.com/post/reverend-raymond-bros hears-makes-a-startling-revelation

Garrison wrote a memo about Thornley being in the Oswald photograph: https://www. onthetrailofdelusion.com/post/reverend-raymond-broshears-makes-a-startling- revelation

Broshears told Hal Verb that Ferrie had the original photograph: Interview of Raymond Bros hears by Hal Verb, December 9, 1968, contained in the papers of Hal Verb.

Thornley letter to Louise Lacey, a friend: http://historiadiscordia.com/the-raymond-bros hears-files-part-00004-the-multiple-wave-oscillator-debacle/

Louise Lacey letter to Thornley: Ibid.

Harold Weisberg on Broshears in New Orleans: http://jfk.hood.edu/Collection/Weisberg% 20Subject%20Index%20Files/V%20Disk/Verb%20Hal%201968/Item%2041.pdf

Broshears on the Stan Bohrman show once again: https://www.maryferrell.org/showDoc. html?docId=103859#relPageId=13; *LA Free Press*, September 13 - 19, 1968: https://www. maryferrell.org/showDoc.html?docId=103859#relPageId=25

Light of Understanding, *August 1968*: https://www.onthetrailofdelusion.com/post/the- good-reverend-writes-about-jim-garrison

Broshears and Jaffe at Long Beach Town Hall: "Garrison Aide Links Dr. King, Kennedy Slaying in L. B. Talk," *Long Beach Independent Press-Telegram*, September 24, 1968.

Broshears interview with the Berkeley Barb: "Life at Stake," *Berkeley Barb*, December 13-19, 1968,   https://www.onthetrailofdelusion.com/post/the-good-reverend-writes-about- jim-garrison

Broshears met FBI Special Agent Irving Dean: FBI memo from SA Irving Dean to SAC, San Francisco, dated April 4, 1969; https://archive.org/details/RaymondBroshears/page/ n73/mode/2up

Broshears wrote to the FBI: FBI memo to Mr. Gale, dated April 15, 1969, https://archive.org/ details/RaymondBroshears/page/n69/mode/2up

FBI report noted the following about Broshears: FBI Air-Tel dated April 7, 1969; https://archive. org/details/RaymondBroshears/page/n71/mode/2up

Broshears letter to Hoover: https://archive.org/details/RaymondBroshears/page/n63/ mode/2up

Broshears then formed the Helping Hands Community Center: Kids on the Street: Queer Kinship and Religion in San Francisco's Tenderloin, Joseph Plaster, 2023;

Broshears quote about brunches: Ibid.

San Francisco's first gay pride parade: https://archive.org/details/Iss09.18/page/n7/ mode/2up; https://www.sfchronicle.com/projects/2021/visuals/archives-first-pride- parade/

"Off Prick Power" sign at gay pride: https://archive.org/details/BAR_19800619/page/n5/ mode/2up; https://archive.org/details/lns-454/page/n3/mode/2up

In 1973, Broshears called the FBI: FBI memo to SAC, San Francisco, dated March 8, 1973; https:// archive.org/details/RaymondBroshears/page/n31/mode/2up

Creation of the Lavender Panthers: "Gay Vigilantes to Fight Back," *San Francisco Examiner*, July 7, 1973.

Lavender Panthers lasted until the spring of 1974: Markowitz, op. cit.

Dick Russell interviews Raymond Broshears: *The Man Who Knew Too Much*, Dick Russell, Carroll & Graf, first edition, 1992, page 575. Unless specified, my references to this book are the first edition.

HSCA interviews Broshears: https://www.onthetrailofdelusion.com/post/raymond-bros hears-testifies-before-the-hsca; https://youtu.be/IfM5F81_v2Y; https://www. onthetrailofdelusion.com/_files/ugd/325b1c_b916c0cf7c8a4373a2569f3b7bb6bde3.pdf

Death of Raymond Broshears: "Heaven Can't Wait," *Bay Area Reporter*, January 14, 1982, https://archive.org/details/BAR_19820114

Garrison wrote two pages on Broshears: pages 120-121, *On the Trail of the Assassins*, Sheridan Square Press, 1988.

Joan Mellen on Raymond Broshears: page 121 of the Kindle edition, *A Farewell to Justice*, op. cit.

James DiEugenio on Raymond Broshears: page 209 of the Kindle edition, *Destiny Betrayed*, op. cit.

Jim Marrs on Raymond Broshears: page 472, *Crossfire: The Plot That Killed Kennedy*, Jim Marrs, Basic Books, 2013.

Broshears quote to Russell about having sex with Leon Oswald: page 576, *The Man Who Knew Too Much*, op. cit.

James DiEugenio on Leon Oswald: page 247 of the Kindle edition of *Destiny Betrayed*, op. cit.

Oliver Stone on the composite nature of Willie O'Keefe: pages 66, 354 and 511 of *JFK: The Book of the Film*, Applause Theatre and Cinema Books, 1992; *https://archive.org/details/jfkbookoffilm doc0000ston/page/511/mode/1up?q=broshears*

Jeffrey Caulfield's book: pages 581 – 590, *General Walker and the Murder of President Kennedy*, Moreland Press, 2015.

Stephen Roy on Raymond Broshears: https://educationforum.ipbhost.com/topic/4458-raymond-broshears/#comment-34083; https://www.jfk-online.com/dbraybropost.html

Steve Jaffe on Raymond Broshears: e-mail to Fred Litwin dated June 11. 2023.

5. He Could Have Been a Contender

The Boston Traveler *articles on Arthur Strout are here*: https://www.onthetrailofdelusion. com/post/arthur-strout-could-have-been-another-perry-russo

Phone call between Lynn Loisel and Arthur Strout: https://www.onthetrailofdelusion.com/ post/exclusive-arthur-strout-calls-the-d-a-s-office; https://youtu.be/MM-XBZhwR_4

Strout had some mental issues: "Strout Fails to Appear in Court," *Lewiston Evening Journal*, April 24, 1967.

The Reverend Clyde Johnson: I tell the Clyde Johnson story in my book, *On the Trail of Delusion*, Chapter 13, "The Ballad of Slidin' Clyde Johnson."

Clyde Johnson's idea about calling Jim Garrison: Memo on Clyde Johnson dated January 16, 1969, from the Edward Wegmann papers; letter from Edward Wegmann to William McNamara, October 6, 1967, papers of Irvin Dymond.

Johnson's story about meeting Oswald, Ruby and Shaw: https://www.maryferrell.org/show Doc.html?docId=55186#relPageId=240

Overt act with Shaw, Oswald and Ruby: pages 64 - 65, *American Grotesque: An Account of the Clay Shaw-Jim Garrison-Kennedy Assassination Trial in New Orleans*, James Kirkwood,

Simon & Schuster, 1970; https://archive.org/details/americangrotesqu0000kirk/page/64/mode/2up; "Two Jurors Selected For Clay Shaw Trial," *The New Orleans Times-Picayune*, January 22, 1969.

Johnson tells the press he is Garrison's ace-in-the-hole: http://jfk.hood.edu/Collection/White%20Materials/Garrison%20News%20Clippings/1969/69-07/69-07-23.pdf

6. Did Rose Cherami Predict the JFK Assassination?

You can read more about Rose Cherami at David Reitzes' terrific website: https://www.jfk-online.com/jfk100cher.html; and I have written several blog posts on Cherami, https://www.onthetrailofdelusion.com/blog/tags/rose-cherami

Opening Scene in Oliver Stone's JFK: page 5, *JFK: The Book of the Film*, op. cit., https://archive.org/details/jfkbookoffilmdoc0000ston/page/4/mode/2up

Rose Cherami illness when she was twelve: Hospital records of Rose Cherami, Social history by Frances Rish, dated April 7, 1961, obtained from a NARA visit on August 29, 2023.

Cherami running away to Houston: Record from the John Sealy Hospital, Case History, obtained from a NARA visit on August 29, 2023.

Rose Cherami married in 1944: Record from the John Sealy Hospital, Case History, op. cit.

Cherami's rap sheet: https://www.jfk-online.com/cheramie-arrest-fbi.pdf; https://www.jfk-online.com/cheramie-arrest-la.pdf; https://archive.org/details/RoseCheramie/page/n3/mode/2up

Cherami taken to John Sealey Hospital: Record from the John Sealey Hospital, Case History, op. cit.

Cherami arrested in Houston: page 185, *Rose Cherami: Gathering Fallen Petals*, Dr. Michael Marcades, Peniel Unlimited, 2020.

Cherami in Tucson, Arizona: https://www.onthetrailofdelusion.com/post/an-important-new-find-regarding-rose-cherami; "Elusive Texas Blonde Finally Nabbed in New Mexico After 80 MPH Chase," *Albuquerque Journal*, May 29, 1957.

Rose Cherami sent to Saint Elizabeth's Hospital: Saint Elizabeth's Hospital Record, Clinical Record, January 31, 1959, obtained from a NARA visit on August 29, 2023.

Rose Cherami's fall and grand mal seizures: Ibid.

Rose Cherami in the fall of 1960: Hospital admission note by Dr. Steele, March 25, 1961, obtained from a NARA visit on August 29. 2023.

While in jail Cherami started another fire: "Woman Faces Arson Charge," *New Orleans Times-Picayune*, December 20, 1960.

Judgment against Melba Marcades in Criminal District Court: Contained in Cherami's hospital records obtained from NARA on August 29, 2023.

Cherami admitted to East State Louisiana Hospital on March 23, 1961: Social History by Frances Rish, April 7, 1961, obtained from a NARA visit on August 29, 2023.

Cherami admitted to seeing visions but denied hearing voices: Ibid.

Permission slip to receive electric shock therapy: Contained amongst hospital records obtained at NARA on August 29, 2023.

June 1961 diagnosis of schizophrenic reaction: June 1, 1961, report presented by Dr. Steele, NARA hospital records.

Magruder calling up Garrison's office: https://www.jfk-online.com/cherdoc0.html; https://archive.org/details/RoseCheramie/page/n55/mode/2up

Dischler called Cherami's mother: Notes of Anne Dischler from the papers of Patricia Lambert, Sixth Floor Museum in Dallas.

Dischler called Don Bowers: Ibid; https://www.onthetrailofdelusion.com/post/did-dr-victor-weiss-talk-to-rose-cherami-before-the-jfk-assassination

November 20, 1963, Fruge called to the emergency ward: Memo from Frank Meloche to Jim Garrison, dated March 13, 1967, on Rose Cherami - https://archive.org/details/RoseCheramie/page/n49/mode/2up; https://www.onthetrailofdelusion.com/post/francis-fruge-s-conversations-about-the-jfk-assassination-with-rose-cherami; Testimony of Francis Fruge, NARA.

April 1967 Fruge report to Jim Garrison: https://www.onthetrailofdelusion.com/post/did-dr-wayne-owens-hear-rose-cherami-predict-the-jfk-assassination; https://www.jfk-online.com/cherdoc2.html

Fruge testimony that this might have been checked later: Francis Fruge interview with the HSCA on April 7, 1978; https://www.maryferrell.org/showDoc.html?docId=220032#relPageId=7

Fruge told the HSCA that Cherami was passing through town: Ibid; https://www.maryferrell.org/showDoc.html?docId=220032#relPageId=5

Cherami says we're going to kill President Kennedy: Ibid.

A month later in his [Fruge's] deposition: Fruge deposition to the HSCA, April 18, 1978, page 8.

Eunice News story on Fruge: *Eunice News*, July 18, 1967; https://www.onthetrailofdelusion.com/post/francis-fruge-s-conversations-about-the-jfk-assassination-with-rose-cherami

George Rennar interview with Bill Boxley: Interview of William C. Wood, a/k/a Bill Boxley by Geroge E. Rennar dated November 4, 1971, page 1; http://jfk.hood.edu/Collection/Meagher%20Sylvia%20Folders/Rennar%20George%201968-1971/Rennar%2007.pdf

Cherami brought to ELSH with a dogcatcher: Notes from Anne Dischler contained in the papers of Patricia Lambert.

Fruge worked narcotics: Eunice News story, op. cit.

Rose Cherami story according to Francis Fruge: See his HSCA deposition and his HSCA interview.

Frederick Turner report from December 10, 1963: https://www.onthetrailofdelusion.com/post/did-rose-cherami-provide-invaluable-information-on-dope-smuggling

1965 FBI memo: Memo from SAC Oklahoma City to SAC Mobile regarding Rozzella Clinkscales [Rose Cherami], dated December 1, 1965.

1978 HSCA investigation of the Cherami story: https://www.maryferrell.org/showDoc.html?docId=1212#relPageId=203

HSCA interview of Dr. Weiss: HSCA Outside Contact Report of Dr. Victor Weiss, dated July 5, 1978; https://www.onthetrailofdelusion.com/post/did-dr-victor-weiss-talk-to-rose-cherami-before-the-jfk-assassination

Dr. Bowers letter to JFK Lancer: Ibid; The letter was included in Michael Marcades book, *Rose Cherami: Gathering Fallen Petals*, op. cit., page 333.

Honesty of Francis Fruge: https://www.onthetrailofdelusion.com/post/the-secrets-of-anne-dischler

August 1965 FBI report about Rozella Clinkscales, aka Rose Cherami: Report of SA James P. Morgan, Jr., dated November 23, 1965, regarding George H. Walker; Rozella Clinkscales.

Argosy Magazine on bizarre deaths: *Argosy*, March 1977; http://jfk.hood.edu/Collection/ Weisberg%20Subject%20Index%20Files/D%20Disk/Deaths/Item%2001.pdf

Conspiracy books claiming Rose Cherami was killed by a hit-and-run driver: Crossfire (On page 402, Marrs writes that Cheramie [sic] was found "apparently after being thrown from a car."; *High Treason* by Robert J. Groden & Harrison Edward Livingstone, Conservatory Press, 1989 (page 122); *Cover-Up* by Gary Shaw (page 57); Oliver Stone's *JFK: The Book of the Film* (page 45).

Jim Garrison claimed Cherami was a victim of a hit-and-run: *Playboy* interview, October 1975, page 175; http://www.whale.to/b/jim_garrison_i.html

Joan Mellen writes: *A Farewell to Justice*, op. cit., page 207 in the Kindle edition.

Gary Shaw's introduction to Michael Marcades book: *Rose Cherami: Gathering Fallen Petals*, op. cit., page 2, and page 11.

Rose Cherami's death certificate: https://archive.org/details/RoseCheramie/page/n43/ mode/2up; https://www.onthetrailofdelusion.com/post/was-rose-cherami-murdered

Documents from the Gladewater Municipal Hospital: Marcades, op. cit., pages 374-382.

Dr. Cyril Wecht on Cherami's wounds: https://www.jfk-online.com/jfk100cher.html

Anthony Summers on the Rose Cherami story: Ibid.

Photograph of Rose Cherami's grave: Courtesy of Fred Litwin.

7. The Man Who Needed Help

David Reitzes has written an important multi-part series on Richard Case Nagell: https://www. jfk-assassination.net/nagell1.htm

I have also written many blog posts about Nagell: https://www.onthetrailofdelusion.com/ blog/tags/richard-case-nagell

I strongly recommend that everybody read this 1982 court case which contains Nagell's psychiatric history: https://www.onthetrailofdelusion.com/_files/ugd/ 325b1c_5ab11974df5b4faabb1bd8bef42a16d8.pdf

Nagell's bank incident: The *El Paso Times* covered Nagell extensively. The September 21, 1963, edition states that Officer Bundren stopped Nagell as he was pulling into traffic in his car. "As I approached the alley, a car was pulling out into traffic. The driver slammed his brakes and when he saw me and then my gun he said, "All right, I give up.'"; here is a link to the El Paso Police Department file on Nagell -- https://ia800500.us.archive. org/23/items/RichardCaseNagelJFKAssassinationElPasoPoliceRecords/Richard-Case-Nagel-JFK-Assassination-El-Paso-Police-Records.pdf

Nagell told Barron that he would hit him: Ibid.

Nagell threat to take a shotgun: "Bank Robber Wants to Kill," *El Paso Herald-Post*, September 21, 1963.

Nagell tried cutting his writs using a tin can converted to an ash tray: "Nagell Pleads Not Guilty," *El Paso Times*, September 22, 1963.

Nagell biographic data: See pages 26 of the 1982 court case linked above; see Chronological Record of Activities; https://www.maryferrell.org/showDoc.html?docId=229958#rel PageId=14; CIA memo "Garrison and the Kennedy Assassination: Richard Case

Nagell"; https://www.maryferrell.org/showDoc.html?docId=229958#relPageId=43; https://www.maryferrell.org/showDoc.html?docId=229958#relPageId=151

Nagell Efficiency Report for April to June 1953: Page 28 of the 1982 court case linked above.

Nagell recommended for promotion to Captain: Page 29 of the 1982 court case linked above.

Nagell's war wounds: Page 3 and page 26-27 of the 1982 court case linked above; page 94 of *The Man Who Knew Too Much*.

Nagell's plane crash: newspaper accounts from the *Baltimore Evening* Sun, late November, early December 1954.

Nagell had a severe cut of the face: "Five Dead in Bomber Crash Here," *Baltimore Evening Sun*, November 29, 1954.

Nagell's examination at Walter Reed by Dr. Edwin Weinstein: page 10 of 1982 court case.

In March, Nagell wished he had died in the crash: Report of SA David Reid, dated February 4, 1964; https://www.maryferrell.org/showDoc.html?docId=48775#relPageId=127

Medical Board recommended in May Nagell be returned to duty: page 9 of 1982 court case.

Nagell's work assignments from 1956 to 1957: https://www.maryferrell.org/showDoc.html?docId=48775#relPageId=15

Nagell's increasing difficulties at work: page 4 of the 1982 court case.

In March of 1957, Nagell made derogatory allegations: page 30 of the 1982 court case.

Investigating officer noted that Nagell was in a highly agitated state: Ibid; Efficiency Report dated March 16. 1957, papers of Dick Russell, obtained on September 29, 2022.

January 1958 official reprimand: page 4 of the 1982 court case.

Nagell accused his commanding officer of bias: Ibid.

Dr. Carl McGahee's examination of Nagell: page 4, pages 31 – 32 of the 1982 court case.

Nagell's February 1958 OER: page 32 of the 1982 court case.

Indorsing officer wrote Nagell lacks maturity: page 4 of the 1982 court case.

Document – Clearance of Account dated February 25, 1958: Papers of Dick Russell, obtained on September 22, 2021, at Baylor University.

In March of 1958, Nagell relieved of counter intelligence duties: page 4 of 1982 court case.

Nagell's panicky gesture: Document entitled "Draper Hawaii From Skith Zama," papers of Dick Russell, obtained on September 29, 2022.

Nagell's top-secret clearance was revoked: https://www.maryferrell.org/showDoc.html?docId=103975#relPageId=36; https://www.maryferrell.org/showDoc.html?docId=55490#relPageId=53

Nagell at Fort Dix: page 4 of 1982 court case.

Nagell's October 1958, resignation: page 33 of 1982 court case.

Nagell's withdrawal of resignation: page 34 of 1982 court case.

Nagell's review for November 1958 to January 1959: Ibid.

Nagell's review for April 1959 to August 1959: Ibid.

Nagell's resignation of August 31st, 1959: Ibid.

Nagell's separation physicals: Ibid.

Nagell honorably discharged: page 35 of 1982 court case.

Nagell's Korean colleague, Ned Glenn: Report of SA David Reid, dated July 24, 1964; https://www.maryferrell.org/showDoc.html?docId=48775#relPageId=208

Nagell's attempt at becoming a policeman: page 5 of the 1982 court case.

Nagell began employment with the California Department of Employment: Ibid.

Nagell applied for disability in January 1960: page 35 of the 1982 court case.

Dr. Trevisano's report: page 5 of the 1982 court case.

Nagell writes to U. S. Senator Thomas Kuchel: pages 35 – 36 of the 1982 court case.

VA award to Nagell in July 1960: page 35 of the 1982 court case; Secret Service Report, dated April 16, 1964, by SA Robert Tomsic on a review of Nagell's medical file, contained in Nagell's Secret Service files, RIF# 154-10002-10330.

Nagell admitted to VA hospital in Los Angeles in May 1962: page 36 of the 1982 court case.

Nagell breaking down door of wife's apartment: Memo: Garrison and he Kennedy Assassination, https://www.maryferrell.org/showDoc.html?docId=4547#relPageId=18; FBI Report of David Reid, dated February 4, 1964, https://www.maryferrell.org/showDoc.html?docId=48775#relPageId=130

Nagell telling people he had been dismissed for telling the press that the Vice Squad was shaking down too man businesses: Report of Psychiatric Examination, June 29, 1966, RIF# 154-10002-10330.

Nagell admitted in July 1962, for a gunshot wound: David Reid report op. cit., https://www.maryferrell.org/showDoc.html?docId=48775#relPageId=130; see pages 19, 36, and 48 in the 1982 court case.

Nagell entered Mexico in August 1962: David Reid report, op. cit., https://www.maryferrell.org/showDoc.html?docId=48775#relPageId=133

Nagell went back in October: Ibid; https://www.maryferrell.org/showDoc.html?docId=48775#relPageId=136

Nagell wrote the military asking for reenlistment: page 36 in the 1982 court case.

Nagell appeared in the FBI office in New York City in November 1962: David Reid report, op. cit., https://www.maryferrell.org/showDoc.html?docId=48775#relPageId=138

Two weeks later, Nagell contacted the FBI office to discuss his divorce: Ibid, https://www.maryferrell.org/showDoc.html?docId=48775#relPageId=141

Nagell phoned the FBI office in Jacksonville in December 1962: ibid, https://www.maryferrell.org/showDoc.html?docId=48775#relPageId=142

On December 20, 1962, Nagell complained of headaches: page 6 of the 1982 court case; https://www.maryferrell.org/showDoc.html?docId=48775#relPageId=91; https://www.maryferrell.org/showDoc.html?docId=48775#relPageId=144

Nagell was given an electroencephalographic examination: page 7 of the 1982 court case.

Nagell was referred to Dr. P. C. Clark: Ibid.

Dr. Clark examined Nagell on January 14, 1963: Ibid.

Nagell sent to staff psychiatrist Dr. M. L. Schwartz: Ibid.

Nagell wrote President Kennedy: page 8 of the 1982 court case.

Nagell contacted the FBI office in Miami on January 24, 1963: David Reid report, op. cit., https://www.maryferrell.org/showDoc.html?docId=48775#relPageId=148

On February 3, 1963, Nagell applied to the Army Board: page 8 of the 1982 court case.

Nagell contacted the L. A. office of the FBI on April 19, 1963: David Reid report, op. cit., https://www.maryferrell.org/showDoc.html?docId=48775#relPageId=150

On June 4, 1963, Nagell appeared at a VA Outpatient Clinic: Richard Case Nagell: Chronological Record of Activities, https://www.maryferrell.org/showDoc.html?docId=189162#relPageId=205

Army replied negatively to Nagell's request: page 8 of the 1982 court case.

Nagell's quote that he fired two shots to keep anyone from following me: https://www.maryferrell.org/showDoc.html?docId=48775#relPageId=153

Nagell's quote that he won't have to go to Cuba: https://www.maryferrell.org/showDoc.html?docId=236078#relPageId=205

Nagell's quote that this is going to be a frame: https://www.maryferrell.org/showDoc.html?docId=48775#relPageId=154

Nagell quote that his motive was he was unhappy with judicial system: Ibid.

Nagell used a piece of tin to cut his wrists: https://www.maryferrell.org/showDoc.html?docId=48775#relPageId=158

Nagell waived a hearing: David Reid report, op. cit., https://www.maryferrell.org/showDoc.html?docId=48775#relPageId=155

Government motion to determine Nagell's mental competency: page 41 of the 1982 court case.

Dr. R. J. Bennett on October 11th: page 130, *My Demons Were Real: Constitutional Lawyer Josepha Calamia's Journey*, Bob Ybarra, Arte Publico Press, 2010.

Court appointed James Hammond to represent Nagell: Ibid, page 131.

Court then appointed John Langford: Ibid.

Nagell tells the FBI he had met Oswald in Mexico City and Texas: David Reid report, op, cit., https://www.maryferrell.org/showDoc.html?docId=48775#relPageId=172

Nagell quote that he knew nothing about Oswald killing the President: Secret Service report dated January 7, 1964, SAIC Oscar Weisheit, RIF# 154-10002-10330.

Marina Oswald was shown a photograph of Nagell: FBI report of David Reid, dated January 24, 1964, https://www.maryferrell.org/showDoc.html?docId=10805#relPageId=3

FBI interview of George Stanga: David Reid report, op. cit., https://www.maryferrell.org/showDoc.html?docId=48775#relPageId=165

Nagell submitted a signed statement to the FBI which addressed his motive: Richard Case Nagell: Chronological Record of Activities, https://www.maryferrell.org/showDoc.html?docId=48775#relPageId=18

Nagell's mother heard about the charges: https://www.maryferrell.org/showDoc.html?docId=189162#relPageId=180; page 47 of the 1982 court case; https://www.maryferrell.org/showDoc.html?docId=48775#relPageId=169

On January 24th, Nagell denied that he had ever been treated by a psychiatrist: El Paso Times, January 27, 1964.

Nagell's claim that the FBI questioned him on subversive activities: Ibid; Secret Service memo from SAIC Weisheit to Chief regarding Richard Case Nagell, dated February 6, 1964, RIF# 154-10002-10330.

FBI spoke to Nagell's wife Mitsuko: FBI report dated June 12, 1964 by James Hoose, Jr., https://www.maryferrell.org/showDoc.html?docId=48775#relPageId=194

Dr. Gustave Weiland agreed with diagnosis: page 42 of the 1982 court case.

Medical officer at Springfield report on March 6th: Nagell v. United States, January 4, 1966, https://casetext.com/case/nagell-v-united-states

Nagell's letter to J. Lee Rankin: https://www.maryferrell.org/showDoc.html?docId=99791#relPageId=1

On March 24th, Nagell told the court he had been without counsel: Nagell v. United States, January 4, 1966, https://casetext.com/case/nagell-v-united-states

Nagell wrote the FBI: https://archive.org/details/RichardCaseNagell/Nagell%2C%20Richard%20Case/page/n243/mode/2up

Mr. Perrenot was allowed to withdraw: Nagell v. United States, January 4, 1966, https://casetext.com/case/nagell-v-united-states

During the trial, Nagell interrupted witnesses: Ibid.

Dr. R. J. Bennett: Ibid.

Dr. Martin Schwartz: Ibid.

Dr. Gustave Weilland: Ibid.

Calamia made a motion for a new trial: Ibid., Ybarra, op. cit., page 137.

Weinstein quote that psychiatrists would be confused: page 10 of the 1982 court case.

Weinstein testimony about Nagell's injuries: Ibid.

Weinstein on the bank incident: Ibid.

Weinstein believed the bank incident was an alternative to suicide: Ibid.

Government psychiatrists changed their testimony: page 11 of the 1982 court case.

Nagell attempt to commit suicide: El Paso Times, June 17, 1964.

Dr. Jo Anne Holzman notes: page 44 of the 1982 court decision.

Nagell's final psychiatric diagnosis: Ibid.

Nagell's examination by H. R. Passaro: page 45 of the 1982 court case.

Judge Coleman's decision: Nagell v. United States, January 4, 1966, https://casetext.com/case/nagell-v-united-states

Nagell refused to be removed from his cell which continued for a week: El Paso Times, April 12, 1966; El Paso Herald Post, April 13, 14 16, and 19, 1966.

Nagell was interviewed on May 31st *by Dr. Robert Murney*: page 45 – 46 of the 1982 court case.

Nagell's examination by Dr, Joseph Alderete: Report of Psychiatric Staff Examination of June 13, 1966, RIF# 154-10002-10330.

Weinstein reiterated his view: page 13 of the 1982 court case.

Weinstein quote on confabulations: Page 51 of the 1982 court case.

Nagell's three made up stories: Ibid.

Alderete testified that Nagell was not in a psychotic state: page 14 of the 1982 court case.

Two other psychiatrists-neurologists now said Nagell was not able to determine right from wrong: ibid.

One of the lighter moments of the trial: El Paso Herald-Post, September 17, 1966.

Letter from Nagell to his sister: correspondence obtained from Bob Nagell.

On January 3, 1967, Nagell wrote Senator Richard Russell: RIF# 180-10090-10208. https://www.maryferrell.org/showDoc.html?docId=99788#relPageId=1&

Nagell wrote his sister to get in touch with Garrison: https://archive.org/details/RichardCaseNagell/Nagell%2C%20Richard%20Case/page/n1/mode/2up; https://www.onthetrailofdelusion.com/post/the-first-garrison-memo-on-richard-case-nagell

Nagell received a one-sentence perfunctory reply: https://archive.org/details/GarrisonPapers/Nagell%2C%20Richard%20%20%282%20of%202%29/page/n15/mode/2up

Nagell sent this reply to Russell on April 1st: https://www.maryferrell.org/showDoc.html?docId=60406#relPageId=67

William Martin flew out on April 10th to Springfield: https://www.onthetrailofdelusion.com/post/the-first-garrison-memo-on-richard-case-nagell

Martin reported that Nagell talked of three plots: Ibid., https://archive.org/details/RichardCaseNagell/Nagell%2C%20Richard%20Case/page/n173/mode/2up

Martin's second interview: ibid., https://archive.org/details/RichardCaseNagell/Nagell%2C%20Richard%20Case/page/n177/mode/2up

Towards the end of April Martin flew back to Springfield: https://www.onthetrailofdelusion.com/post/the-first-garrison-memo-on-richard-case-nagell; https://archive.org/

details/GarrisonPapers/Nagell%2C%20Richard%20%282%20of%202%29/page/n73/mode/2up

The next day Martin met with Robert Nicholas: https://archive.org/details/GarrisonPapers/Nagell%2C%20Richard%20%282%20of%202%29/page/n73/mode/2up

Nagell then passed by the office: Martin memo to Jim Garrison, dated May 11, 1967, https://www.onthetrailofdelusion.com/post/the-first-garrison-memo-on-richard-case-nagell

Nagell stalked out: Ibid.

Martin then immediately wrote Nicholas at a letter: letter from Martin to Nagell, dated April 25, 1967, Ibid.

Nicholas letter to Martin dated April 28, 1967: https://archive.org/details/GarrisonPapers/Nagell%2C%20Richard%20%282%20of%202%29/page/n83/mode/2up

Nagell wrote Martin in May about writ of habeas corpus: https://www.onthetrailofdelusion.com/post/the-first-garrison-memo-on-richard-case-nagell

On June 7, 1967, Nagell gave Martin a letter of introduction: Ibid.

Martin wrote Nagell to inform him of what had happened: Ibid, https://archive.org/details/RichardCaseNagell/Nagell%2C%20Richard%20%282%20of%202%29/page/n43/mode/2up

Nagell replied that there was no point in continuing: letter dated June 30, 1967; https://www.onthetrailofdelusion.com/post/the-first-garrison-memo-on-richard-case-nagell

Nagell wrote his sister: Ibid.

Nagell's habeas corpus memo: https://archive.org/details/GarrisonPapers/Nagell%2C%20Richard%20Case/page/n115/mode/2up

Tom Bethell's letter to Richard Popkin: letter dated September 22, 1967, https://archive.org/details/RichardCaseNagell/Nagell%2C%20Richard%20%282%20of%202%29/page/n3/mode/2up

Bethell's diary entry: entry for September 22, 1967, https://www.jfk-assassination.net/bethell2.htm

Nagell story appeared in print in Ramparts Magazine: "The Garrison Commission," Bill Turner, January 1968, page 56, https://archive.org/details/turner-william-w.-the-garrison-commission-ramparts-vol.-6-no.-6-jan.-1968-pp.-43-70/page/55/mode/2up

Nagell would later claim the article was completely erroneous: Memorandum of conversation dated March 10, 1969 in the American Consulate in Barcelona, RIF# 180-10090-10208; see also, https://www.maryferrell.org/showDoc.html?docId=103975#relPageId=3

On April 3, 1968, Fifth Circuit reversed Nagell's conviction: Richard Case Nagell, Appellant, v. United States of America, April 3, 1968, https://law.justia.com/cases/federal/appellate-courts/F2/392/934/27920/

Nagell met with Jim Garrison in Central Park: pages 183 – 186, *On the Trail of the Assassins*, op. cit.

The next day Garrison spent six hours talking to Nagell: pages 67 – 72 of the New Orleans conference, https://archive.org/details/NewOrleansConference921196812Of17/page/n77/mode/2up

Nagell claimed to be hit by a car without lights: CIA memo – Garrison and the Kennedy Assassination, December 10, 1968, https://www.maryferrell.org/showDoc.html?docId=101530#relPageId=7

Nagell appeared at the American consulate in Zurich: CIA document, Staff Cable re: Richard

Case Nagell, June 6, 1968, RIF# 104-10012-10091, https://www.maryferrell.org/show
Doc.html?docId=109802#relPageId=2

Nagell boarded a train headed to West Berlin: Stasi documents on Richard Case Nagell. All the
Stasi documents will be made available on my website in the document section.

Nagell was charged with espionage: Ibid.

Nagell's four-page handwritten statement: I will also be posting this on my website.

Nagell's 26-page psychiatric examination: I have had this report professionally translated and
this will also be uploaded to my website.

Nagell's return to West Berlin: Secret Service memo from SAIC O'Malley to SAIC Towns
regarding Richard Case Nagell, dated June 19, 1969, NARA.

Nagell's examination by Dr. George Babineau: Psychiatrist's Report on Richard Case Nagell, US
Citizen Released by GDR, dated October 29, 1968, papers of Dick Russell, https://www.
maryferrell.org/showDoc.html?docId=48775#relPageId=79

Nagell's examination by Dr. Benjamin Kagwa: page 15 of the 1982 court case.

Nagell examined by Dr Iris Norstrand: Ibid.

Nagell showed up in New Orleans just before the Shaw trial: page 229, On the Trail of the Assassins, op. cit.

Why Nagell did not testify at the Shaw trial: https://www.onthetrailofdelusion.com/post/
why-didn-t-richard-case-nagell-testify-at-clay-shaw-s-trial

Nagell visited the Zurich consulate on February 27th and 28th: Department of State telegram,
RIF# 104-10305-1005, https://www.maryferrell.org/showDoc.html?docId=229958#rel
PageId=69, March 1969 cable on Nagell's visit, papers of Dick Russell; Some of the
documents related to Nagell's European visits are here: https://www.onthetrailofdelu
sion.com/post/richard-case-nagell-visits-europe-in-1969

Nagell went to the Barcelona consulate: Memo dated March 10, 1969, regarding Nagell's Demand
That Department of State Locate His Family, papers of Dick Russell, RIF# 154-10002-10330.

Nagell returned to the consulate on March 12th: Ibid, including the section titled, "Subsequent
Actions and Meetings with Nagell."

Nagell in Madrid: Department of State telegram subject, Welfare: Richard Case Nagell,
April 18, 1969, papers of Dick Russell, RIF# 154-10002-10330.

Department of State telegram providing guidance on dealing with Nagell: Department of State
telegram, March 26, 1969, papers of Dick Russell, RIF# 154-10002-10330.

Nagell visited the embassy again on April 3rd: State Department telegram dated April 18, 1969,
papers of Dick Russell, RIF# 154-10002-10330.

Nagell's last meeting with the consul was on April 7th: State Department telegram dated April
8, 1969, papers of Dick Russell, RIF# 154-10002-10330.

On April 10th, Nagell appeared at the Berlin station: Report dated Mary 2, 1969 by Thomas
Hench, 766th Military Detachment, https://www.onthetrailofdelusion.com/post/is-
this-document-the-smoking-gun-on-the-richard-case-nagell-story

Nagell then went to the West Berlin Police Office: Report dated April 15, 1969, signed by
Pickardt of the Berlin police, papers of Dick Russell, RIF# 154-10002-10330.

Memo written by John Hanley of the Secret Service: papers of Dick Russell, RIF# 154-10002-
10330.

Nagell was taken to Hospital Wilmersdorf for treatment: Berlin police report dated April 22,
1969, papers of Dick Russell, RIF# 154-10002-10330.

Nagell went to the New York Regional Office of the VA: Secret Service report dated May 21, 1969, by Special Agent Robert Doule. papers of Dick Russell, RIF# 154-10002-10330.

Article about Nagell in The Family: https://www.maryferrell.org/showDoc.html?docId=103975#relPageId=27

Nagell's three-page addendum: https://www.maryferrell.org/showDoc.html?docId=23829#relPageId=9

Bruce Flatin on Nagell's article: Letter contained in the papers of Dick Russell, RIF# 154-10002-10330.

Nagell ad in the East Village other: Memo dated September 2, 1969, regarding Item in East Village Other, RIF# 104-10310-10144, https://www.maryferrell.org/showDoc.html?docId=12652#relPageId=1

Nagell was back in Zurich in mid-April 1970: https://www.maryferrell.org/showDoc.html?docId=55490#relPageId=37

Routing sheet from a 1970 dispatch: RIF# 104-10122-10445, https://www.maryferrell.org/showDoc.html?docId=31052#relPageId=2

Nagell was granted legal custody: page 54 of the 1982 court case.

I asked his son Robert about this: e-mail from Robert Nagell on June 7, 2024.

On January 2, 1973, Nagell filed an action to get full disability: page 55 of the 1982 court case.

Weinstein wrote the Department of Justice on July 23, 1973: page 56 of the 1982 court case.

On November 23, 1973, the Board informed Nagell: Ibid.

In June 1975 conspiracy author Richard Popkin: https://www.maryferrell.org/showDoc.html?docId=9966#relPageId=19

Popkin was the author of The Second Oswald: Avon Library-New York Review Book, 1966, https://archive.org/details/secondoswald0000popk

Dick Russell flew to San Diego to visit Popkin: page 49 – 50 of The Man Who Knew Too Much, op. cit.; "The Man Who Had a Contract to Kill Lee Harvey Oswald Before the Assassination of President John F. Kennedy," *Gallery Magazine*, March 1981; contained in *On the Trail of the JFK Assassins*, Skyhorse Publishing, 2008, Russell, page 152.

Russell quote that there would a "concerted effort to discredit Nagell": Ibid.

In September 1975, Russell's attorney filed a document that listed the facts: https://www.onthetrailofdelusion.com/post/richard-case-nagell-s-lawsuit

Quote from the July 2, 1982, court decision that Nagell was entitled to a full pension: page 19 of the 1982 court case.

The government appealed but on March 2, 1983, the Court of Appeals affirmed the judgment: https://openjurist.org/706/f2d/320/nagell-v-us-1-73

Bob Nagell quote about the settlement: e-mail from Robert Nagell, June 7, 2024.

One of Russell's last conversations with Nagell: page 694 of *The Man Who Knew Too Much*, op. cit.

Russell quote "quote the raven, 'nevermore'": "From Dallas to Eternity" Dick Russell, Boston Magazine, November 1993, https://archive.org/details/nsia-RussellDick/nsia-RussellDick/Russell%20Dick%2019/page/n7/mode/2up

On October 31, 1995, Jeremy Gunn sent Nagell a letter: https://www.maryferrell.org/showDoc.html?docId=204526#relPageId=1

Horne comment on Gunn letter: https://drive.google.com/file/d/1GgKtzftg0P56QKtb9q64R6vBxcK6Be9z/view?usp=sharing

Nagell autopsy: https://drive.google.com/file/d/1xmPAxaBAIwn05ZmhnnW7_Ntt6Ej ZGhz7/view?usp=sharing

Nagell smoked continuously at Bay Pines: https://www.maryferrell.org/showDoc.html? docId=48775#relPageId=147

Tom Samoluk flew to Los Angeles: https://www.onthetrailofdelusion.com/post/richard-case-nagell-s-nonexistent-evidence

Possible JFK Records Formerly in Custody of Richard Case Nagell: https://www.maryferrell.org/showDoc.html?docId=201180#relPageId=1

Dick Russell claimed that Nagell had made arrangements for this to surface: page 58 of *The Man Who Knew Too Much*, op. cit.

Dick Russell quote about sending a detailed outline to Nagell: page 81 of *The Man Who Knew Too Much*, op. cit.

Bob Nagell on his father's possible CIA/KGB connections: e-mail from Robert Nagell on June 8, 2024.

Dick Russell recounts a conversation with Nagell in 1978: page 47 of *The Man Who Knew Too Much*, op. cit.

8. Did French Intelligence Solve the JFK Assassination?

There are two primary sources on *Farewell America*. Warren Hinckle, former editor of *Ramparts Magazine*, wrote about his experiences in his memoir, *If You Have a Lemon, Make Lemonade*, W. W. Norton & Company, 1990, pages 245 – 268; https://archive.org/details/ifyouhavelemonma0000hinc/page/244/mode/2up; Hinckle also wrote this as an article, "The Mystery of the Black Books," April 1, 1973, *Esquire Magazine*.

Bill Turner wrote "Farewell America," *The Rebel*, February 13, 1984; https://www.jfk-online.com/farewellturner.html, and then also a chapter in his memoir, *Rearview Mirror: Looking Back at the FBI, the CIA and Other Tails*, Penmarin Books, 2001, pages 114 – 131; https://archive.org/details/rearviewmirror00will/page/114

Jim Garrison called Bill Turner: Hinckle, page 245, Turner, page 116; Turner puts the date in February 1967 which cannot be true. Hinckle puts it at the summer of 1968 which also cannot be correct.

Jim Rose going to Mexico City: Hinckle, pages 249 – 250.

Steve Jaffe meets broadcaster Ed Foley: memo from Stephen Jaffe to Jim Garrison, dated March 20, 1968 regarding meeting with Ed Foley on November 16, 1967, http://jfk.hood.edu/Collection/Weisberg%20Subject%20Index%20Files%20Original/J%20Disk/Jaffe%20Stephen%20-%20Jim%20Rose/Item%2003.pdf

Jaffe quote on Foley: Ibid.

On January 3, 1968, Jaffe and Foley met with Vince: memo from Stephen Jaffe to Jim Garrison, dated January 26, 1968 regarding an interview with Jim Rose on January 3, 1968, http://jfk.hood.edu/Collection/Weisberg%20Subject%20Index%20Files%20Original/J%20Disk/Jaffe%20Stephen%20-%20Jim%20Rose/Item%2001.pdf

Sheinbaum sent Rose to Bill Turner: Memo from Bill Turner to Jim Garrison, dated January 9, 1968, regarding a contact by former CIA agent, https://archive.org/details/GarrisonPapers/Cabell%2C%20General%20Charles%20P/page/n87/mode/2up

Rose showed Turner a clipping from the Fresno Bee: Turner, page 118, op. cit. Turner puts the date in January 1966 which would predate the Garrison investigation.

Rose had excised his name with a razor blade: Ibid.

Lindsay Gazette: https://cdnc.ucr.edu/?a=d&d=LG19650310.1.8&e=-------en--20--1--txt-txIN--------

Turner quote about clearing Rose for action: "Remembering Jim Rose," *Probe Magazine*, May – June 2000.

Hinckle quote on Jim Rose loving adventure: Hinckle, page 247, op. cit.

Rose met two girls in Mexico City: Gary Schoener memo on new info in case of Richard Case Nagell, July, 1968, http://jfk.hood.edu/Collection/Weisberg%20Subject%20Index%20Files/R%20Disk/Rose%20aka/Item%2002.pdf

On March 9, 1968, Garrison gave Turner $300 for Rose: Bethell diary entry for March 9, 1968, https://www.jfk-assassination.net/bethell7.htm

Bethell thought it was a waste of time: Bethell diary entry for March 26, 1968, https://www.jfk-assassination.net/bethell8.htm

Jim Rose and Dan Bohring: RIF# 104-10435, 1003, CIA Cable: Following Information Volunteered by AMGARBON, https://www.maryferrell.org/showDoc.html?docId=8297#relPageId=2

Harold Weisberg on Rose's activities: http://jfk.hood.edu/Collection/Weisberg%20Subject%20Index%20Files/G%20Disk/Garrison%20Jim/Garrison%20Jim%20File/Item%2018.pdf

Garrison read the manuscript on flight to Los Angeles: memo from Steven Burton to Harold Weisberg, dated December 25, 1968, regarding James Hepburn, http://jfk.hood.edu/Collection/Weisberg%20Subject%20Index%20Files/H%20Disk/Hepburn%20James/Item%2028.pdf

Garrison was enthusiastic about the book: Ibid.

Garrison met with Burton, Jaffe and Field at her house: Ibid.

Western Union telegram: http://jfk.hood.edu/Collection/Weisberg%20Subject%20Index%20Files%20Original/J%20Disk/Jaffe%20Stephen%20-%20Jaime%20Hepburn/Item%2002.pdf

Text of The Plot: *Farewell America*, James Hepburn, Frontiers, 1968, https://archive.org/details/farewellamerica0000hepb/mode/2up

Quotes from Farewell America:

The Committee: Chapter 13, page 281.

Quote about the collaboration on which the Committee was dependent: page 287.

Committee turned their attention to political camouflage: Ibid.

Cost of the assassination between $5 and $10 million: page 293.

One person following Kennedy's trips in 1963: page 298.

One plan was to shoot Kennedy in his car on a highway: page 343.

Quote about Jesse Curry: page 347.

The attack was carried out by a team of ten men: page 353.

Attack on General Walker had been simulated: page 338.

Quote on Oswald considering himself well-covered: Ibid.

Rose Cherami story was included: page 349.

Ruth Paine described as a lesbian: page 328.

George de Mohrenschildt: page 333

George de Mohrenschildt on Farewell America: https://www.maryferrell.org/showDoc. html?docId=10087#relPageId=256

Clay Shaw named as an intermediary: page 337.

Two paragraphs about H. L. Hunt: pages 251 – 252.

Quote about Hugh Hefner: page 246.

Three Dallas policemen were murdered: page 347.

Quote about Rush to Judgment *being a scholarly work*: page 328.

John Locke quote about Farewell America: https://web.archive.org/web/20040204180958/ http://mcadams.posc.mu.edu/fa.txt

Jaffe traveled to Europe the second week of May: memo from Steven Burton to Harold Weisberg, dated December 25, 1968, op. cit.

Jaffe was picked up by Herve Lamarre: Steve Jaffe described his trip to Europe in detail in a discussion at Maggie Field's home which was taped. Here is a link to a transcript of the Steve Jaffe tape from December 16, 1968. I have a copy of this tape and I will be uploading it to YouTube, http://jfk.hood.edu/Collection/Weisberg%20Subject%20In dex%20Files%20Original/H%20Disk/Hepburn%20James/Item%2077.pdf

Jaffe's description of Herve Lamare: This document contains Jaffe's report to Garrison from his trip to Europe as well as other associated documents, http://jfk.hood.edu/Collection/ Weisberg%20Subject%20Index%20Files%20Original/J%20Disk/Jaffe%20Stephen%20-% 20Jaime%20Hepburn/Item%2007.pdf

Information in The Plot: Ibid.

Jaffe reported that the manuscript was written by one man: Ibid.

On June 21, 1968, Jaffe met with Philippe: Ibid.

Philippe was a careful study: Ibid.

The highlight of Jaffe's trip: Ibid.

Jaffe and de Gaulle: Jaffe presentation at the 2022 CAPA Conference.

2020 Survey by Dr. Mantik: https://web.archive.org/web/20220522003528/https://theman tikview.com/pdf/JFK_Survey.pdf

Jaffe meeting with Ducret: Jaffe presentation cited above.

Lamarre and Jaffe at Interpol: See the Jaffe document on his trip to Europe, and the Jaffe tape.

Burton wrote that while in Geneva, Jaffe was in Lamarre's hotel room: Addendum to Hepburn memo, December 25, 1968, http://jfk.hood.edu/Collection/Weisberg%20Subject%20In dex%20Files/H%20Disk/Hepburn%20James/Item%2028.pdf

Jaffe sent two telegrams to Raymond Marcus: The papers of Raymond Marcus.

Lamarre asked Jaffe about getting a copy of the Zapruder film: Jaffe tape recording.

Jaffe told Burton that he returned with substantial evidence: Burton memo of December 25, 1968, op. cit.

Times-Picayune *article on "Foreign Group Has Facts"*: http://jfk.hood.edu/Collection/Weis berg%20Subject%20Index%20Files/H%20Disk/Hepburn%20James/Item%2036.pdf

Author Edward Jay Epstein wasn't impressed by Garrison's foreign agents: letter to Elmer Gertz, lawyer for Gordon Novell, dated August 3, 1968, contained in the papers of Elmer Gertz, Library of Congress.

L'Amerique Brule: My Book

Jaffe asking for details about people inside the limits of New Orleans: memo from Stephen Jaffe to

Jim Garrison, dated August 4, 1968 regarding Frontiers Establishment Publishing Co. Representative, http://jfk.hood.edu/Collection/Weisberg%20Subject%20Index%20Files/H%20Disk/Hepburn%20James/Item%2017.pdf

Lamarre said the book would be released in the U.K.: Ibid.

Lamarre gave copies of the book to Jaffe, Garrison and Mark Lane: Steve Jaffe tape, op. cit.

Garrison said, "let's hope the book does some good.": Ibid.

Verschworung [Farewell America in German]: https://www.buecherdorf.at/politik-zeit geschichte/33943-verschwoerung-die-hintergruende-des-politischen-mords-in-den-usa.html

In the beginning of November, Jaffe called Burton: Burton memo dated December 25, 1968, op. cit.

On November 14, 1968, Burton called Fred Newcomb: Memo regarding ad for film *Farewell America* by Fred Newcomb, undated, http://jfk.hood.edu/Collection/Weisberg%20Subject%20Index%20Files/H%20Disk/Hepburn%20James/Item%2010.pdf

Farewell America LA Free Press *ad*: http://jfk.hood.edu/Collection/Weisberg%20Subject%20Index%20Files/H%20Disk/Hepburn%20James/Item%2060.pdf

Jaffe had a scuffle with Lou Ivon: https://archive.org/details/nsia-SchoenerGaryRCorrespondence/nsia-SchoenerGaryRCorrespondence/Schoener%20Gary%20R%20185/page/n1

Jay Singer article in the LA Free Press: http://jfk.hood.edu/Collection/Weisberg%20Subject%20Index%20Files/H%20Disk/Hepburn%20James/Item%2059.pdf

On December 13, 1968, the film Farewell America *was shown*: Memo from Burton dated December 23, 1968, regarding *Farewell America*, http://jfk.hood.edu/Collection/Weisberg%20Subject%20Index%20Files/H%20Disk/Hepburn%20James/Item%2029.pdf

One massive error was the inclusion of the 'walkie-talkie man': Ibid.

Jim Garrison and the Zapruder film: see *Twenty-Six Seconds: A Personal History of the Zapruder Film* by Alexandra Zapruder, Twelve, 2016, page 198 – 201; "A Tale of Two Subpoenas," by Mark Lane, *Midlothian Mirror*, April 25, 1968, also reprinted in the *LA Free Press* of April 12, 1968, https://archive.org/details/nsia-LaneMarkBiographyFiles/nsia-Lane MarkBiographyFiles/Lane%20Mark%20Biography%2033/mode/1up

On December 16, 1968, a meeting was held at Maggie Field's house: http://jfk.hood.edu/Collection/Weisberg%20Subject%20Index%20Files%20Original/H%20Disk/Hepburn%20James/Item%2077.pdf

Here is an excerpt from a transcript of the tape: I will be uploading this tape to YouTube.

Marilyn Newcomb wrote that Jaffe then said that Lamarre had gotten a copy from Garrison's office: http://jfk.hood.edu/Collection/Weisberg%20Subject%20Index%20Files/H%20Disk/Hepburn%20James/Item%2009.pdf

Weisberg also wrote that "Ray Marcus had earlier told me of three occasions on which Jaffe had told other he had given a copy of the Z film to Lamarre": http://jfk.hood.edu/Collection/Weisberg%20Subject%20Index%20Files%20Original/J%20Disk/Jaffe%20Stephen/Item%2019.pdf

Newcomb memo on Zapruder film going to Canada to be copied: http://jfk.hood.edu/Collection/Weisberg%20Subject%20Index%20Files%20Original/J%20Disk/Jaffe%20Stephen/Item%2002.pdf

Lamarre told Jaffe he had put Clay Shaw into the film "as a courtesy to Jim Garrison": see the memo of the tape of the meeting at Maggie Field's house.

Maggie Field went to Paris and met with Lamarre: http://jfk.hood.edu/Collection/Weisberg%

20Subject%20Index%20Files%20Original/H%20Disk/Hepburn%20James/Item%2026.pdf

New York Times *article on* Farewell America *from January 1, 1969*: http://jfk.hood.edu/Collection/Weisberg%20Subject%20Index%20Files/H%20Disk/Hepburn%20James/Item%2071.pdf

An article in the South Carolina Anderson Independent *newspaper*: "Conspiratorial Theory: Some People Will Believe Just About Anything," February 18, 1989; contained in this file, https://www.cia.gov/readingroom/docs/CIA-RDP80-01601R000800290001-5.pdf

La Presse *serialized* L'Amerique Brule: Part one was on February 10, 1969, *La Presse was* Montreal's largest circulation newspaper, page 7, https://numerique.banq.qc.ca/patrimoine/details/52327/2681826?docsearchtext=L%27amerique%20brule%22

Herb Caen on Farewell America: *San Francisco Chronicle*, April 20, 1973.

Hinckle quote on who was responsible for Farewell America: Hinckle, op. cit., page 260.

Quote about Charles de Gaulle in Farewell America: Hepburn, op. cit., page 175.

French Communist party placed a role in the resistance: The KGB in Europe and the West: The *Mitrokhin Archive*, Christopher Andrew and Vasili Mitrokhin, Penguin, 2000, page 600.

In 1945 alone, KGB agents resident in Paris: Ibid., page 198.

At least fifty KGB agents resident in Paris from 1946 – 1958: Ibid.

Quote from Ivan Ivanovich Agayants: Ibid.

Bogus memoirs and other intelligence work: page 601

KGB penetration of French intelligence continued during the 1960s: page 608.

In 1961, the French blamed the CIA for a coup attempt: https://www.onthetrailofdelusion.com/post/jfk-revisited-misleads-on-supposed-cia-support-of-the-1961-coup-attempt-in-france

Paese Sera *story on CIA involvement*: https://www.google.ca/books/edition/Communist_Forgeries/gZ4KeT5i_nkC?hl=en&gbpv=1&dq=%22Is+Il+Paese+a+communist+paper%22

Paese Sera *was also involved in an operation to claim that Clay Shaw was working for the CIA in Rome*: https://www.washingtondecoded.com/site/2020/11/litwin.html; You can read more about Permindex here, https://www.onthetrailofdelusion.com/blog/tags/permindex

Edward Jay Epstein on Vosjoli: https://web.archive.org/web/20110412125154/https://www.edwardjayepstein.com/diary/devosjoli.htm

Philippe de Vosjoli article in Life Magazine: https://www.cia.gov/readingroom/docs/CIA-RDP70B00338R000200170118-8.pdf

CIA memo on assassination buffs being supplied money and circumstantial evidence by the KGB: https://www.maryferrell.org/showDoc.html?docId=51188#relPageId=4

Shamrock also said there had been a KGB commission to investigate the JFK assassination: https://www.maryferrell.org/showDoc.html?docId=192786#relPageId=3

In 1978, Vosjoli was contracted by the HSCA: HSCA Outside Contact Report, dated May 9, 1978, by James Kelly, NARA.

Chart of the assassination in the book Executive Action: https://archive.org/details/executiveactiona00free/page/60/mode/2up

9. The Bolton Ford Incident

The major documents quoted in this chapter can be found here: https://www.onthetrailofdelu sion.com/post/lee-harvey-oswald-was-not-impersonated-at-bolton-ford

Bolton Ford quote for the trucks: ibid.

FBI report on Oscar Deslatte: https://www.maryferrell.org/showDoc.html?docId= 10477#relPageId=681

Deslatte denied the incident ever happened: mentioned in a memo written by James Alcock from an interview with Fred A. Sewell, on Mary 2, 1967.

Sewell remembered that the man said his name was Lee Oswald: Ibid.

Question from Garrison to Sewell about Oswald or Lee Oswald: Ibid.

Second interview with Fred Sewell: Memo written by Kent Sims dated February 14, 1968, about an interview with Sewell conducted that day.

Garrison quote on discovering Banister was behind Friends of Democratic Cuba: Garrison, op. cit., page 58.

Dialogue with Jim Garrison and Frank Klein: Ibid, pages 58 – 60.

Garrison quote about CIA psychological profile: Ibid, page 60.

William Corson on the CIA psychological profile: *The Armies of Ignorance: The Rise of the American Intelligence Empire*, William Corson, Dial Press, 1977, page 30, https://archive.org/details/armiesofignoranc008072/page/30/mode/2up

Bolton Ford in JFK: JFK: The Book of the Film., op. cit., pages 76 - 77.

Garrison quote about the man with a scar: Garrison, op. cit., pages 57 – 58.

Schulingkamp v. Bolton Ford: https://casetext.com/case/schulingkamp-v-bolton-ford-inc-1

Delphine Roberts, President of the National Confederation for Conservative Governments: you can see some of Roberts' politics here, https://www.onthetrailofdelusion.com/post/did-delphine-roberts-see-oswald-in-banister-s-office

Afterword

James Douglass' chronology of the assassination and Nagell: Douglass, *JFK and the Unspeakable: Why He Died and Why It Matters*, Orbis Books 2008, op. cit., page xxvii.

Douglass devotes five pages to Nagell: Ibid, pages 153 – 158.

Douglass repeats Russell's claim that there was something suspicious about Nagell's death: Ibid, page 157.

James DiEugenio also spends five pages on Nagell: *Destiny Betrayed*, op. cit., pages 93 - 98.

DiEugenio on Nagell's mental health: "The Life & Death of Richard Case Nagell," Probe Magazine, November – December, 1995, https://www.kennedysandking.com/obituar ies/the-life-death-of-richard-case-nagell

Dick Russell's smoking gun: Quote is from page 54 of the first edition of *The Man Who Knew Too Much*, https://www.onthetrailofdelusion.com/post/is-this-document-the-smoking-gun-on-the-richard-case-nagell-story, Dick Russell also has a second smoking gun which is debunked here, https://www.onthetrailofdelusion.com/post/dick-russell-s-second-smoking-gun-on-the-richard-case-nagell-story

Russell was taken in: Ibid.

Russell also believed Nagell when he said he had met Fidel Castro: page 429 in the first edition of *The Man Who Knew Too Much*, https://www.onthetrailofdelusion.com/post/did-richard-case-nagell-warn-fidel-castro-about-the-assassination

Russell added in a footnote: page 773 of the first edition of *The Man Who Knew Too Much*.

1993 article "From Dallas to Eternity" in Boston Magazine: http://jfk.hood.edu/Collection/Weisberg%20Subject%20Index%20Files/R%20Disk/Russell%20Dick/Item%2006.pdf

Russell spoke at Judyth Vary Baker's conference: https://youtu.be/pY2DIx0EmvY?si=xJUpbmr7_KVJCw77

More on Judyth Vary Baker: https://jfk-archives.blogspot.com/2010/09/judyth-vary-baker.html; https://www.jfk-assassination.net/judyth.htm

Russell on Broshears: The quote "they never tried" is Russell's, found on page 368 of the second edition of *The Man Who Knew Too Much*, Carroll & Graf, 2003.

Broshears' HSCA deposition: https://youtu.be/IfM5F81_v2Y?si=h0qDPVyQsdlw79OF, https://www.onthetrailofdelusion.com/post/reverend-raymond-broshears-talks-to-the-hsca

DiEugenio also believes Raymond Broshears: page 148 in the first edition of *Destiny Betrayed*, Sheridan Square Press, 1992.

DiEugenio quote about Broshears "spoke about a Leon Oswald": page 248, *Destiny Betrayed*.

Douglass on Rose Cherami: Douglass, op. cit., page 245.

DiEugenio on Rose Cherami: Here is another example of where James DiEugenio gets this story wrong -- this blog post examines his misuse of a newspaper article, https://www.onthetrailofdelusion.com/post/did-dr-wayne-owens-hear-rose-cherami-predict-the-jfk-assassination

HSCA staff report on Rose Cherami: https://www.maryferrell.org/showDoc.html?docId=1212#relPageId=201

Frank Meloche memo: https://www.onthetrailofdelusion.com/post/did-rose-cherami-watch-the-dallas-motorcade-on-television

Joan Mellen recreated this very scene: page 206 of *A Farewell to Justice*.

Douglass accepts Cherami's assertion that Oswald and Ruby were lovers: Douglass, op. cit., page 246.

Vince Palamara on Bootsie Gay: page 173, of *Honest Answers About the Murder of President John F. Kennedy: A New Look at the JFK Assassination*, Trine Day, 2021.

Palamara on Richard Case Nagell: Ibid, page 106.

Palamara agrees that Nagell was one of the most important witnesses: Ibid, page 97.

Palamara on Rose Cherami: Ibid, page 106.

Palamara on Cherami's death: Ibid, page 176.

Article on DiEugenio's website about Crafard: "The Tippit Tapes: A Re-examination" by John Washburn, April 30, 2024, https://www.kennedysandking.com/john-f-kennedy-articles/the-tippit-tapes-a-re-examination

Here is the document in question: https://www.maryferrell.org/showDoc.html?docId=232910#relPageId=309

Then his article veers into silliness: Washburn, op. cit.

DiEugenio presents the Bolton Ford episode: page 109 of *Destiny Betrayed*.

Palamara on Bolton Ford: page 163 of *Honest Answers*, op. cit.

DiEugenio on Farewell America: Pages 281 -283 of *Destiny Betrayed*.

Rob Reiner's podcast series Who Killed JFK?: https://www.iheart.com/podcast/1119-who-killed-jfk-127000428/

Gus Russo on William Harvey: e-mail from Gus Russo on August 28, 2024; you can read more about William Harvey here, https://www.onthetrailofdelusion.com/post/was-bill-harvey-in-dallas-in-november-of-1963; and here, https://www.onthetrailofdelusion.com/post/a-reply-to-jefferson-morley-on-bill-harvey, and here, https://www.onthetrailofdelusion.com/post/jefferson-morley-is-wrong-on-william-harvey-again

Jaffe quote to Jefferson Morley: https://youtu.be/w2IBeqr0BJI?si=mg6R2TrvUSCklNcQ

Jaffe on why Harvey's name did not make it into a contemporaneous memo: e-mail from Stephen Jaffe dated August 4, 2024.

Jefferson Morley on JFK assassination records: https://jfkfacts.substack.com/p/rfk-jr-joins-trump-in-call-for-full

Bugliosi offered some important advice: Endnotes, page 5426 in the Kindle edition of *Reclaiming History: The Assassination of President John F. Kennedy*, W. W. Norton & Company, 2007.